D1093149

PILGRIMAGES IN
CHESHIRE & SHROPSHIRE

BEESTON CASTLE

A pilgrim descendant of the Norman Earls of Chester gazing from the ruined fortress
over the rich lands of which his fathers once were lords

PILGRIMAGES

IN

CHESHIRE & SHROPSHIRE

By

FLETCHER MOSS

Author of " A History of Didsbury," " Didisburye in the '45,"
" The Chronicles of Cheadle and Gatley,"
" Folk-Lore, Old Customs, and Tales."
Member of the Councils of Manchester and Withington.

Published by the Author from his home *The Old
Parsonage, Didsbury ;* and from his town office in
The Spread Eagle Hotel, Hanging Ditch, Manchester.
June 1901

E. J. MORTEN (Publishers)
Didsbury, Manchester, England.

First Printed 1901
BALLANTYNE,
HANSON & CO.

Reprinted 1972
E. J. MORTEN (Publishers)
Warburton Street,
Didsbury,
Manchester 20

ISBN o 901598 36 4

Printed by Scolar Press Limited
Menston, Yorkshire, U.K.

"*GOD SAVE YOU, PILGRIM!*
Whither are you bound?"

ALL'S WELL THAT ENDS WELL.

Preface

THE tale of pilgrimages which comprises this book originally appeared in the *Manchester City News*. There were forty-one articles written during the last three summers and autumns. They are now revised, in their former order, and illustrated by photographs, the greater part of which have been taken by X, whose name and identity are now published for the first time.

When I was writing the history of Cheadle and Gatley I was greatly helped by an old friend, James Watts, the lord of the manor of Cheadle Bulkeley, who became much interested in the work. He had inherited from his father, Sir James Watts, whose ancestors in the male line had lived and died in the old parish of Didsbury for many generations; but his mother's name was Buckley, and her grandmother was Mary Hyde, who was descended from the Hydes of Hyde on her father's side, and on her mother's from the Hollingworths of Hollingworth. A few generations take the pedigree to Alice Rode of Rode, whose grandmother was Alice Moreton of Moreton, whose mother was Alice Brereton of Brereton, whose mother was Agnes Legh of Adlington, and once in the county families, according to the county historians, the ramifications of pedigree are endless.

When James Watts, otherwise the X of these rambles, found that he really could claim descent from the old families whose names were the same as their lands, he became greatly interested, sparing no pains or expense to hunt up the old records and the old halls; my knowledge of Cheshire and the adjacent country to the south of it being brought to help; and gradually photography was more and more used to secure some permanent record of what is fast tumbling to decay or spoilt by the destroying hand of the "restorer."

In my book on "Folk-Lore" are accounts of five lonely pilgrimages I had previously taken. The chief one was the great day's work of going from Standon Hall to find the Royal Oak at Boscobel. Others were to see the Grand Old Man at Hawarden, and Barthomley Church, the place of the massacre on Christmas Eve in the Civil War. To the battlefield of Blore Heath and the ghost-haunted Combermere Abbey I had often been in days of yore.

This preface may end with the words of lament I used to end the tale of a pilgrimage when the ways of the modern tourist were not so well known to me.

There are thousands of cyclists who leave Lancashire for Cheshire any fine summer's day. They visit a country studded with works of art, solemn temples embellished with monuments of our fathers, of beautiful architecture, sculpture, and carving, all hallowed by the long associations of history. This interest and this beauty, like that of so much of the open country, seems lost to the modern tourist. Wisdom may cry aloud, though none regardeth her. Turn in to this old church where in its quiet shade we may rest and dream awhile. Here are the tombs of the Crusaders. Here are the effigies of men who fell in the fierce slaughter on Flodden. Here are memorials of those who fought the death-grip battles with France and Spain. And nearer still, here are "the bruised arms hung up for monuments," the actual weapons of Cavalier and Roundhead, when our present liberties and peace were fought for and ensured. Here are heroes—for "peace hath her victories no less renowned than war"—heroes from all down the long roll of England's glorious history. Is it nothing to you, oh all ye that pass by? And the hurrying cyclist gasps—"Which is the best pub for a shandygaff?"

FLETCHER MOSS.

The Old Parsonage,
    Didsbury.

Contents

CONTENTS

List of Illustrations

FULL-PAGE ILLUSTRATIONS

xiii

ILLUSTRATIONS

b

ILLUSTRATIONS IN TEXT

ILLUSTRATIONS xvii

ILLUSTRATIONS

PILGRIMAGES IN
CHESHIRE & SHROPSHIRE

INTRODUCTORY

OUR pilgrimages began on this wise.
A kindred spirit to be known as X had become infected with the harmless, interesting form of ancestor worship known as pedigree-hunting—a strong desire to see where and how his forefathers lived, the rock from whence they were hewn, or the hole in the pit from whence they were digged, or into which they were put when they were done with. The country for forty miles south of the Mersey was well known to me. We had both taken to cycling, one of the best inventions of this generation, discarded our horses for ever, though we had been horsemen all our lives, and pitying old Chaucer and his crew, whose troubles with their horses and bad roads were so lightly glossed over, we wandered forth on bikes, with railway trains at times to help us, in search of ancient halls, which the destroying hands of time or man have not yet swept away, or quiet country churchyards where we may read about the many virtues of our forefathers, or even see their gorgeous images sculptured in marble, or painted and faded on panel, and thankfully reflect how much better it is to have them lying peacefully there, than to have the poor relations who are so common nowadays and are not always so good as they might be.

A

When we went on our first day's pilgrimage we never thought of the many more which were in store for us, of the interesting knowledge that was to be derived from them, or of the vast amount of enjoyment there was to be obtained from them.   We heard the local legends, we read the local histories, and gradually it became our constant practice for me to be the scribe and write down what was worth recording while X took photographs, more and more carefully, until at last the snapshot camera was never used, and the half-plate size with tripod was lugged about where'er we went.

These notes on the way, with pictures of the places as graven by the sun, are here reproduced so that others may have some idea of the scenes they cannot see and the happy days in which they could not join.   These are not all the records of what has been done, they are only part, and life is far too short to see the beauties of this English land ; but when the summer comes upon the earth again we hope to wander on and note some more, for the toil has proved to be a pleasure and the work is rest.

AN APPLE ON A TOWER

DUTTON HALL

IN our studies of the history of Cheadle in Cheshire,
I found that the manor is mentioned in the
Domesday Book, although the historians have
all stumbled over the entry. Gamel the Saxon
held it as a free man, and then comes a long gap in
its history—nearly two hundred years—when a younger
son of the Duttons of Dutton is said to have acquired
the manor by marriage, and to have taken the name
of Geoffrey de Chedle. From him X claims descent.
A long descent through six hundred years and many
female lines; but females are as necessary to a descent
as the more orthodox and rarer males, and as he owns
the Cheadle Bulkeley share of the manor the case is
the more interesting, for the lands he holds his ancestors
held before him, and the first recorded one of them
came from Dutton. As I knew the whereabouts of
the old hall at Dutton and the occupier thereof, it became our fixed intention to go on pilgrimage to the
place as soon as possible.

To help us on our way we went by the morning
train from Cheadle to Warrington, having for our sole
companion a golf caddie, who gave us his views of life.
He says he carries "things" for "toffs' and gets four-
pence a round, but if he had a badge he would be
paid ninepence, and wouldn't he save some brass? He
proudly told us he had more than ten pounds in the
bank already; and when I remarked that was more

than many of the "toffs" had, he said, "Oh, ay; but they've got to pay me, chus 'ow."

Leaving the train at Arpley we went on the Chester road over the Mersey and the Ship Canal to Walton. Here is a showy, pretentious-looking church that seems to lack the "calm repose and peace divine" of our ancient parish churches, and when we learnt that it was a brewers' church—one of the investments brewers make for another world—a smell of sour beer seemed to come over all, and we hurried on. By the roadside are flat stone seats without backs, but with deeply chiselled inscriptions which would cost far more than the worthless seats. We approach Norton Priory, and the name brings back to memory some of its shameful history, with the bitter strife and religious hatred that raged around it. The lands of Norton and many surrounding manors were once given in pure alms, and if that and similar gifts had not been robbed there would be no need of poor-rates in Cheshire to-day. The bluff and bloated King of England sent orders to his sheriff, Sir Pears Dutton, to take the abbot of Norton with his head-men and "without any further delaye cause them to be hanged as most arrante traytores in such sondrey places." Whether they were hanged or not history does not confirm, neither does it say, nor do we know if the final clause in the founder's charter, the curse on the violator, has been fulfilled. The founder prayed that the blessings of Heaven should rest on those who maintained the charity, and any violators of it should be punished with Pilate and Judas in hell.

Trundling our bicycles up the steep ascent we come to Halton Castle, once a stronghold of the robber barons who took toll of all wayfarers. X wishes to go right up to it, for he says his ancestors owned it. I feel rather frightened that he may claim all the countryside. There does not seem much of the ancestral hall about this place, but these barons of old had numerous families, both legitimate and illegitimate, mostly the latter, and it would be difficult to escape having them for ancestors.

Down the country lanes we make our way towards a worn-out hall that not even the country-folk seem to have ever heard of. Morphany is not even mentioned in Ormerod's well-known county history. It is not in the maps, but out of the world apparently. I knew it because for many years the cheese made on the farm was sent to our firm to sell in Manchester—the more remote the farm, the more difficult it was for new-comers to find.

At last we stand by an ancient oaken door with immense curled hinges and studded with huge iron bolts. The daub or clay which fills up the ornamental quatre-foils and the oaken framework of the house is tumbling in decay. Briars flourish amid the weatherworn stones of the great chimney, stonecrop and house-leek adorn the roof, and the whole place looks lost, forlorn, and desolate. After much knocking, a dejected voice comes from some bushes at the corner asking what we wanted. " Th' front dur wunner hoppen; it anner hoppent for yeears." We are allowed to photograph, and X photo-graphs diligently all day, but the light was not good, the folding camera new, and the films not sharp enough, therefore none are here reproduced. There is a hen-coop by the front doorstep with five goslings, all of which are of different sizes, and look the picture of misery. They have no chance of washing themselves or keeping them-selves tidy. There are two old bumble-footed cocks, with swelled heads and limbs, and about two feathers and a half in their tails. They are evidently suffering from rheumatism and vermin, and any aristocratic fox would turn up his nose and his brush at the smell of them.

We bump along the cobble-paved lanes from Morphany Hall for miles until we get to the good high-road
again and find our way to Dutton Hall, a rambling pile
of many ages whose end is on the steep bank of the
Weaver, and whose fields around show the fat stock and
fertility of Cheshire. The name is doubtless derived
from *dun tun*, the town on the down; as Halton is the
high town, Norton the north town, and Walton the well
town, or possibly the walled town.

There is here one of the most beautiful old halls that
I ever saw spoilt—a magnificent carved oaken hall cut
up into three storeys and little bedrooms. It must have
been at one time like a small cathedral made of oak.
Lofty, clustered columns, with a most beautiful roof in
the attics, where the starlings build, and the lovely
bosses or carved flowers and mouldings are gone. In
the bedrooms you may read bits of deeply-cut inscriptions on the oaken cornice; then you have to go into
the next room, and the next, and so on, to follow up
the writing. A long account in wonderful carving and
spelling commemorates the building of the house in
1539 "bi the especiall devising of Sr piers dutton . . .
and after long sute before all the nobulls and jugs
(judges) of this realme bi the space of vii yeres and
above the same Sr piers was appioted heir malle . . .
of all duttons land and so adiuged. . . ." This is sup-
plemented by the beautiful entrance, over which there
is plainly inscribed, "Syr Peyrs Dutton Knyght Lorde
of Dutton and my lade dame julian hys wiff made this
hall and buyldyng in ye yere of our Lorde God
mcccccxlii who thanketh God of all." He certainly
had need to thank God for all, though one would have
thought that, considering he had gotten it by robbing
the charities, the poor, the sick, and the church, the less
said about it the better. For this was the same Sir
Peter above mentioned who went to hang the abbot of

PORCH OF DUTTON HALL

Norton, and it is evident his wealth and power came from the robbery of the religious houses, the great source from whence nearly every one of the proud families of Cheshire derive their wealth. He reminds me of one of the head-men in the Church and State party in Manchester, who told me that his chief reason for going to church was to pray that the horse he had backed might win its race.

Inside the outer doorway, which is filled now with slight modern work, is an enormously massive old oaken door, deeply carved, with the usual smaller door as part of it, evidently the great door of the abbey of Norton. Above and round it are large carved bosses, having sacred signs, the five wounds, a scapegoat, camel, bear, &c., and again, "Who thakyth god of all xxxix." Stupendous hinges, gorgeous coats-of-arms, carved columns and rare old work are there, the stolen spoils of the once great neighbouring abbey.

This grand house was probably "warmed" at the marriage of the two daughters of Sir Piers Dutton on the feast of St. John the Baptist in 1542, when all the musicians and minstrels of Cheshire marched in procession before the happy couples. For the lords of Dutton had the licensing of the county minstrels from those far-off days when Randle, Earl of Chester, was in jeopardy by the wild Welshmen, and Roger Lacy, sur-named Hell or Hellfire Roger from his fierce spirit, with his steward Dutton of Dutton, gathered all the rabble of Chester Midsummer Fair, males and females, fiddlers and tinkers, and rushed to the rescue. That was the Randle who bought all the land between the Ribble and the Mersey for forty marks of silver, the equivalent of about a hundred sacks of flour as nearly as I can reckon it, and as each sack of flour should make a hundred loaves of bread the reader may reckon for himself, and also remember that the value may go

up in the future as much as it has gone up in the past.
Therefore, what may that bit of land be worth some
day? The Earl of Chester, in gratitude for his deliver-
ance, conferred on his rescuers the right to license all
the gentlemen and ladies of easy virtue, learnedly styled
"omnium leccatorium et meretricum," in the county of
Chester, to practise their vocations. In process of time
it came to pass that musicianers were not necessarily
rogues, though they were so considered in Elizabeth's
time, the exception being in Cheshire, where they were
licensed as described below in the next century:
" . . . all and every useinge and p'fessinge ye noble
art, ye worthy science and high misterie of musique
and minstrellzie . . . pub'cly here to drawe forthe their
sundry instruments of musique and minstrellzie and to
play heere pub'cly unto ye court house. This omitt
you nott as you will at yo'r perills aboyde ye rebuke
of ye Court, ye forfeiture of your instruments, and
imprisonments of your bodyes. God save ye Kinge's
Ma'ty, his most hon'ble counsell, and the Lord of
Dutton, and send us peace. Amen." Then they had
to go to church and play "a sett of lowd musique
upon their knees," singing "God bless the King and
the heir of Dutton." Of course it all ended with a
dinner just as if they were common councillors, and
the music would no doubt be of a very miscellaneous
character.

Some thirty or forty years since there was a sign
on a doorpost in Manchester, "Lamb and Dutton,
Solicitors." Some one was said to have gone at night
and painted out the letter D and put M. Then the
sign was "Lamb and Mutton, Solicitors." Funny folk
said the alteration might be more complete, for according
to "Æsop's Fables" it was not the lawyers who were
converted into lamb and mutton, that being a much
more likely fate for the clients.

After being hospitably entertained and much interested in Dutton Hall, I asked the way to Crewood
(pronounced Crude) Hall, and was shown it on the
opposite bank of the Weaver. Down the big fields
of mowing grass we trundled our bicycles, and lifted
them over the fences where no bicycle ever went before
or probably will ever go again. At the bottom of a big
hill we got on to the towing-path of the canal, and rode
along it where a chance wobble might have "chucked
us in the cut." We crossed the Weaver by the wooden
bridge used by the canal horses, and ascended the
opposite bank. By a picturesque private road we found
our way to Crewood Hall, which is mostly modern, but
has a very good porch built of stone for the first storey,
with a timber-built gable above. On an immense stone
which forms the outer lintel of the porch is a weather-
worn superscription, in more or less high relief, com-
memorating the building of the house by the proud lords
who then owned it. The date is 1638. The shield of
arms has quarterings almost worn out, and of which my
knowledge is small, but perhaps the engrailed cross,
like unto one we had seen in the morning over a public-
house door, was of the Brookes who now own Norton
Priory, and others were the badges of the Duttons
and the usual "romping" cats or lions rampant, the
cognisance of so many Cheshire families. There are
the letters G G for Gilbert Gerard, and in immense
capitals across the stone JEHOVAH JIREH (God
provides). To my slight knowledge of building it
seems that it would cost as much to reproduce that
stone as to build many a modern jerry house. A
beautiful araucaria stands by the porch. We rest and
chat and photograph, and see some good old-fashioned
furniture. It seems some one owns the place still, and
there is no use our claiming it, so we ask the way
for The Forest, meaning to strike into the great

road from Chester, or the railroad at Delamere or Cuddington.   All of which we safely did; and thus ends our first day's pilgrimage.

A CHESHIRE INN

The inscription on the gable reads : "In the year 920
King Edward the Elder founded a city here and called it Thelwall"

BUNBURY CHURCH, BEESTON CASTLE, UTKYNTON HALL

THE central point of this long midsummer day's pilgrimage was Beeston Castle, the picturesque, enchanting, castled crag, round which all southern Cheshire seems to gather. Weeks would not suffice to see all that is in this fair land, and many volumes on it might be written.

We went by early morning train to Nantwich, and I, an old campaigner, not knowing how we should fare or whither we might get, made a good sandwich of the cold fat chawl which with new milk is my time-honoured breakfast, to cheer me on the way; but X, being unprepared, was advised to lay in something in the town. At one shop he bought cheese and at another he bought bread. Not being used to marketing he asked for a loaf, and they gave him a four-pound one, saying they did not cut it. So we cut it in the street, and he gave the half away at once, and left the other half on Beeston Castle. Then he bought some parkin, when he heard the town was noted for it, a few pounds more, all helped to load, and we went to church, where morning service was going on, though there was no congregation unless a solitary female who dotes on the parson may be called one, and piles of charity bread for the morrow's doles were being brought in. A few hurried glances at the handsome church and carved work were all that we could spare, and the quaint old houses in the little town we had not time to see.

What a sleepy place it seemed, and yet what stirring times it has gone through! In this church were fifteen hundred prisoners kept in prison, short of food and water and the necessaries of life. By the side of the chancel they tumbled the warm body of Captain Steele into his grave when they shot him for the betrayal of Beeston. There they shot Lieutenant Higgins for being Irish and deserting, and hanged two Irishmen. A prisoner was found to have the Church surplice in his breeches. Perhaps he was trying to keep it clean from the polluting touch of the Puritans. In the market-place those Puritans actually made a county squire and a woman, who were taken in adultery in the Vicarage on the Sabbath day at the time of divine service, do penance at the cage in the market-place with the paper of their condemnation pinned on their breasts. This old wich or salt town was the scene of a battle more than eight centuries ago, and was twice leagured round for months in the great Civil War, when its men and women manned the walls day and night. But we must leave this history and get on with our work.

I had instructions to buy a local paper containing an account of a marriage in the family, and then we cycled over some of the biggest boulder-stones in any pavement. That is the cyclist's equivalent, when on pilgrimage, to doing penance by having peas in the shoes. On the road to Tarporley we passed cottages on banks by the roadside smothered with roses and honeysuckle, and X said they were just the places he should like to live at. Then we came to the lordly hall of Dorfold, and he made the same remark again, so I commented on the breadth of his views. Dorfold Hall as seen from the road is a perfect Elizabethan mansion, with a profusion of projecting gables, big windows, twisted chimneys, and steep roofs. It is furnished in accordance, and Lord Leighton, the late

President of the Royal Academy, said it was the most
"harmonious" hall of the period that he knew. We had
to be content with looking at it from the road, and then
we travel on to the fine old Norman church of Acton.

Here the inevitable repairs were going on, and very
little Norman work is left, but there are some sculptured stones that were there before the Normans were
heard of. There is an ancient font, possibly Saxon,
that until lately was used as a pig trough. That little
tale turned my thoughts to the human nature in the
public men of all time. Some pious party would give a
new font to the glory of God and themselves. Some
one else would get the job of making it, and some one
else—probably a churchwarden—would get the old font,
which would then be worth very little, but which he
might take away and use as a swill trough for the swine.

There is a grand monument to a Sir William Man-
waring or Maynwaringe. The name is spelt in about
thirty different ways, but the pronunciation should always
be the same, *i.e.* as if it were spelt Manering. This
member of the family is said to have endowed the church
with a piece of the true cross, and when he went to the
wars in France he left written instructions that his
"picture in alabaster" was to be set up in Aghton
Church, and here it is, much defaced, for the schoolboys
sat near to it for untold generations, and they did their
very best to spoil it, far more than was done in the Civil
War, though the church was made into a garrison and
the parson's widow was shot. At the back of the
monument are the paintings of priests who were to
pray for him who was past praying for. Above them
are emblazoned shields of arms, and over all is the
family crest. The crest should be an ass's head, but in
this case the flattering sculptor has made it as like to a
horse's head as he could. The motto is "Devant si je
puis," the Norman French for "Forward if I can," and
the poetic or legendary explanation of it is that an

ancestral Mainwaring in the Crusades had his horse killed and could only get an ass, which he mounted, crying, "Devant si je puis"; and to this day the sign of the Mainwarings is an ass's head.

From the grand old church at Acton we journeyed on to the still grander one at Bunbury, dedicated to St. Boniface, the patron saint of innkeepers, celebrated for its wakes, junketings, and bear-baitings, also for having both rector and vicar. In the days of its glory Bunbury was all inns and church. Many of the former are gone, and about one mentioned in history no one could tell me anything. When writing about the Royal Oak I had found in contemporary tracts that when Giffard of Chillington, whose servant had guided the king and his party to his house at Whiteladies, had left the king, he and the Earl of Derby were made prisoners, and were being taken to Chester Castle, when they stopped at an inn at Bunbury, and Giffard escaped from the inn when the soldiers and prisoners baited and boozed. That was the day after Worcester fight, and they had been riding all night. Giffard was never taken again, but the Earl of Derby, as is well known, was soon beheaded.

The splendid church of Bunbury was rebuilt for a collegiate church about 1386 by Sir Hugh Calveley, who obtained leave from King Richard the Second, but the grant was overweighted by a clause whereby prayers were to be offered up for ever, not only for the repose of the souls of the founder and his ancestors, but for the repose of the king's soul and all his blessed or unblessed ancestors, murderers and thieves as most of them were. The task was hopeless, the load enough to sink any ship, and all is quiet now. Under the boy king, Edward VI., the tithes were grabbed, and leased, and sold, and muddled with paltry doles given instead to a preacher or rector, a vicar or curate, a schoolmaster and an usher. We roamed through the church as we liked, thankful there was no one to disturb

CHURCH OF ST. BONIFACE, BUNBURY

us. It is all in beautiful order. The prehistoric or
ancient stone coffins and mutilated effigies of warriors
and pilgrims that were worn out and buried before this
church was built, are ranged inside, ticketed, and
labelled with short historical notes.

That quaint chronicler, Froissart, made Sir Hugh
Calveley one of his heroes. He was of pure Cheshire
breed, and his name is redolent of the county and its
chief industry. It should be pronounced Cauvley. The
Cheshire man calls his calf a cauf, and speaks of the
calves' ley. The family badge is a calf—appropriate for
any one who is fond of new milk. Sir Hugh was one
of the thirty Englishmen chosen to fight the duel with
thirty Bretons, when the fierce order was given, "If
thou art thirsty drink thy blood." He was deputy-
governor of Calais when he burnt the French ships in
Boulogne harbour and seized immense booty. He
spoiled Estaples, from whence the English took everything they could carry. For forty years he was a sore
thorn in the side of the French, and the consequence
that chiefly concerns us now is, that the richest spoils
of France were lavished on the old church at Bunbury
and the sumptuous altar-tomb of its benefactor.

When the warfare is accomplished and the fire of life
is dying down, what is to be done with the money? If, as
is most likely, this monument is a fairly correct likeness
of Sir Hugh, he must have been inches over six feet in
height. The grim old warrior lies with his hands joined
in prayer. The hands are immense, with bony knuckles,
white and rigid with hard gripping of sword-hilt or
battle-axe. The big jaw shows protuberant through
the camaille's links, and the moustache curls over it.
The nose is broken; perhaps it was broken in life.
The jewelled armour, harness, and trappings are beautifully chiselled in the marble. The surcoat is emblazoned
with calves, and the monument is in fairly good preservation, though the colouring and gilding, with some of

the embellishments, are gone.   It must have been a
wondrous work of art when perfect some five hundred
years ago, and a special sermon might here be preached
on *sic transit*, for pieces of this precious alabaster have
been chipped off and stolen, pieces even of the sword
were ground down to powder to make a holy charm and
cure foot-rot in sheep!. There is another costly monument, burdened with Latin inscriptions and shields of
quarterings, of one of the last Beestons of Beeston, who
died at the age of 102, and who in his day had given
his little help in the greatest sea-fight of all time, when
the English terriers worried the Invincible Armada of
Spain, till the storms arose which shattered it.

In a much more humble grave in the churchyard is
the author of " Providence Improved." He was a native
of the village, and, as his tombstone says, "a painefull
schoole Mr. and a godlie minister." His troubles with
the Quakers who came to argue with him when he was
preaching are amusing to read, for he called them a
giddy sect, and spake hard things of them, but the
history of his times and place is very painstaking, and
therefore valuable.

It was noon when we left Bunbury's beautiful church,
and all the morning I had hoped that we should have
our midday meal on Beeston's "castled crag." So
thither we wended our way and stabled our steeds (alias
bicycles) within the outer gateway of the castle. On
the very top of the rock there is a famous well, but the
attendant says we cannot draw the water, and it is
bad, and there is none, and he sells aerated waters.
These gassy aerated waters remind me of one of the
dark questions in Job: "Why should a wise man fill
his belly with the east wind?" X says that all his doctors
strongly recommend them, and he enjoys them with
cheese and parkin, leaving his half-loaf of bread on the
rocks. He gives me a bit of his two pounds of parkin,
and it seems to consist of lumps of raw oatmeal in black

treacle. I think of the colouring matter from the feet of the niggers of Barbadoes who trod out the sugar-cane and made the treacle black, and throw my piece to the jackdaws. I decline his soda-water, saying I have no doctors and am content with my chawl, and under the shadow of a great rock I go to sleep. Then mine own familiar friend whom I trusted took advantage of me while I slept and photographed me. But I also took a grand photograph of him when he stood on the brink of the precipice with a sheer descent of probably two hundred feet to a farmhouse straight down below him. It is now reproduced to form the frontispiece of this book, but at the time I labelled it "Earl Randle watching the invasion of the Welsh under Llewelyn, or Owen Glyndwr, or some of the tribe of Jones." For X prides himself on his descent from the robbers who built the castle, and the doomed race ("doomed" is the word) is nearly extinct.

As I have elsewhere written some notes on the history of Beeston Castle, it must suffice here to say that from the days when the Crusaders planned these towers and battlements on the model of Byzantium or Constantinople, until the day when Cromwell shattered dungeon and keep and barbican in dust, its history is interesting, and to-day the ruined fortress, the towering isolated crag rising so abruptly from the fertile fields of Cheshire, is most eloquent of other times and other manners.

Here are two bits of English history worth noting together. At Beeston Hall near to the castle, in the Civil War, Prince Rupert, the nephew of the king, the dashing cavalry general, rested and dined, and then burnt the house and its contents, hanging about a dozen simple countrymen who were not quick enough in obeying his commands. To-day there is in Germany another Prince Rupert, a lineal descendant of the king, who should to-day be sitting on the throne of England if

B

kings ruled by right divine, or Conservatism was to continue unchecked.

One bit of life conjured up most vividly the mediæval joys of the chase, for a heron came flapping past with its long legs stretched past its tail, and so near that I could see its eye; and oh! to have seen the dash of a peregrine falcon in pursuit. The picturesque and delightful hawking parties of old are gone with the mailed knights in glittering armour, with fluttering crests and pennons. Instead of them a tourist in fancy flannels comes to me and says he has known me for years and will show me Woolton Hill, near Liverpool, and the iron tower at New Brighton, which he says is the tallest structure in England. He seemed to be one of those townsfolk in Liverpool who look upon New Brighton as one of the foretastes of Paradise. I did not swear, but I looked the other way. Over the Eternal City, with the square grey tower of Saint Werburgh's Abbey, beyond the woods of Hawarden, there rose tier upon tier of the mountains of Wales stretching to the west and south farther than human eye could see—a wondrous vision of an enchanting land.

Dreams are sweet, but life is short, and we were fully thirty miles from home. Again we "wenden on our pilgrimage." Through Tarporley town. There was no time to stop, no time to see the church, for had we not that morning seen the noble churches of Nantwich, Acton, and Bunbury? Our next object must be the historical Hall of Utkynton. The ways were steep, the wind was strong, the sun was hot. If we did have to go down hill a notice-board was generally there to tell us it was dangerous. X said we were always going up hill, and the wind was always against us, and it affected his chest. I told him it was the three bottles of soda water with the pound and a half of parkin and the cheese that he had had at Beeston that were on his chest. If he had had some good fat bacon he would have been lubricated inside and out like a well-oiled machine. We struggle on up these sandy forest lanes in glorious air and scenery. We wonder whether tea can be "begged, bought, or stolen" at Utkynton. When we get up to the old place we find only an unprotected female in possession; all who can be spared are in the hayfield, for it is the sixteenth of July and a glorious hay-day. We see the rare curiosity

OAKEN PILLAR IN CENTRE OF UTKYNTON HALL

nowadays, a big oak tree, in the hall or house-place, that supports the house, though we do not like to ask to see above how its branches support the roof. The chapel, we are told, is used as a cheese-room, and we wonder which use is the best—this or that. There is good old furniture and mullioned windows, and terraced gardens. X again assures me that it is just the very place he wants to live at. Those terraced gardens sloping steeply down the valley, with the pleasant forest hills beyond, open to the sun and sky, should still be very beautiful. There is the ancient sun-dial, and the tiny low-walled garden close to the hall, where my lady doubtless kept her pet flowers and fragrant herbs, the little plot she called her very own, from which she gave her bosom friends a nosegay—rosemary, that's for remembrance ; pansies, that's for thoughts ; the violets withered when father died—gillyflowers, lilies, carnations, lavender, sweet marjoram, tansy, lad's love, and balm.

Long after the glory had departed from Utkynton there was a good collection of armorial bearings on stained glass, which are now preserved at Vale Royal, and Earl Randle's horn, the badge of the forester's office, so long held by the Dones, is probably held by the Earl of Haddington, the present chief forester. The house was plundered in the Civil Wars by the ferocious royalists, and some treasure was hidden in the forest, which tradition says has never been found. If some reader of these lines be in haste to be rich, let him go to Delamere and dig in the forest for this long-lost treasure. It will pay him better in health and pocket than backing horses.

The ancient family of Dones, hereditary Foresters of Delamere, were necessarily a rough and quarrelsome breed. They had power of life and death in the forest, or if they had not legally full power, they were not within taking it. There are documents now at Chester showing how they hanged or beheaded men first and justified the deed after. Payment of a fine would commute many sins. The savage forest laws made their hand against every common man, and every common man's hand against them. At the battle of Blore Heath they, with their relatives and retainers, fell wholesale, and their power was weakened. Their crest of arrows, or shield of arms with arrows on a bend, with the family

motto, "Omnia mei Dona Dei," may still be seen on many
a sculptured stone or painted window. The biggest
rogues generally take the most religious mottoes. We
lately saw how Sir Piers Dutton robbed the religious
houses and charities, and from their spoils built Dutton
Hall, inscribing over its portals his name, with the pious
phrase, "Who thanketh God of all." The Dones, the
tyrants of the forest, the wild country extending for
many miles in Cheshire, the stern, fierce foresters who
would hang a man and seize his goods if he infringed
their forest laws, took for their motto, "Omnia mei
Dona Dei" (All that is mine is the gift of God).

The waifs and strays in the forest were seized, and
even the poor herdsmen's swarms of bees. When seiz-
ing goods the foresters would probably lapse into the
vulgar tongue and render the motto of their master's
house—"Them's mine, we'n Done 'em." They claimed
the right shoulder of every deer killed in the forest, and
the right to search any man's house or oven in quest
of venison. If any were found, the forester got the
man's best beast, and everything else was confiscated
to his lord, the Earl of Chester. What a nice chance
it would be for the ancestors of our hard-swearing police
to show their intelligence by swearing that mutton was
venison if it had a little nice currant jelly to it. It would
be almost necessary to taste, and if it all disappeared
they could swear to anything. It is worth noting how
all that was most valuable then is worth little now.
Even two hundred years ago coal could not be gotten
in all the forest district; therefore turbary was valuable.
Foreign feeding-stuffs were unknown; therefore pannage was wanted for fat bacon. Sugar was very scarce;
therefore honey was prized and bees-wax useful. The
right of puture, or the temporary boarding of agents of
the lord at the house of a tenant, is not quite extinct
even now, for I know of a place where it is regularly
observed.

The derivation of the name Done is an interesting puzzle, for the natives pronounce the word with the *o* long, and it was formerly often spelt Donne.   It would not be from *down* or *doune*, for Downes is another common Cheshire name.   It may be from the word *done*, as one would say, " He's done him."   There was a poet in the family once, and when his father, who was an old man, said, " Sam, thou'st 'ad a good schoolin', better till me ; canst oo mak me some varses for my greve, for I shanner last much longer."   Sam seemed pleased with his expectations, and sat up all night at the job so as not to keep his father waiting. Then he produced the following lines, the first two of which rhyme when spoken by the natives :—

> " Here lies Samuel Done,
>   Who is very well known,
>   So there needs be no flam ;
>   He's a plague to his wife
>   All the days of her life,
>   And a rogue to his poor son Sam."

The father looked for the poker, while the son sidled towards the door, doubtless thinking he had better get on with his work : and so had we with ours.

There was no tea to be gotten at Utkynton, but at the little hamlet of Cote Brook we found a good Samaritan who made us tea, with fresh eggs and pre-serve, and then charged one shilling.   We each gave her a shilling, but she brought sixpence each back, saying she meant one shilling for the two, which she said was quite enough, and she refused to take more, apparently thinking that we were making fun of her, which certainly was not the case.   The fun was between ourselves, for I poured out the tea, and as I like mine in about equal proportions of tea, sugar, and cream, I was treating X to the same mixture.   He was horrified, for his doctors had persuaded him that sugar would be

dreadful for him, and he must not touch a single piece.
I refrained from further allusions to the pound and a
half of parkin and the cheese and the soda-water, but
could not help reminding him of the epitaph in country
churchyards :—

> " Physicians sore
> Long time he bore."

That was the first of the afternoon teas that were in the
future to be such important additions to our pleasure,
and yet often so difficult to get.

From Cote Brook we journeyed on to Little Budworth, passing through another glorious bit of "the
forest primeval," where the sinking sun lit up the ruddy
boughs of the fir trees and the feathery twigs of the
birch, where the sandy ground was covered with bracken
and bramble, and rolling on in contentment unalloyed
we gradually gained our home and rest.

THE FOREST

THE GROSVENORS — ALDFORD — FARNDON—HOLT—MALPAS

MALPAS, the birthplace of the author of the well-known hymn—

"From Greenland's icy mountains,
From India's coral strand,"

was the goal of our pilgrimage on the sixth of August, and by an early train to Chester we landed at the ancient city shortly after nine o'clock, in dull and gloomy weather. A farmer had journeyed with us during the latter part of the ride, and as I have more faith in the weather forecasts of an old farmer, or even of an old farmyard pig, than in the so-called scientific reports, we asked his opinion, and were told that "it 'ud be main fair while dinner time," but he would doubt it after. As the oracle had spoken our next uncertainty was as to when was dinner-time, and it was obviously better for us to put off dinner until our journey was done, and then let it rain as much as it liked.

After a hurried visit to the Cathedral, with glimpses of the Norman work and carving of the old Abbey, X had to find a confectioner from whom he could buy cakes, for he had again played the part of the foolish virgin and come without oil; that is, he may have had oil for his lamp, but he had none for his body, and the fat bacon sandwich to supply the oil for the body was almost necessary when no one knew where we might get to after seeing Malpas.

Through the streets of Chester we follow the tram lines over the Dee and up to the gates of Eaton.

Through the park we go as if we own it. We come
to a richly ornamented lodge covered with sculptured
shields, the armorial ensigns of the ancestors of the
Grosvenors. It is new, staring, and glaring, "the boast
of heraldry, the pomp of power." We pass other lodges,
or gentlemen servants' houses, horses, deer, cattle, and
pheasants. At a gigantic obelisk we turn and go
straight for the golden gates that might fly open for us
if we were millionaires, but as we are only cyclists they
do not move, and we have to shy off to the right and
merely catch a glimpse of the colossal statue of Hugh
Lupus, that is, Hugh fitly named the Wolf, the first
Norman Earl of Chester. He is on his heavy war-horse
with his falcon on his fist, and X says that although he
(X) is only riding a bicycle he is a descendant of Hugh
Lupus as much as the Duke himself is. "If this," I
say, "is another of the estates that should have come to
you, let us go and claim it now we are here; we might
get some lunch." He says he does not want it. It is
too grand for him. His father often stayed there as a
guest, but he prefers some old manor-house with many
corners and big chimneys, with perhaps a moat, and certainly a ghost. Oh yes, a good ghost is worth a deal
of money. Who cares to dwell in marble halls, with all
the bother of vassals and serfs? Give me the lowly old
parsonage, with the roses and the jessamine looking in
at the windows, and above all the charm and the peace
of home. Our talk glides on from ghosts and heraldry
to horses, for are we not passing the home of Bend Or?
There are millions who have heard of Bend Or, many
of whom would sooner see him than anything else the
proud halls of Eaton could show, even including the
owner thereof. His name is a mystery to most of them;
therefore here followeth a short account of its origin.

In 1386 there began a great trial which lasted three
years, and in which three hundred of the earls, abbots,
and lords of England took part. A Sir Robert Grosvenor of Hulme was sheriff of Cheshire. He had mar-

ried an heiress, as the Grosvenors often did. It was long before they married the Eaton property, and centuries before they married Westminster and gave their name as descendants of the Belgreaves to the aristocratic suburb of Belgravia. Sir Robert had for his coat of arms a shield—"d'azure oue une bend d'or," that is to say, a blue shield with a bend of gold. The bend or band of gold was like a broad golden ribbon one might wear athwart one's breast. Sir Richard le Scroope said those were his arms, and therefore that Sir Robert Grosvenor was (to use a Manchester term) infringing his trade-mark. There was any amount of hard swearing in the case. Even the Abbot of Vale Royal swore to what he could not possibly know and what was certainly untrue, for he swore that the Grosvenors came in at the Conquest bearing those arms, although armorial bearings were not then known. The other side swore the Grosvenors were never heard of until quite recent times and had appropriated their mark. Chaucer the poet, the patron saint of pilgrims, was on their side—let us note that—and they won. The Grosvenors were told they must show the difference on their shield by having "a bordure d'argent," or border of silver, which they declined. So they had to give up the Bend Or.

Now, in 1877, it came to pass that Sir Hugh Lupus Grosvenor, first Duke of Westminster, had a very promising racing colt to which he wished to give some distinctive name; and mindful of his ancestor's trial he gave it what might have been the unlucky name of Bend Or, a name the British public could not understand, and they promptly corrupted it into Ben Door, for they would "back Ben with Archer up" to any amount. Aided by all that wealth and skill and Archer's jockeyship could do, the colt won all before it, though many good judges considered its rival, Robert the Devil, to be a better horse. Bend Or transmitted its good qualities in a still greater degree to its son Ormonde, a horse I made a special pilgrimage to see before it went to South America, for by many racing men it was said to be the best horse ever foaled.

The name of Grosvenor itself has a complicated history, for discarding the tales told at the trial about the arms, which tales it is evident were not believed at that time, there is, according to Ormerod, no contemporary record of anything more like the name than Venator (*i.e.* Hunter), until in 1234 the deed of purchase of Hulme (Peover) recites that Gralam de Lostock conceded or sold Hulme to " Richardo filio Ranulphi Grossovenatoris," that is, to Richard the son of Ranulph

HULME HALL MOAT

Grossovenator, apparently the Latinised form of a surname which ultimately became Grosvenor and apparently was derived from a nickname, as so many surnames were derived in those days, the nickname meaning the gross or fat venator or hunter. One hundred and fifty-two years had rolled away between the purchase of Hulme and the trial about the right to the arms, and the family of Grosvenors had got on in the world. There is still a perfect moat at Hulme, with a beautiful stone bridge, and an old hall containing parts of another much older, with immense oaken arches and

beams.   It lies away in the fields, two miles from everywhere, for I made another pilgrimage to find and see
it before I wrote these lines.   It has long since ceased
to be owned by the Grosvenors, though one would have
thought that some of their wealth might be well ex-
pended in maintaining the moated hall, the first landed
estate connected with their name in Cheshire, as a model
ancient hall.   More than five hundred years have gone
since their trial, and the latest augmentation to the
emblazoned shield of the now ducal house of Westminster is the cognisance of the Confessor, one who
lived long enough ago to be accounted in England both
king and saint.

Can anything be more delightful than gliding through
a well-kept park, on a fine summer's day, with good
company, conversing of an historic and romantic past?
Our latest improvement on the doings of our ancestors
has been to discard horses.   Though we have ridden
scores of thousands of miles on them, we now look upon
them as a primitive and somewhat barbarous means of
travelling.   Hugh Lupus encased himself in iron and
terribly overburdened some poor beast of his day.   His
descendant who is with me has his iron made into a
bicycle, and rides comfortably upon that.   What a job
it would have been to have got Hugh Lupus with his
horse and armour across the Dee! but we merely trundle
our bikes over some more iron called the Ironbridge,
and, glancing at the Elysian fields of the boating parties,
we roll on again towards Aldford, the old ford.

Here are remains of a castle, and an old church
"restored" until, to use a vulgar phrase, it looks as if it
"stunk of brass."   A gaudy church, with polished granite
columns instead of the massive Norman, Early English,
or Decorated Gothic that most probably beautified the
original simple village church.   There seems to be
nothing old left about it excepting the remains of the
ancient preaching cross and a mutilated recumbent statue
lying in the grass—some one on whose form and features

the family or friends wished to confer immortality, and now the well-worn effigy is trampled on by village children in hob-nailed boots, and they put pebbles on the eyes, and where the arms are still meekly folded across the breast. It may be the memorial of some pilgrim who was on the land before even the Grosvenors were heard of, for if tradition had connected it with them it would be deemed almost worthy of worship. We sit on the steps of the cross in the hollows made by the knees of the pilgrims of centuries ago ; for these topmost steps are worn in the middle, not at the edge. There we sit and rest, and moralise, and eat gooseberries.

This manor of Aldford has had its chequered history. It was owned and forfeited by the young Brereton upon whom Anne Boleyn smiled, and that was too much for his head, for he lost it in more ways than one. The estate was given and forfeited, and given and forfeited, for the kings and queens of England then played with their subjects as cats play with mice, and each petty lordling copied his overlord. In this manor they claimed the special privileges of free duel and the ordeal by fire and by water. That is to say, if one man accused another of any crime, the accused could challenge him to single combat and fight it out. If man or woman were accused of having too much knowledge, or of witchcraft, there was the simple and ready ordeal by fire or by water. If by fire, it was tried if the man's flesh would burn, and if it would burn he was innocent ; but if not, he was guilty and must be stoned or pressed to death. If some poor old woman were accused of being a witch, or of overlooking some neighbour's cattle, or of casting an evil eye, or of muttering, she could easily be tried by water in the nearest pit. Her thumbs and big toes were tied together, and she was " chucked i' th' pit." If she sank she was innocent, but if she did not sink quickly or struggled much she was certainly guilty and must be killed at once as a warning to others not to look sly or to mutter. What wonderful things

our ancestors did, and not very long ago! A few
generations have been brought in their turn and laid
under the sod, and now we are quite surprised at them.
They ought to have known better, and we are so
superior. But our gooseberries are all done, and we
must get on.

From Aldford we journey on to Farndon, another
ancient place at which to cross the river. The name
was probably Ferry Town originally, for the oldest
spellings give it Ferenton—the local pronunciation
seems more like Fern. The long and beautiful bridge
across the river is the great feature of the place, and on
the opposite side is the Welsh town of Holt, an English
name meaning a hold or stronghold. There have been
centuries of feuds between the rival towns, and even
now I thought there was a Welsh accent in the speech
of those across the border.

We visit the church at Farndon, and find it open,
beautiful, and interesting. There is a notice-board
describing one old monument that had been dug up
after long burial, and saying there were two others
of similar date, but they had been broken up a few
years since to mend the roads with the bits. There
is an exceptionally beautiful stained-glass window
with portraits of the officers and typical men in the
various branches of the Royalist army at the siege of
Chester in the Civil War. Their arms and accoutre-
ments are minutely given, and are therefore most
valuable to show the costumes of the period. The
wonderful boots of the officers are worth special notice.
They are light yellow, and wide enough at the top to
hold a peck of apples round the calf of the leg. They
were probably the ancestors of the modern top-boots,
having their tops turned inside outwards. Over them
falls fancy lace, and all the colours of the rainbow seem
to be in the gentlemen's sashes. The breeches are
gorgeous, the feathers in the hats prodigious, and the
long hair of the cavaliers falls over their shoulders. In

the top corner of each little portrait picture is the totem,
or shield of arms, to testify to their respectability and
to show the illiterate who they were.

A rather good satire was here unconsciously perpetrated between us. X called to me from one aisle of
the church, "Here is another of your relations," and I
—mindful of having too many poor relations—said,

FARNDON BRIDGE

"Has he any brass?" The very suitable answer was,
"That's just what he has. He's all brass. Nothing
but brass." For behold, it was merely a brass tablet—
another memorial to one of the great clan of the Fletchers
whose pilgrimage was finished and whose record was
written on brass. There may be some readers who do
not know the meaning of the word Fletcher, and others
who do not consider the important work of these
fletchers in the history of England during centuries of

warfare.   The fletchers were the fledgers or featherers
of arrows, the important part of arrow-making, and
it was the Cheshire arrows that decided the battles
of Flodden, Crecy, Poictiers, Agincourt, and others.
Therefore the fletchers were workmen of the highest
skill, who largely contributed to the success of Cheshire.

From Farndon Church we walk down the steep
slope to the bridge and up again to Holt Church,
another fine old building, undergoing the too frequent
alterations or repairs.   I ask for Cornish Hall, a place
from whence many tons of cheese have come to Manchester.   As it is only a mile or so on the road towards
Wrexham, we are soon bowling there, and find a fine
old Jacobean house with many gables, good oak staircase, and remnants of a moat.   We are told that Queen
Elizabeth and Oliver Cromwell have slept in the house.
This does not mean that they slept there together, for,
of course, the queen would be there first.   Any other
arrangement would be very shocking.   The Sovereign
is the Lord or Lady of the Manor, and there used to
be a mayor and corporation.   The district is called the
Royal Vale and the most important produce of it is
strawberries, for which this time we are too late.

The master is not at home, so we return to Holt
and sit on the parapet of the bridge and have our
lunch.   It must not be called dinner, for the farmer
feared rain at dinner time and the weather continues
gloomy.   The scene is very beautiful and tranquil, with
the rival towers and churches on either hand, the clear
water of the river flowing under the arches, the distant
hills and woods, the waterfowl, the fishermen, and the
cattle in the water.   The stone seats are rather hard,
and we might fall backward into the river, but it is all
very pleasant, and we enjoy our chawl sandwich.   A
drove of pigs comes past.   They are unconscious that
we are eating one of their relations.   They seem to be
like ourselves and want something to eat.   They are
evidently intent on that above all things.   Ignorance

with them is bliss, or they might be thinking that the greatest happiness the future has in store for them is that they may fatten quickly and be well cured, so that civilised man who likes to eat the flesh of dead pigs can have some good fat bacon. X says if I talk such stuff he will have no more of the sandwiches ; for he was nurtured delicately, whilst I was reared as my fathers were.

He goes below to where a man was fishing, and photographs him and me as I sit at lunch on the parapet of the bridge wondering whether I should fall into the water.

The church clock strikes one, and even our long day is flying ; so off we go for Malpas. The name of the place is said to be derived from the Latin, which is very unusual. It signifies the bad pass, and the original name had a similar meaning. The pronunciation is Maupas, as

MALPAS
The black speck near to the gig is a kitten that
was nearly run over

the Cheshire men pronounce *l* as *u*. The church is a grand specimen of the pre-Reformation churches. Just inside the doorway is a wonderfully fine oaken chest, covered with gracefully flowing ironwork. It is difficult to tell which is iron and which is oak, for they almost seem to have grown together. It is said to date from the twelfth century or thereabouts, and to have been made to hold " Peter's pence." It would certainly hold bushels of pence, enough to satisfy any reasonable Peter, if any one ever is satisfied with riches. In the crypt below the altar there is another

C

old chest of similar size, which is said to have been a coffin. It appears to have been a "dug-out,'" that is, simply the trunk of an oak tree hollowed out. It has apparently outlasted even the bones of the body that was buried in it. Perhaps the bones have been long since scattered on the earth to enrich the grass and fatten the cheese. The little secret stairway to the crypt is interesting, and the oaken roof of the nave is grand. Is there skill enough in the present day to do such work for love or money?

The east window is in memory of Reginald Heber, Bishop of Calcutta, who is best known as the writer of the hymn "From Greenland's icy mountains." He was born in the higher rectory here, his father being one of the rectors. From time immemorial Malpas was blessed or otherwise by having two rectors at once, but the parish is now subdivided. The old stained glass that used to be in the east window, dated 1596, and signed Jacob Harmansz, was knocking about as lumber for some time, and is now in the west window of the north aisle. Some of it was stolen recently. X knows a man who has some, but it is customary to lay all similar charges to Cromwell or the Puritans.

Here is a note about longevity connecting recent times with the Civil War. A man named Povey, aged ninety-four, was buried at Malpas in 1723. When young he was in the service of the Viscount Cholmondeley, and had helped to bury the silver plate and money under the gravel walks or in the pits at Bickley Hall when the Puritan soldiers were expected. Long afterwards the plate was safe but not the money, though no one knew who took it. When very old Povey married again, and had a daughter who lived to over eighty. She was naturally fond of repeating what her father had told her as to what he had seen and done in the troublous times of one hundred and fifty years before.

The registers of Malpas tell a sad tale of the plague that was once rife in Cheshire. At Didsbury they buried

about a dozen Blomeleys with others " ex pestilentia
eodem morbe eodem die eodem sepulchre," meaning
that several had the same disease, the same day, the
same grave.   At Malpas a large family named Dawson
were all swept away.   A brother named Richard, being
left "sicke of ye plague and prceyving he must die
at yt time, arose out of his bed and made his grave

PETER'S PENCE CHEST, MALPAS

and cast strawe into it . . . and went and layd him
down in ye. sayd grave, and caused clothes to be layd
uppon him, and so departed out of this world : this
he did because he was a strong man and heavier than
his nefew and another wench were able to bury.   Then
ye nefew John . . . haveyng layd him down in a dich
died in it yt nyht.   Then Rose, ye servant, ye last

of yt household, died also." A woman named Mawde Clutton died, and afterwards her child died also. The entry relating to it ends, "Its aunt and another wench buried it. Nihil pro eccl'ia." What? "Nothing for the church." Two rectors, with probably as many curates and half-a-dozen churchwardens and officials, and nothing for any of the idle lot. They evidently felt wronged at getting nothing for nothing and neglecting their duty. "Its aunt and another wench buried" the poor little plague-stricken orphan, did they, and the "ecclesiastics" stood idly by? Wherever could the poor thing hope to go to?

Adjoining the churchyard is the site of the castle, the first church having probably been within the castle walls. The sexton tells us the place is now only used for dancing! Longfellow should have known of this when he wrote the charming poem of "The Norman Baron":—

> "In his chamber, weak and dying,
>   Was the Norman Baron lying:
>   Loud, without, the tempest thundered,
>   And the castle turret shook.
>   *   *   *   *   *
>   In the hall the serf and vassal
>   Held that night their Christmas wassail;
>   Many a carol old and saintly,
>   Sang the minstrels and the waits.
>   *   *   *   *   *
>   Tears upon his eyelids glistened,
>   As he paused awhile and listened,
>   And the dying Baron slowly
>   Turned his weary head to hear.
>   *   *   *   *   *
>   All the pomp of earth had vanished,
>   Falsehood and deceit were banished,
>   Reason spake more loud than passion,
>   And the truth wore no disguise."

That Baron freed his vassals and villeins when he could no longer keep them, when all earthly things were slipping from his grasp for ever. The Barons de Malpas never freed theirs. But through centuries of struggling they freed themselves, and now they vote by ballot—another dreadful innovation. The grass-grown site of the dungeon and castle of the Norman Baron is reserved as a place on which the village maidens may dance and play. What a great fact! Is it something towards the fulfilment of the famous vision when the swords are to be beaten into plowshares? The mighty are indeed fallen, for under our feet is the dust of generations of both lords and slaves, and of the castle itself we do not see one stone left standing upon another.

These Barons de Malpas were a bad breed. The first was a bastard son of Hugh the Wolf, and great-nephew to the bastard king. History gives few examples of greater thieves or greater tyrants. The proudest of our nobility are proud of inheriting their virtues and estates. After centuries of improvement in Christianity and civilisation, these Barons de Malpas claimed the right of presenting the heads of accused persons for judgment at Chester Castle. That is to say, they cut off their victims' heads first and asked for justice afterwards, doing in grim earnest to obnoxious persons what the clown in the pantomime does in mimicry when he cuts off a policeman's head and says, "Oh, I beg your pardon!"

But the long summer's day is too short for all these memories. We want our tea, and we shall have to get home, and it begins to rain. We find a place for tea, and the rain, as if mindful of the farmer's words, falls heavily. A local paper shows us that a train will soon leave Malpas station for Chester. The station is more than a mile from the town, and the train should leave in five minutes. The tea is not ready, the weather looks worse, so we fly without tea, for which we pay half-price. The train, of course, is late, and we get to Chester just in time to miss a train for Manchester. We find there is another nearly due at Liverpool Road Station, so there we hurry. It is the first time we have seen this place, and we hope it is the last. The various platforms are down steep steps far from the offices. There is no one to tell us anything. A crowd of people stand in the wet, for there is scarcely any shelter. Everything is marked M. S. and L.—Muddled, Slow, and Lazy. We have to stand in torrents of rain, and the train is three-quarters of an hour late. The guard is labelled M. S. and L., and he acts up to his badge, for he almost refuses to let us lift our own bicycles into the van. At last we get off, and change carriages at Altringham. We are taken as far as Baguley and told to get out. Again we stand in the wet for about half-an-hour for an express that the porters say is coming every minute. We deplore our fate and resolve never to travel by the M. S. and L. Railway again.

Finally we land home in safety after a memorable and happy day. We had travelled over a hundred miles, about a third of the distance being on the cycles. The time taken had been exactly twelve hours, and in all that time neither of us had had one single drop to drink!

FARNDON BRIDGE

THE OLD HOME OF THE EGERTONS

ON September 17, 1898—one of the hottest days of the summer—we travelled by train to Whitchurch, intending to cycle down the valley of the Dee to Shocklach, and then find our way up the Broxton hills to Egerton, the lonely spot from whence numerous families of Egerton derived their name. At Whitchurch, or the "white church," we did not see anything particularly interesting, and had little time to stay. The church was entirely rebuilt nearly two hundred years since, and therefore the charm and grace of the old Gothic is gone. There are remains of an inscription round the doorstep, saying it was the burial-place of Talbot, the great Earl of Shrewsbury, but the inscription is nearly worn out, and we must leave it for another day. It is a pity a few shillings-worth of mats are not put for its better protection.

From the outskirts of the town we see the tower of Malpas church, four miles away, and as there does not seem to be any good road to our left we make for Malpas, intending to see more of that most interesting church, as on our former visit, it may be remembered, the rain came down heavily. After taking many photographs of Malpas we journey on to a place with the common name of Chorlton, and find our way in faith along lanes that twist and wind in every direction. At each lane end or corner we want to ask our way, and there is no one from whom to ask, unless it be a cow, or worse still a cow's husband. I do not like the latter gentry, for when a child I was always told that when

any one looked very cross they looked as "pleasant as
a cow's husband."

Through miles of lanes we roll along until we suddenly see a tiny church in a field, probably half a mile
from any house. Ormerod's "History" has a drawing
of the doorway, and says it is Saxon work. The church
is dedicated to St. Edith, a Saxon saint, for "Edith"
means "the blessed." Longfellow says :—

> " She who comes to me and pleadeth
> In the lovely name of Edith
> Will not fail in what is wanted.
> Edith means the blessed."

The church is on the Welsh border, remote from
everywhere, and we
are charmed with it,
and photograph it
all round. My anti-
quarian friends say
the round-headed
doorway, with zigzag
and coil, or rope or-
nament, is probably a
local or country form
of Norman. The
stones are square
and rough, with big
joints. The belfry
end is of later date,
for it has shields of
arms on it. The
arms appear to have
been a chevron be-

DOORWAY TO ST. EDITH'S, SHOCKLACH

tween three animals' heads, but they are almost obliter-
ated by the weather. If the arms are a chevron between
three bulls' heads, they are the arms of the Bulkeleys of
Bulkeley, a small neighbouring manor, from whence

the Bulkeleys of Cheadle Bulkeley came.   The chancel
end is later again, probably Decorated.   The whole
place is very primitive, reminding me of St. Tudno's
chapel on the Great Orme's Head.   The walls are very
thick, with castle-like windows and one bit of old glass.

We recline on an altar-tomb, and eat our lunch in
the most perfect summer's day and the most tranquil
pastoral scene it is possible to imagine.   It is noon, and
hot, and the stillness of autumn is coming on.   There is
no sound of bird or beast, and we rest and are thankful.

ST. EDITH'S, SHOCKLACH

The old custom of strewing the graves with rushes is
here observed.   There was once a castle near by, but it
is gone.   The name of the place is, perhaps, derived
from the slutch or mire, that may be very bad even now
in wet weather, for we must be near the river, and the
soil looks sticky.   I conclude, therefore, that the name
of the place is merely another form of " Such slutch," for
the Domesday spelling is Socheliche, and " Lache "
means slutch, or miry, heavy dirt.   It also interests me
to note that the names engraven on the tomb on which
we lie are Caldecots of Caldecot.   That is another form
of Coldcot, and thereby hangs a tale.

Exactly twenty years ago one of the principal pictures in the Christmas number of the *Graphic* was an old-fashioned hunting-party in front of a house, which I at once recognised to be Standon Hall, the place I have so often written about. Then I learnt that the artist was a young man in a bank at Whitchurch, named Randolph Caldecott, who was intimate with some of my cousins, and who had been to Standon and sketched the house. Shortly after I recognised, in his illustrations to Washington Irving's " Bracebridge Hall," the gates of Combermere Abbey, and found he had been to the house of another cousin, who was steward there. Then he became famous, and now his genius sheds interest on the place whence the Caldecotes or Caldecotts of Caldecott sprang.

There seems to be little there now beyond a rambling picturesque hall, and we journey on to the Cock at Barton. This is the model of a good old-fashioned inn. We ride into the yard, and enter by the back door into a kitchen—a large timber-framed thatched building, open to the roof, with a fireplace built round with bricks in the middle of the room. It is a good untouched specimen of the rough buildings of two or three centuries ago. Previously to the manufacture of bricks, which in country districts were not common until about two or three hundred years since, on account of the scarcity of fuel, there would have been no chimney. The smoke would have had to wind its way out of the room wherever and whenever it best could get out. The taproom is also quaint, with a heavy oaken beam over the ingle nook, on which are the arms of Leche of Carden. The parlour is filled with first-rate, genuine, old oaken furniture, which is quite a treat to see. There are prints of the first Lord Combermere, Sir Watkin, and others, who were old men when I was a lad. Of course we want tea, but there is no fire, for the day is very hot, and to save time we are content with our usual dose—a bottle

of soda-water for X and a pint of milk for self.   The
weary pilgrim is photographed in the ingle nook, but, as
he has no long churchwarden pipe, he lacks the solemn
pomposity and the sublime air of foolish dignity that
characterises churchwardens or councillors when they
take their ease in their inn.

A flight of rounded stone steps leads up to the front
door of the Cock at Barton, which both inside and outside is one of the nicest and most picturesque country

THE COCK, BARTON

inns any pilgrim could wish to find.   It must be owned
by some fine old county family who are in keeping with
the place ; otherwise they would have modernised it, or
built a staring ugly new thing, or sold it to a brewer.
As it is, it is a charming little roadside hostel, and the
owners are the Leches of Carden, whose large rambling
black-and-white house we soon see in a beautiful park
on the lower slope of the Broxton hills.   The house
stood the usual siege in the Civil War, and has long
been owned by the Leche family, the first of whom was

a leech or surgeon to King Edward the Third, who
retired on an annuity or rent on the mills on the Dee.
He was probably a leech only in name, and gave the
king nothing but advice, keeping his blood-sucking
stock-in-trade safe in a bottle, for both he and the king,
his patient, lived to be old men.　Carden, Cawarthyn,
Kaurthyn, or Cawarden, is spelt in many ways.　The
last looks like Hawarden, which is not very far away,
but spell it as you like if you will but see and admire
the country.

We trundle up, up, up, in magnificent scenery, with
wonderful views behind us.　The hills, resplendent with
heather and bracken and gorse, are before us, and behind
us is Wales and the great vale of Chester.　X complains
of the wind always turning against us when we have to
trudge up hill.　I remind him that he generally complains of the wind going the wrong way when he has
had soda-water, but I cannot get him to take milk, and
he says I shall be wanting tea directly.　That is very
likely, but first let us find Bulkeley Hall, where the
Bulkeleys of Cheadle Bulkeley came from ; also Egerton
Hall and Chapel, for X numbers the ancient lords of all
these manors, including the original Egertons, among
his prolific ancestors, and he really and actually did
inherit the lordship of Cheadle Bulkeley.

We find Egerton Green a rambling district, too
aristocratic for cottages, shops, or public-houses.　The
difficulty is to find any one from whom to ask our way.
When we see some country folk, there is, I suddenly
find, danger of misunderstanding.　For when I ask for
an old chapel, they are for sending me to some barn
where Farmer So-and-so "makes prayers"; and some
of them know "nowt about ranters, or chapels ayther."
I ask for the nearest public-house, and they stare in
astonishment, and then chuckle with sad, derisive laughter, as if their heaven were very far away.

We tour on towards Cholmondeley Castle, and the

country becomes more aristocratic than ever.   Then we fortunately meet a smart young man, who seems to be an upper groom or footman from the castle, and he takes us to be gentlemen, and politely tells us all about the country.   He says that Egerton Hall and the old chapel are about a mile and a half down a lane, the first house in it; that Bulkeley Hall is in the opposite direction, and we had better go to the former, then come back to where we were, and go through the grounds of Cholmondeley Castle, past the castle and stables.

As prudent managers we must consider our means of retreat and our bread-basket.   Broxton is the nearest railway station, being about four miles away, but it is not on a main line.   Beeston Castle station is on a main line, but is six or seven miles off.   Nantwich and Whitchurch are farther again.   We decide to try and catch an express to Crewe from Beeston when we have done, and meanwhile we are reduced to our last apple, and are ravenously thirsty.   X asks me if I want tea.   I feel like Esau when he bartered for porridge, but although X's name is a translation of Jacob, he has no porridge to barter, except a porridge of ancestors, and they are no good to me.   I would rather have a good dish of tea than a field full of them.   The rabbits and squirrels are running about the road, and I remember that when at school we killed a squirrel with a stone, and ate the poor little innocent for supper, making its skin into a purse ready for money, if ever we had any.   These want catching and cooking, and we have no time or wish for the job.   Let us endure a bit longer and fly down that winding, rambling lane to Egerton Chapel, and see for ourselves from whence these Egertons came.

Tired and thirsty, we mounted our bicycles again, and bumped and jolted down the lane for a long mile, and then came to a sudden steep dip in the road and a corresponding ascent, on which was an ordinary-looking red-brick farmhouse that, to a practised eye, was evidently on the site of the place that we were in search of —the old home of the Egertons. The fold, or farm-yard, would be more than an acre, being plainly the courtyard of the old hall. On one side was a long range of shippons or cowhouses, and at the other side and end were remains of the moat, on which the geese were placidly floating. Beyond were fine old walnut trees, and in another corner, down by the moat, was a dilapi-dated ruin.

This ruin has been a good building of stone; it is now roofless and neglected, surrounded by overcrowded, straggling trees. When Ormerod wrote his "History" in 1814 he described this chapel as he saw it, and when he wrote his "Additions" in 1819 he mentions that it had then been repaired, and surrounded by a plantation. That was probably done through his notice of it. Then his reviser and enlarger, writing in 1884, does enlarge, and says, "Great care has been taken of it ever since." He evidently wrote to the parson or the steward for his history. There is no roof whatever to the chapel, though there are some old oak beams rotting on the floor. There are corbels projecting from the walls, as if there had been a low room underneath with a fireplace. The east window has been of three lights trefoil-headed. The date is said to be about 1360. The north doorway, of stone, is deeply recessed, with mouldings terminating in heads now much worn away. They may have been the likenesses of legendary saints or family heroes; their present use seems to be for the cart colts to rub their shaggy manes against. One end of the building is in danger of tumbling down, and the whole of it is most shamefully neglected. If most of the overcrowded trees that were planted in 1819 were cut down, the fabric made secure, ivy planted in places, and a small piece of the moat taken round the site so as to make it an island, the work need not cost more than one or two hundred pounds, and the place might be made a thing of beauty, a sacred shrine for the great family of Egerton, an historic spot for any of the name; for this is the old home of the race, and the house that was consecrated for and by their fathers' worship five hundred years ago, is roofless and desolate, a picture of the abomination of desolation.

Let it not be thought that the Egertons are poor. They have thousands of acres in these parts that are worth a hundred times what they were worth a hundred years ago. Land in this old parish of Didsbury that was worth £10 an acre will now sell readily at £1000 an acre, and of this increasing value there seems to be no end.

As one whose public duties bring him into continual conflict with agents who, with or without their overlord's consent, persistently obstruct sanitary regulations for the good of their tenants and neighbours, I have often wondered how it is, and why it is, that such great power for good or evil should be possessed by our landed aristocracy. The Egertons are among our richest land-owners. Let us see what is the meaning and derivation of their name. Whence first came the Egertons; or in the language of the old book, where is the rock from whence they were hewn, or the hole of the pit whence they were digged, and how has their enormous wealth been gotten?

Egerton is a small manor and township in South Cheshire, adjacent to two other small manors, Great and Little Edge; and the simplest, and therefore the most probable derivation of the word is that some wandering pastoral Anglo-Saxons fenced their huts round, and called the place Eggeton, or the town on the Edge, the Edge being a ridge or hill, and spelt in olden times Egge. When it became customary to have two names, custom gave the name of a place to the owner of the place, and in 1295 the Sheriff of Cheshire was a Philip de Eggerton, the first historic person of the name. According to the pedigrees as published, which are

doubtless true in later times but fictitious in earlier
times, there has never ceased for six hundred years
to be an unbroken, lineal, legitimate, male descent of
Eggertons or Egertons of Egerton, most of whom have
been christened Philip, down to the present Sir Philip
Egerton, of Egerton and Oulton. This unbroken descent
is more remarkable than it may appear to those who
are not acquainted with genealogy. For several of our
county families bear historic names, when they have not
in their veins one drop of the blood of that historic
family whose name they "assumed" when they "dropped"
into their estates. Another and elder branch of the
Egertons ended in the male line with the first Earl of
Wilton, who died in 1814, leaving only a daughter,
upon whose issue the earldom devolved. The Egerton-
Warburtons of Arley are also of unbroken male descent,
for when a younger son of the Egertons married the
heiress of the Warburtons, he and his descendants used
the double name.

Of far more importance have been the younger
branches of this family through an illegitimate line.
In the reign of Henry the Eighth a son of Eggerton
of Eggerton went to the wars, for this family has produced many a soldier and many a priest. His grandfather, John, had fallen at Blore Heath. He was named
Ralph, or Rauffe, as it is still written in the remains of
his sumptuous oratory at Bunbury, and those who wish
to know how to pronounce the name Ralph may learn
thereby. For capturing the French standard at Tournay
Ralph Egerton was made standard-bearer of England,
and endowed with the Ridley estates of Sir Edward
Stanley of Holt, whose treachery had won the battle
of Bosworth for Henry the Seventh, and whose reward
was confiscation and death from the mean miser whom he
had helped to the throne of the "crooked Boar." Ralph
Egerton, like Sir Hugh Calveley, lavished the spoils of
France on the church of Bunbury, for all that art and

skill could do in architecture, carving in wood or stone, painting on stone or wood or glass, was done to beautify the Egerton Chapel, and though the vandalism of later times has swept most of it away to make room for an organ, there are remnants left to please those who are pleased with beautiful things, and to make us wonder at the art of our half-civilised forefathers.   The tomb of

the founder is gone, but on the wall is a brass depicting a knight on his knees with a standard, and from his mouth issues a scroll with three short words something like "Firm, Fast, Finem," meaning, of course, firm to to the end.   I forget the exact words, forget even whether they are Norman-French or Latin, for in these accounts I trust to my memory, helping it with Ormerod's "History," and some-

CURIOUS CARVED DOOR TO EGERTON CHAPEL, BUNBURY

times they both fail me.   On every coign of vantage amidst the relics of carved work is painted the pheon, or arrow-head, the ancient badge of the Egertons, which on their shield of arms now shows the difference of their lion rampant from the lions rampant of other folks.   For there is no commoner crest or arms than this fearful wildfowl, and none more appropriate to the rampant orator of a council, or the fiery politics of a rabid Tory, when he jumps on his feet to wave his fists and roar.

Sir Ralph Egerton charged one-third of his estate to

D

build and maintain his splendid chapel, and to build
houses for two "honest and virtuous preests," who were
to pray for his soul and for the souls of all his kith and
kin for ever, with sundry charities.   If those who got
the estates did not find the honest and virtuous priests
to do the praying, they might have maintained the
chapel for the prayers or meditations of others.   His
wishes were soon despised, and little remains but bits
of stained glass, painted sculptured stone, and carved
oak.   His son had an illegitimate son, who was educated as a lawyer, made chapter clerk of Chester,
knight of the shire, and finally Lord Chancellor of
England.   In his days Cheshire was rent in pieces,
and he seems to have picked up a good many of the
pieces.   At the confiscation of the religious houses
many of their spoils were given as an endowment to the
cathedral of Chester.   But, unfortunately, and whether
by accident or design it is not known, the word
"Chester" was omitted from the charter at the chief
point in the clause reciting the gift.   This flaw becoming known, presumably through those who should have
concealed it, for the ex-chapter clerk appeared as counsel
for the opponents, many long years of litigation followed,
for neighbouring landowners grabbed the endowed lands,
and finally, after bribing Queen Elizabeth's favourite,
the Earl of Leicester, her "Sweet Robin," to act as
receiver, they got them subject to a small chief rent.
In those troublous times the value of the rich lands of
Cheshire was depreciated almost to nothing, from the
repugnance many had from trafficking in land stolen
from the old religious houses, or wrung from the new,
reformed, and Protestant Church in her direst hour of
need, and from the general insecurity of tenure.   The
Lord High Chancellor invested largely, for who would
be likely to dispute titles with him?   And with the
tenacity of his race he stuck to the land.

Fifth in descent from him came the great Duke of

Bridgewater, the father of inland navigation, who enriched his country as well as himself by his great canal.   He was the last in direct male line, the subsequent Earls of Ellesmere having taken the name of Egerton when inheriting through the sister of the great Duke.   Another

EGERTON CHAPEL, EGERTON HALL

branch of the family was settled at Tatton, for the last Brereton of Tatton had left his estates to his half brother-in-law, the Chancellor, and again the male line ended in the fifth in descent, Samuel Egerton of Tatton, who also left his estates to his sister, who was the widow of Tatton of Wythenshawe.   She and her children took the name of Egerton, and from the eldest son is descended Earl

Egerton of Tatton, while the descendants of a younger son retook their proper name of Tatton of Wythenshawe.

There are many other branches of the family, and to ordinary mortals the wealth of the Egertons would seem to be beyond the dreams of avarice. Yet the spot where their fathers worshipped in the old home of the race is forlorn and desolate. Is there none who will save the ruins, let light through the tangled thicket of overgrowth, reserve an acre encircled by the brook, plant it with yew tree and cedar of Lebanon, and let the daffodil, the gillyflower, the lily, and the rose, blossom in their season, making the desolate place into an isle of beauty?

X tried to photograph the remains of the chapel, and I talked to the farmer, who asked what we charged for taking photographs. Plates and time were short, or we ought to have bargained for our tea, but I know the "pictures" farmers like. They want themselves and the "missus" in the middle, with about a dozen fat pigs and fat children, a few cade lambs and poultry in front, some milch cows showing big udders, with mares and foals behind, and a background of big ricks and fruit trees—a variety of little details that would take time to arrange, and we are in a hurry. I see it is a cheese farm, and ask the farmer if he makes his cheese coloured, and if it is smooth-skinned, or open-meated. He suddenly becomes suspicious, and says he has none to sell, he sends it all to Hanging Ditch. He is evidently down on trusting me, and thinks wonders of Hanging Ditch. If he knew it as well as I do he might know it as a place where cheese goes bad, and debts sometimes go bad, and where there are rats and rates, and factors wear out their lives in trying to earn their bread and cheese.

X asks me if I do not want my tea. This interesting question is repeated every few minutes. I have complained before about being in a land that is poetically said to be flowing with milk and honey, when you cannot get any of either the one or the other. A pint of new milk and half a pound of fresh honey would be grand, but it cannot be gotten, and I cannot live on blackberries and butterflies. Therefore, what is to be done? The country is dreadfully aristocratic; there are no inns and few cottages. We must catch the express at Beeston Castle Station, and there there is a public-house; but we have to find and photograph Bulkeley Hall, and the long, hot, glorious summer's day is drawing to its close. We fly through the grounds of Cholmondeley Castle, past the stately stables, out into the park, scattering rabbits and water-hens, who little know how hungry and thirsty we are, or they would hurry away a bit faster. We find Bulkeley Hall, the ancestral home of the Bulkeleys of Cheadle Bulkeley, and of Beaumaris. We conform to the country pronunciation, and ask for "Buukley," or the natives would only stare at us. It appears to be almost a replica of Cheadle Bulkeley Hall, that now stands in Cheadle village, which was built about 1760 by Thomas Egerton, a scion of the direct male line of the Egertons, who was rector of Sephton, Warrington, and Cheadle, three very rich "cures of souls."

We fly again until we come to a full stop in a sandy lane, and have to walk. Then it is downhill, good roads, and superb scenery for miles. Some of the hills are marked dangerous. X puts his feet on the rests, "coasts," "scorches," and shouts, "What is the good of being a magistrate if you cannot——" The rest of the sentence is lost in the distance as he flies downhill and round the corner. I wonder what his wife would say if she saw him. Whatever would she do? I must do something quickly, or one of us will be lost, so I hurry after him, and we get safely to Beeston Castle Station with five minutes to spare. A porter takes the cycles, and X gives him a big piece of silver, telling him to run into the hotel, and tell us when the train is coming. He says he cannot do that, but he pockets the tip before saying it, and then tells us the train is due, and may be in any minute. We rush across the road to the hotel, ask if we can have any tea, hot or cold. We are told "No," they cannot make so many teas. Then I say, "Give me a pint of milk, and my friend some soda-water." The answer comes without hesitation, "The milk is all sour, you cannot have any." Then it is my turn to turn sour, for the practice of delaying or refusing teas even at hotels is much too common. Fortunately, a waitress comes downstairs with the remnants of some-body's tea on a tray, and out of a teapot I get half a tumbler of tea, which I fill up with cold water and drink, and then get some more in a cup with milk and sugar. So the milk had not all gone sour ; but they call it cream. We rush back to the station, only to wait half-an-hour, for the express is behind time, because it is Saturday. We get to Stockport in the dark, and as we have no lamps, the cycles are put outside a cab, and jolting in a "growler" across the ruts and in the smells of Stockport is a wonderful contrast to the air and scenery of the Bickerton Hills, and the gliding downhill through Paradise.

SWINYARD'S MOATED HALL

VALE ROYAL

A HAPPY band of pilgrims of the Lancashire and Cheshire Antiquarian Society having obtained leave to pay their respects to the relics and remnants of the once-celebrated Cistercian Abbey of Vale Royal, I made one of the party, cycling alone from home to meet them at the abbey.

The present structure is a curious medley of a house, showing very little of the strange, eventful history of its predecessors. The front door is undoubtedly the old front door of the abbey. Such doors were only made for abbeys and churches where they could get oak about a foot in thickness, and carve at it for ages. The place was nearly all rebuilt once or twice, and is now rather bare and lonely looking, the owner being in Africa on a hunting excursion. The once magnificent Gothic abbey is all gone, and very little of its contents is left, but some very fine old glass, and an oaken chest similar to the front door, with figures on the sides that are carved in relief two or three inches deep. There is a magnificent barbaric display of arms and armour, and trophies of the chase; two lions fighting being particularly striking. On the beams of the great hall are the names and the arms of the Cholmondeleys and their family alliances. The great name of Cholmondeley is there spelt in many ways, as befits the delightful spelling of our ancestors, who had not to pass any standard in scholarship, but you must please always to pronounce it

as if it were spelt Chumley. There is an extraordinary
collection of ancient stained glass. Some windows show
the history of the abbey, and they were particularly interesting, but I had no means of photographing them,
and there was no one to explain them. The following
is a short history of the place.

On August 2, 1277, or almost exactly 621 years
before our visit, King Edward the First laid the founda-
tion-stone of the abbey on the site of its high altar. He
did this in fulfilment of a vow that he made when in
danger of shipwreck on returning from the Holy Land.
The historian records that before the fabric was built it
could be seen glittering and illuminated at night, and
sweet music was always heard on its site. The charter
says : " Edward, the illustrious king . . . for the health
of our soul and the souls of all our antecessors and successors . . . give to them and their successors serving
God in free, pure, and perpetual alms . . . all those
lands." Then they had a great feast at which they ate
porpoises. As time went on the abbots " waxed fat and
kicked." One of them is said to have been so holy that
when souls could not rest in purgatory, his benediction,
if they could get it, would send them straight to heaven.
They seem to have been very like the parsons of to-day
and of all religions, always striving for more power,
begging, and quarrelling. They had exclusive powers
and jurisdiction in their own territories over any one,
and claimed that if any of their tenants or men were
accused elsewhere, they could have their cases brought
to their own courts for trial. When a native died,
the abbot was entitled to his best beast for heriot, and
a share of his goods. Then the Church had its pick,
and the widow or family got precious little, and were
often thankful to keep their teeth or their skin whole.
A man might not let his daughter be married without
"squaring" the abbot, and the abbot fixed the price.

Trifles were not overlooked, and these blessed fathers had the right to buy all fowls and ducks at twopence each.

But the day of retribution came. The people had often risen in arms against them; they had shot the abbot's horse, they had played football with a monk's head; but the powers that were were always against them, until those powers turned against one another. When the great robbery of the religious houses and charities was perpetrated, the abbot was accused of many crimes, but the most deadly and never-to-be-forgiven sin was that he said "the Kynge's grace was not lawfully married." Fancy any one daring to say that the one supreme head on earth of the Church of England was not lawfully wed! Of course he got hanged. The historians are very quiet on the matter, and slide quickly over it, for they also take care to keep on the side of the powers that be. The abbey was dissolved and confiscated, and the building and site given to a young man named Holcroft, who was described as being an esquire of the body to the great king. What might have been meant or included in the term "an esquire of the body" I do not know, but, like the king's, the breed soon went out.

One of the most noteworthy things these abbots did was when the thirteenth abbot, John Buckley (perhaps Bulkeley), went to repel the invasion of the Scotch, and fought at Flodden at the head of three hundred of his tenantry. Another little note interesting to me is that one of the dispossessed monks, named Thomas Fletcher, got a pension given to him of six pounds a year for life. He must have been something special. At the foundation of the abbey some of the land taken was from Nicholas Baret, and there is mention of a Henry Mous; so I am probably finding some ancestors.

To return to the exquisite stained-glass window

which commemorates the origin of the abbey—it is in
the great hall over the front door. At the top is the
Deity enthroned in heaven, and surrounded with legions
of angels, some of whom are bringing a spirit or vow
from below, where there is a ship in a tempest containing
a gigantic figure of a king with the model of an abbey
in his hand. Connecting the upper and middle parts
are the words, "De profundis clamavi" (Out of the
depths I have called), and the window evidently represents the king trying to bribe the Almighty by the
promise of an abbey.   Edward, who is sometimes called
the first really English king, is known to have been
long-headed as well as long-legged, and he doubtless
thought that if he took the Almighty into partnership,
and showed Him how He could make money by the
transaction, he would be saved. Edward would also
know there were other agencies at work.   Round about
we see devils blowing winds and waves, and at the
bottom of all there is the old lad himself with a rope
trying to pull the vessel down to the bottom of the sea.
I was quite pleased to see him, for I had not heard or
seen much of him for years.   Rector Kidd used to
delight in preaching about him when I was a boy, but
nowadays the parsons all over the country seem to
ignore him, and preach against one another.   The old
gentleman is very eager and determined to get the king
and his crown with abbey and all.   His men work with
one will, and his tail curls with excitement until there is
possibly danger of it getting in a knot.   Now the devils
we meet in public life generally have their tails wrapped
up, or hidden in their dress, but this is the identical
old Scrat that we were so familiar with in childhood's
days.

I was much interested in the whole affair, when
suddenly a dreadful thing occurred.   The blind ran
down with a crash, and there was no one anywhere near

to me or the window. Was that the work of the angels above, who might be thinking I was ridiculing the picture, or of the devil below, who might think I was admiring it and ridiculing him? The truth will never be known, but the curtain or blind had fallen, and I could see no more of the representation. I have had too much experience of this world to neglect the warning, therefore I went across the room to inspect the opposite window. There the earthly king is enthroned in glory with the charter of the abbey in his hand, and before him are the abbot and his retainers, all on their knees with their hands upraised in prayer. A scroll above the crown in Latin tells us: "Ego Edwardus, the first after the Conquest, in fulfilment of my vow, built the abbey, and now give it. . . ." There is a strong family likeness in the abbot and his followers, especially about the noses; they are all very well off for nose, and those likenesses were probably taken after they had had the porpoises and the burgundy.

I puzzled a little time, wondering whether these portraits were authentic and contemporary. Those of the abbot and his retinue may be, but not that of the king. There are not the strongly marked features of the man whose last act was to cause his son to take an oath that he would boil his father's body as soon as the breath was out of it, send the heart to the Holy Land, and carry the bones in triumphal procession before his army to overawe those turbulent Scots. The weak and wicked son broke his oath, and lost Scotland. The father was buried in Westminster Abbey, where he had long before hung as trophies, memorials from the Holy Land, the golden crown of Wales, and the sacred stone of Scotland. Round his tomb was written, "Edvardus Primus Scotorum malleus hic est. Pactum serva" (This is Edward the First, the hammer of the Scots. Keep your promise). The father kept his promises but the son never kept his.

The one had a long, glorious life of success, the other one of failure and ruin. Nearly five hundred years after his death some sacrilegious meddlers, with the consent of the clergy, dug up this hammer of Saracens, French, Welsh, and Scots, to see what he looked like, and he was there still, with his "long shanks," in his royal robes, and the corpse, though shrunken, measured six feet two inches in length. This was the man who bargained with God in his prayers, and kept his promises. The first King Edward of the mixed blood that made Englishmen. His predecessors had been Norman, Saxon, or British, but he was English in birth, breeding, and name, and perhaps the greatest king that England ever had; and one of his memorials is what is left of this abbey of Vale Royal.

There are other views of heaven, and my poor thoughts get lost in wondering how many heavens I have heard of. First, there is the well-known heaven of the parsons, where every one wears a surplice and sings psalms for ever and ever, with occasional processions and crowns of gold for those who are extra good. Then there is the rich man's heaven, where money is made faster and faster, where the mills are larger, where the machinery turns quicker, where there are no strikes, and no bad debts, and where profits are continually bigger and bigger. That is the ideal heaven of some whom I have known. Then there are the happy hunting-grounds of the Indians and the sportsmen, and the lord of Vale Royal has evidently been in his heaven, for the place is crowded with the skins and heads of animals. No animals are safe now, for the resources of civilisation arm men with rifles, and bullets of three metals, steel-tipped, to drill through the hide and bones, copper-bottomed, to drag behind, and with leaden middles, to distribute themselves in bits about the poor animal's heart and interior. Lastly, there is the heaven of the

overworked, those who lie in bed on Sunday till dinner-
time, and of the poor "slavey," who cannot even do
that, and whose epitaph is—

"Then weep not for me, and mourn for me never;
I'm going to do nothing for ever and ever."

This abbey of Vale Royal might have been, and
doubtless in many cases was, a heaven on earth. It
was planted in the pick of the land, in one of the fairest
scenes, in one of the most favoured bits of the earth.
If the men in it and around it had been content to till
their fields, and to cultivate their gardens, to tend their
flocks and herds, and to beautify the house of their God
and their common hall with all that the fine arts could
give them, the best that cultured skill could work in
architecture, carving, painting, or literature, what could
be better, and in what way could they be happier?
Their own records show how the domineering spirit
of the priesthood and the old priestcraft alienated the
people from them, and their crimes bore fruit in the
great crime that drove them forth and robbed them,
scattering and shattering the good work that many
honest labourers had wrought upon for centuries.

My tale of Vale Royal is ended. I should like to
have stayed there longer, to have seen more and to
have written more; but our time was short, and we
could not go again. Precious little is left of the once
glorious abbey. A curious four-sided cross on a tall
column stands on a knoll that is called the Nun's Grave.
White cattle were kept until recently in memory of the
white cow with red ears, which legends say returned
when all was stolen, that she might sustain the starving
brethren, and there are eagles kept in cages, and fed on
cats and rabbits, that they may do their share to fulfil the
words of the prophet. For hath not the great prophet
Nixon prophesied that when an heir should be born to

his master's house an eagle should perch thereon, that all the world might know that a male child was born, a future lord of Delamere? And if there were no eagles ready the expected child might be a wench.

Probably Flibter Moss

A VAGABOND IN THE STOCKS

In the good old times it was the law and the custom to put wayfarers or idlers who went coshering about without visible means of subsistence into the stocks until they got work.

TABLEY OLD HALL AND MERE

TABLEY OLD HALL

MY first pilgrimage this year (1899) was on Friday, the fifth of May, to Tabley. I did not expect to get into the old Hall, but I wanted to arrange about sending some cattle to ley in the park, also to examine a grove of old yew trees that I once saw there, and to see again even at a distance the heronry and the wild-geese. The time for the leying of cattle here begins on old May Day, or the first of May according to the old Kalendar, that is now the twelfth of May. Readers of folk-lore will remember how their ancestors "got done" out of eleven days.

The journey had to be taken alone, for X was cumbered with the cares of business, and although poverty is no crime, it is often inconvenient. A good old proverb tells us—

> " For age and want save while you may ;
> No morning sun lasts all the day."

I went quietly along, and rested on the seat that is by the roadside on Bucklow Hill. There I had peeled an apple when a young cyclist came and sat down beside me. I offered him a piece, which he declined, saying he was very fond of apples but could not eat them. I said "Why?" He replied that he had no teeth for eating apples. My next question was, "What did they rear you on?" It seemed a puzzler. He was a nice-looking lad, with gorgeous stockings, and knew how to roll up a cigarette, but had apparently been brought up with a bottle, and given bread and butter and tea for breakfast. Something was said by them of old time about "the children's teeth being set on edge," and nowadays we are finding young men whose fathers provide them with plenty of money and finery, but not teeth enough to eat an apple!

At the second lodge to Tabley Park on the Chester road the traveller may see a fine specimen of that beautiful shrub, Darwin's berberis; its deep orange-coloured flowers are now in perfection. There are few parks anywhere that are more crowded with objects of interest than that of Tabley. The medieval moated hall, the sanctuary for birds, the meres, and the fine trees with the heronries, gooseries, and waterfowl of many cries and varied plumage. To me it is the perfection of a retired spot. But then it cannot be seen or appreciated, for tourists no doubt give trouble until now most elaborate restrictions are enforced. For instance, a printed list of rules says (*inter alia*), "In no case is it permitted for sketches or photos to be made in the Park or of the old Hall, and no eating is allowed on the premises. No children or dogs can possibly be admitted. Visitors are also requested not to touch anything or to loiter behind the guide." What harm could it do to any one or anything to take a sketch or a snapshot?

At the first lodge, the keeper had been very uncivil; now a farm-bailiff walked me into the park a few yards and showed me that there really was grass for cattle. He said, in fact, there was plenty, for few men would send beasts there when they were not allowed in the park to look after them. He would look after mine for me and send word if they died. When I asked him to look at the old Hall with its herb garden and the grove of yews, he appeared frightened and said he should get "sacked" at once if he took me anywhere, and he seemed rather afraid that I might overrun him. After my return home, I wrote for special permission to inspect and photograph the old Hall. A reply came to the "Reverend" Fletcher Moss, curtly refusing, but as I had been there several times before when the place was owned by the late Lord de Tabley, a liberal-minded

TABLEY OLD HALL

gentleman of artistic and literary tastes, who not only escorted our Antiquarian Society even over his private house but allowed the Photographic Society to photograph everything, therefore I am enabled to give a short account of this interesting old hall with its appearance at that time.

According to Sir Peter Leycester, the careful and painstaking pedigree recorder and historian of his part of Cheshire, who was born in the hall A.D. 1613, it was built about 1380. Most of the original building must have perished, but the central hall with its gallery and open stairway is probably the one then made with the readiest and best material they had, namely oak. The column as shown in the accompanying picture is doubtless part of the original structure. The Jacobean mantelpiece is dated 1619. There are many scars and holes in the doors and panelling, which are said to have been made by spears or bullets or arrows, and the whole place, standing as it does in its little island home with only a chapel to keep it company, is very interesting.

The wild cherry-trees were laden with blossom, and the woods carpeted with anemones, not a single flower of which I touched. A water-hen croaked from the reeds, and a flash of light blue showed me that stately and picturesque bird, the heron, fishing by the water-side. As long as his dagger-like bill was pointed towards me he was almost invisible, but when he turned his head the pearly-grey breast and long crest-feathers were plainly seen. He flew off to his nest in the chestnut trees, and I thought of a distant piece of road from whence the heronry can be seen. The bird life was most abundant, and over all other sounds there constantly came the resonant trumpet-like note of the Canadian gander.

I longed to sit down and eat my other apple, but could not do so without breaking three of their printed rules all at once, and that seemed very dreadful, and might end in my being locked up. So I went back to

E

the road and sat on a heap of broken stones and enjoyed myself.   Numbers of chaffinches came and chirped
about me, and flat black spiders, with four legs on each
side, ran over me.   I wondered whether the bishop
knew how many legs these spiders had, and if it mattered
anything to the spiders whether he knew or not.   One
of them was getting in my trousers pocket, but when he
found there was precious little money there, he was soon
off, like the rest of the black-coats.

The broken stones on which I was reclining looked
as if they had come from the Clee hills beyond Ludlow.
They would average about a fourth or a fifth of the size
of those that are put on our roads, and the Cheshire
roads are much better than ours.

Three tramps came by and looked suspiciously at
me, as much as to say, "Theer's a cove wi' a bike.   It's
bloomin' time bikes was kept for aw o' us instead o' us
traypsing fro one workus to another, wearing out our
own bloomin' boots."   I felt rather like a tramp, for I
should have to go miles for tea or anything to eat, as in
that aristocratic neighbourhood tourists are sent empty
away even when willing to pay.   What a blessing it is
we have a right to the road, and can breathe the pure
air even if it comes from off the park, and bask in the
sun heedless for one bright May day of the little losses
and cares of life !

Round by the Smoker and by the back of Tabley
Park I got to Knutsford Heath.   How can I pass
over the old racecourse, the only one on which I ever
contended for a prize, without the memories being revived ?   More than thirty years have gone.   The place
was then an open sandy common, the motley crowds of
gypsies and tinkers and roughyeds are gone, and nurse-
maids with perambulators abound.   The scum of the
country would then close round you with, "What's th'
odds agen thee, mester ? Gi' us a wrinkle w' ut ?"
There was the joy of him who rejoiceth to run a race—

A VERY ANCIENT SPECIMEN OF THE CHESHIRE HALL

the yells for the vanquished, "the inhuman shout which hailed the wretch who won."

And then the quiet ride home to Didsbury on horseback through the ford of the Mersey, and now I am told that it is untrue that I or any one else used to ford the river, and I have come down to a bicycle, and roll along by Tatton Park and Ashley, where the vicarage garden is bright with purple aubretia and euonymus, and down the steep hill to Castle Mill, where oldish girls with high-heeled shoes are hobbling painfully downhill, and young ones are picking marsh-mallows for May decorations.

At home, and eventide, when helping to put the poultry safe for the night, I noticed an old goose turning her eye upwards, and after some searching I saw a few birds at an immense height (probably a thousand feet), the time being soon after seven and the evening light and very bright. My man said he could see they had long necks stretched out like geese, but I could not see that. Their wings also seemed narrower and more curved than the straight wings of geese. But whatever they were they were of large size, and their course was due north. Ere another day would dawn, if there were any dawn or dark at the height at which they were, they would be in Iceland or the Arctic regions. What guided them in their trackless lofty flight? I am too old a bird to believe that any of our little landmarks were noticed by them, and if darkness comes over the earth, it matters nothing to them. Their thoughts are not as our thoughts; they swerve not either to the left or to the right, and their guide might be the Pole-star.

WILD-GOOSE

GAWSWORTH

GAWSWORTH is so exceptionally beautiful, with its ancient church and halls embosomed in lofty trees and faithfully reflected in the placid pools, that the artist and the tourist delight to go there. The antiquary may muse over the remnants of the many stately monuments of the vanished Fittons, the lover of heraldry may here study all the coats of arms of all the Cheshire families in bewildering profusion of quarterings, and even the simple-minded may try to imagine what that church was like when from floor to ceiling, walls, windows, roof, and all were ablaze with the colours of the rainbow, for all that art and skill in their palmiest days could do to beautify it was freely done.

X, who rejoices in so many ancestors, numbers among them a family named Orreby who owned Gawsworth before the Fittons were heard of, and therefore it was right and proper for him to make a pilgrimage to the graves of his forefathers, and to burden himself with a half-plate camera and all accessories to record some mementoes of the spot.

We took the great south road as far as Monks Heath, then turned to the left towards Macclesfield, but again turned to the right at the first lane end, and passed by woods where all the birds were in the joy of their springtide. After passing a forge or smithy we went straight on by Henbury Hall, when we should have turned to our right, but a new signpost pointing down this lane had shown us the word Siddington, when on

GAWSWORTH CHURCH

GAWSWORTH RECTORY,

WITH LOCKED GATE AND NOTICE OF MODERN VERSION OF TEXT ABOUT TRESPASSERS

the other side of its same arm was the word Gawsworth. Arrived at the cottage by the church gates we
found men working at fortifications round the churchyard, and notices saying no one could be admitted who
had not previously received the sanction of the rector
and churchwardens. As we had not had any notice of
this notice it was impossible to comply, though I had
no doubt the rector would admit us if he could be found.
Therefore I went to the rectory, but found the garden
gate locked, with a big notice on it, "Private grounds.
Trespassers will be prosecuted."

humorous

I rang the bell three times, but there was no answer.
I hesitated whether to keep on ringing, for there was
evidently some one inside the house, when a man who
was working at the fortifications and was careful to lock
the churchyard gate after him as he went in or out, sent
a stable boy to me, and from him I learnt that the rector
was in the house, but "when 'e's lock'd issel in 'e wunner
come out." I asked if there were no maid-servants to
answer the bell, and the answer was, "'e wunner let 'em."
When I said something about the ordinary civilities or
courtesies of life, the poor lad only seemed ashamed for
his master, so the next thing we did was to rig up the
camera in the road and photograph the rectory, taking
care to focus for the notice on the gate.

This public notice is a plain statement which must
be either true or false. If it be the latter, why does a
minister of the gospel blazon it forth on a public road?
If it be true, what does he do when in conducting the
public worship in the church he and the congregation
(who have seen the notice) come to the oft-repeated
words, "Forgive us our trespasses as we forgive them
that trespass against us"? Do all parties to the prayers
and the worship mutually understand the old satire that,
when the priest teaches the people, they are to do as
he tells them to do, not as he himself does. We were
told that the rector is a new-comer to the district,

and that he had been chaplain to a prison. It seems very likely, for the high spiked palings that now keep people from the church, there being a double row of them in places, and the locked gates, are all more suggestive of a prison than of the House of God, which should be free to all.

No one is more cognisant of the nuisance there may be from too many tourists than we are at the Old Parsonage, Didsbury, for at each of the churchyard gates is a notice-board with an untrue statement on it, as if truth were an insignificant detail, and people ask for the keys of the church, and we have to give long tedious explanations as to the best ways of getting them ; but we try to be patient, and protect the flowers, or tell the visitors to come on Sundays when churches and religion are in use, for in some parishes there is one day reserved for them.

Fortunately the best positions for photographing Gawsworth Church and halls are on the road, where every detail of them may be seen reflected in the clear water of the pools. Only two of these ancient fishponds are left. The sites of others may be seen, for the fish-eating Churchmen of old had many ponds, not only for variety, but that some might be run dry and ploughed up to breed finer fish. The woman at the cottage told us she had notice to quit after living there for nearly twenty years, rearing a family and eking out a living by showing the church. X had set up his camera and was about to take the cap off when some one frightened the wild-ducks on the pool, and all the reflections in the water were destroyed. A little patience set that right. Again all was ready, when some dense smoke rolled over everything, quite stopping photography. The smoke evidently came from a rubbish heap in the rectory garden, and X, who was very religiously brought up, burst out, saying it was that something parson doing it on purpose. He had been thinking of the words another

THE OLD HALL, GAWSWORTH

parson lately used when speaking of the Sultan, but I
was alarmed that his placid temper should be so ruffled,
and suggested we sang a hymn, something about

> "Where every prospect pleases,
> And only man is vile."

Time and patience brought satisfactory exposures,
and we sat by the water-side, eating apples and talking
politics. There is a beautiful church that was once by
force stolen from the Roman Catholics. It is now kept
locked up at the caprice of one man, who, according to
Crockford, receives more than £1 per annum per head
of the population of the parish. One of the ancient
inscriptions in it was "Orate pro aia Georgii Baguley
rectoris hujus ecclesiæ qui rectoriam de novo construxit"
(Pray for the soul of George Baguley, rector of this
church, who built the rectory anew). Other times bring
other manners; other prayers are now wanted, and one
more restitution, and that is the church to be free and
open to all.

Let us leave these priests and talk of the lords or
squires. We cannot talk of the people, for their records
and the remembrance of them is forgotten. The Orrebys
are vanished as though they ne'er had been. The
Fittons have left many memorials of themselves. The
name is still common. It is even now over the village
post-office. The way they adapted their family motto
to their name is amusing. In early days they were
Fytons, and their motto (a very good one) was "Fyte
on." Then they became more religious, and on one of
their sumptuous monuments in the church they were
said to be "Fittons to wear a heavenly diadem," that is,
"fit ones" for heaven. Then they got classical as well
as rich, and composed "Fit onus leve" (weight makes
smooth), a good motto for a steam roller.

The clan of the Fittons suffered severely at Blore
Heath. The squire was a young man who took sixty-
six men into the fight, and only half of them returned

again.   He and his younger brothers escaped, but three
of his uncles were left on the steep banks of the brook
where those little red and white roses grow.   The last
of the name who held undisputed possession of Gawsworth died at the siege of Bristol on the Royalist side.
He had settled all his estates on a cousin named Fitton,
but many years after his death a son of his sister Pene-
lope, who became Lord Gerard and Earl of Macclesfield,
produced a will of his uncle's in his favour, and got
possession.   Many years of litigation followed, and
the dispossessed Fitton, who had become Lord High
Chancellor of Ireland and a papist, was by James the
Second made Lord Fitton of Gawsworth when James
was king no more, and chance or fate decreed that
the deed should be dated on the first of April.

The Gerards soon came to an evil end, for even at
the next generation there was no male heir, and the
co-heiresses married Lord Mohun and the Duke of
Hamilton, who, not content with quarrelling at law,
fought a murderous duel to the death in Hyde Park.
Lord Mohun being dead, his second stabbed the
wounded Duke of Hamilton "to make sure," and fled
the country, but four years after he was burnt in the
hand and branded for his share in the little tragedy.
The lands of the Fittons passed away from them and
aught that was akin to them for ever.   Many of their
splendid monuments and effigies are still in the church,
others are gone, some of them even in our own time,
when an ignorant parson destroyed more than all the
roughs ever destroyed.

As we sat talking by the side of the pool, big fish
at times swirled upwards in the water, and a lonely
orphan wild-duck paddled about until its turn came to
be devoured.   We had been there nearly two hours,
and only two persons had passed on the road; the
parson had not "unlocked issel" or ventured forth; and
the big carp that, according to a certain Lady Peggy
nearly two centuries ago, were then as big as some of

MARTON HALL

WELLTROUGH HALL

the lords, were getting more restless. So we thought we had better go, and turning for Congleton we struck across to the south road at Marton, and photographed the old hall there.

As X had adjusted the camera, and was taking the cap off for a short exposure, I noticed three shepsters fly on to the far gable of the house for an instant : the same instant or second that the exposure was made, for I wondered whether they could possibly be taken. There they are, in the picture, one on the pinnacle and two on the ridge of the roof, near to where the gable joins the main building.

We also found and photographed another of the ancestral halls of the Davenports, that numerous and powerful family in Macclesfield Forest and borderland. Welltrough or Wheltrough is a picturesque house on a hill, with part of the moat still in existence and on the side of the hill. If this is the hill in this neighbourhood called Tunsted which I have read about, its name alone denotes great antiquity.

The Marton Oak, which stands a few yards up a lane, is a noted tree with enormous, hollow, riven trunk. Some think it really is two trees, but the outside remnants may have got farther apart with age. It has been used as a tethering-place for the farmer's bull, and if the bull did injure the old tree he kept off the tourists, who might have done worse.

THE MARTON OAK

YEWS—SPEKE HALL

WHITHERSOEVER we have gone on our pilgrimages, whether to ancient church or hall or lowly thatched cottage, there have we generally found yew trees or the remnants of them. Sometimes there is a mere shell, a charred and hollow trunk; at others, a magnificent tree, as stately as a cedar of Lebanon; at others, a clipped and tortured thing. They are generally planted close to the building, as if they were specially venerated. How is it our most poisonous tree—for excepting part of the fruit the tree is poisonous throughout, the wood, bark, leaves, and kernel being poisonous to most animals, including man—should be so taken care of? It was undoubtedly protected by many of the kings, for it furnished the mighty bows of the famous English archers, whose bows should be at least as tall as the men themselves, and able to bend in a semicircle. Often, when sitting under an ancient yew in some Cheshire churchyard, I have thought its boughs may have furnished bows for Flodden, that fierce fight so long exulted in and mourned for, for in Cheshire there was scarcely a parish from which there was not one dead.

Yews are not found among the prehistoric monuments or stone circles, but they are almost invariably found by the oldest churches, or by any very old building, and they seem to have acquired a semi-sacred character, many people even now wishing to be buried under their shade. After some cogitation I believe the churches originally came to the yews, not the yews to the churches,

SPEKE HALL

SPEKE HALL: THE END OF THE HOLYROOD PANELLING

just as the earliest churches were built by wells or where
water bubbled forth. So also they might be built where
some famous preacher preached, and the best place for
that in primitive communities would be under a spreading
yew tree, whose boughs might bend under scores of sit-
ters but would not break—"a pillared shade upon whose
grassless floor" the audience might sit and listen. It is
recorded how in more modern days Wesley, Knox, and
Fox the Quaker did so preach, and some at least of the
original yews that sheltered the builders of Fountains
Abbey are even now still standing, centuries after that
stately abbey rose in all its splendour and beauty and
fell again, and the generations of its workers are
forgotten, and the spoiler's seed and breed are rooted
out, and many other kings and queens and great folks
have arisen and strutted and fretted their little hour on
the stage and are gone, while the old yews still brave
the storms and linger calmly on.

It was at Speke Hall, one of the most charming
ancient manor-houses in existence, that my attention
was particularly drawn to yew trees.

Speke is a wonderfully fine old black and white house
of many gables, enclosing spacious courtyard or quadrangle, a very difficult place to photograph, for underneath the yews the shade is dense. Across the front
there runs the plain inscription, "This worke, 25 yards
long, was wholly built by Edw. N. Esq. Ano. 1598."
The stone bridge is still intact but the moat is dry,
transformed into a garden fair. One side of the great
hall is panelled with lofty wainscoting carved in many
compartments, bearing the solemn warning, "Slepe not
till U hathe consederd how thow hathe spent ye day
past If thow have well don thank God If othrways
repent ye." This panelling with the library was part
of the sack of Holyrood in 1543 by Sir William Norres.
Many specimens of armour and fine old chests are scattered around. Upstairs are quaint old bedsteads, carved

and dated, one of 1583, with watch-pocket in the wood. The floors are of clay, and the walls of wattle and daub. Many rooms look ghostly, with their time-worn, faded tapestry, and one grey lady in particular may at times be seen looking through the window down into the moat for the child heir of the house who once was drowned there. Perhaps she put him in and cannot rest. In Saint Raymund's room, where is his bed with name and arms, there should not be a ghost. On a window-sill I note a lodging-place for owls, and little boards are put to hold the swallows' nests. It is a charming, quaint, old, haunted house, and behind it is a grove of trees carpeted with hyacinthine blue in the spring, and beyond again is the sea, the estuary of the Mersey in its widest part, with a little worn-out pier, the ideal spot for smugglers and romance.

When first I saw the place it was on one of the pleasant and instructive little excursions of the local antiquarian society. Our cicerone was pointing out the many beauties of the place, the spoils of the palace of Holyrood, the ancient armour, harness, and furniture, and when we came to two immense yews in the court-yard or quadrangle, whose boughs extend over the roof of the house, perches for the peacocks when they are tired of flaunting their beauty in the sun, he bade us observe that the two yews were male and female, the female being the lesser tree, good evidence of the care the builders of the house and planters of the trees took in their selection. Until then I did not know the yew was diœcious, and I had not any opportunity to ask him how any one could tell the male from the female. But again I marvelled at the builders and gardeners of those days as compared with the rubbish we have now. Then they built and planted what would last three hundred years. As many days just to get everything and every-body sold is now considered quite sufficient.

I wrote to nurserymen for female trees, but they

evidently did not know what I meant, though they would sell anything. So I wrote to our old friend Leo Grindon, the well-known botanist, who searched his own works and those of other people, and said that he could not tell the difference between the male and female trees, unless they were in fruit or flower, which was not the time of the year when they could be moved, and that they would then be almost necessarily old trees. Afterwards I learned that all Irish yews were females, the upright growing ones being called Irish, as they originally came from Ireland. It is also said that if male and female have grown long together, as have those at Speke Hall, they are married, and if one be killed the other will probably pine away and die, which sounds nice, though it be more than is expected of their betters, even in our civilized heathendom. Dean Swift had heard of this folklore, for he mentions two yews with classical names, and says that the parson cut one down to mend his barn, whereupon the other fell sick and died, so there was no excuse needed to burn it.

Folklore also says that lightning will not strike a yew tree, that no heat hurts it or no frost, and that it is a palm or symbol of immortality. Experience has shown that their average growth is a foot in the diameter of the trunk, or, which is about the same, a yard in circumference for every sixty or seventy years, according to situation or advantages. This gives a means of approximately estimating the age of any existing tree, and they probably are in their prime at from two to three hundred years old. In some church registers records of the measurement of yews in the churchyard are kept, and this Whit week I noted full particulars of those comparatively young trees that are now in the Old Parsonage garden. There are few fine yews left in this neighbourhood. One that sheltered the last cottage where split oak trees went from floor to ridge, was bought with the house and land by a man who boasts that he only cares for what pays, and now the house and tree are down, and a part of the trunk, two feet in diameter, and of deep purple or maroon colour, is made into a gatepost and whitewashed.

Soon after the last sentence was published, an old man called to ask me where this gatepost was, and he bought it to make into a sideboard, though the seller did not bless me.

Cheshire owed much of its wealth and power all through the medieval wars to its archers with their tough yew bows.   Four thousand of them were requisitioned by Richard the Second to guard the freedom of debate in Westminster Hall, and the authorities of Chester passed stringent laws that children should learn archery even when only six years old, and that they should shoot on Sundays, it being the first item in Sunday-school teaching.   In many villages (of which Didsbury is one) a field near the church is still known as the shooting-butts.

All the poets mention the yew.   Chaucer spelt it *Eu* or *Ew*.   In the earliest English manuscript it is said to be *Iuu*.   To me it seems probable that the words bough and bow were originally the same, for a Cheshire countryman calls them each boo, and would make a bow of a bough of a yew, or a yewen bou. Shakspere's knowledge of the yew and its folklore is well shown in his witch's concoction of a charm in the caldron, or making the hell broth boil and bubble :—

> "Liver of blaspheming Jew,
> Gall of goat and slips of yew,
> Sliver'd in the moon's eclipse,
> Nose of Turk and Tartar's lips."

The yew being slipped or slivered off during an eclipse would be supposed to be more poisonous than usual, and quite nasty enough for any doctor's physic.   Gray's immortal Elegy has :—

SPEKE HALL FROM THE MOAT

SPEKE HALL.

" Beneath those rugged elms, that yew tree's shade,
   Where heaves the turf in many a mould'ring heap,
Each in his narrow cell for ever laid,
   The rude forefathers of the hamlet sleep."

A similar line is in Samuel Rogers's " Pleasures of Memory " :—

'· The churchyard yews round which his fathers sleep."

Wordsworth described the yew as—

". . . a living thing,
Produced too slowly ever to decay ;
Of form and aspect too magnificent
To be destroyed.

.   .   .   .   .   .

" beneath whose sable roof
Of boughs, as if for festal purpose decked
With unrejoicing berries, ghostly shapes
May meet at noontide—Death the Skeleton,
And Time the Shadow."

Tennyson wrote in " In Memoriam "—

"Old yew, which graspest at the stones,
   That name the underlying dead,
   Thy fibres net the dreamless head,
Thy roots are wrapt about the bones.

O not for thee the glow, the bloom,
   Who changest not in any gale,
   Nor branding summer suns avail
To touch thy thousand years of gloom."

Later on, in the same poem, he found out his mistake and wrote—

" To thee, too, comes the golden hour,
   When flower is feeling after flower,
   But Sorrow—fixt upon the dead,

And darkening the dark graves of men—
What whisper'd from her lying lips?
Thy gloom is kindled at the tips,
And passes into gloom again."

THE YEW TREE'S SHADE

SPEKE

BATTLEFIELD—HAUGHMOND ABBEY—
HODNET

"From this worm-eaten hold of ragged stone
To that royal field at Shrewsbury"—

THAT is, from this old parsonage at Didsbury to
the battlefield by Shrewsbury—we had to cross
all Cheshire, and the quickest way to do it was
to go by the morning express to Shrewsbury,
and then to cycle homewards along the road to the
north. For it was from the north that Hotspur's army
came, and most of the gentry of Cheshire with their
retainers were with him in the great battle that was
fought in the summer of 1403, the first fight in those
Wars of the Roses that wasted the lives and work of
Englishmen for nigh a hundred years.

King Henry the Fourth had recently seized the
government and had his relative and predecessor quietly
murdered. Mortimer, who had probably the best claim
to the throne, was a prisoner in Wales of the noted Owen
Glendower, who had consoled his prisoner by giving
him his daughter in marriage. The Earl of Northum-
berland's famous son Hotspur had taken the Earl of
Douglas prisoner at Holmeden Hill, and then quarrelled
with the King about the prisoners. These various fac-
tions united against Henry, agreeing to divide England
amongst them—the Percies to have all the land north
of the Humber and the Trent, Glendower to have all
west of the Severn, and Mortimer the rest.

Their rendezvous was to be at Shrewsbury, and
Hotspur as usual was off in hot haste, but the King
got there a few hours before him and seized the city.

Glendower had not come; he was probably weaving spells or calling for spirits. Hotspur said he was as tedious as a tired horse or a railing wife. The King had taken the precaution to disguise himself while in battle, and to have several of his knights to represent him. Hotspur and the Douglas, the two most renowned warriors in Christendom, vowed to kill the King, and foot by foot they forced themselves like a wedge into the thickest of the King's army, killing every one of those knights and the royal standard-bearer; but the King himself was missed, and at last by some chance arrow or spear the furious Hotspur fell. That ended the fight, for Hotspur's army melted away, and the Scotch followers of Douglas were butchered almost to a man. Two hundred of the gentry of Cheshire are said to have been slain, for they were on the side of their Earl, the murdered King whose treasure had been kept at Beeston Castle, and therefore there may have been a thousand Cheshire men whose bones were heaped together and buried in trenches over which the railway now runs and the lonely church of Battlefield stands.

The fame of this battle comes by the pen, not by the sword, for it has been made the scene of what is perhaps the greatest of the immortal dramas of Shakspere, and it will be known through all time to come that hither went Hotspur—

> " Whose spirit lent a fire
> To the dullest peasant in the camp ; "

Douglas, a name renowned

> " Through all the kingdoms that acknowledge Christ ; "

The great magician, damn'd Glendower,

> " At whose birth the goats fled from the mountains ; "

Prince Hal, the madcap riotous youth, the mighty conqueror, the poet's own ideal prince,

> " Dropt from the clouds
> To witch the world with noble horsemanship ; "

And the King, wan with care, who could not sleep:

> "O gentle sleep,
> Nature's soft nurse, how have I frighted thee,
> That thou no more wilt weigh my eyelids down,
> And steep my senses in forgetfulness?"

Also that fat rogue Falstaff, larding the lean earth as he walked along, with his troop of scarecrows, the cankers of a calm world and a long peace. Only a shirt and a half to the company, the shirt having been stolen, and the half one made of two napkins. The "press" money had gone in drink, and as for their poverty he did not know how they had come by it, and in their leanness had certainly not taken after him. Hither to Shrewsbury came we also, and, like Shakspere's gentleman, who

> "Stopp'd to breathe his blooded horse,
> And ask the way to Chester,"

we started for the north, and though we have abjured even blood-horses, and had no armed heels to strike into the sides of our poor bicycles, we went off towards Chester at a pace that would soon have blown Hotspur and his mailed chivalry on their undersized cart-horses.

Battlefield church stands lonely amid the fields near by the main road and railway going north from Shrewsbury, and about three miles from the town. At the time of the battle the country was probably open common, and it is likely that the King when hard pressed would vow all sorts of things to Heaven with a share in the profits if he won the battle. There was a church and college and hospice, which last might be a hospital or hostel or both. They were all on two acres of land surrounded by a moat, and have all vanished excepting the tower and some little of the church. There is a much weather-worn statue of the King under a canopy over the east window, and inside is an ancient oaken Pieta. In a side chapel is old glass

representing the King looking desperately scared, a
priest with a bad smell under his nose looking with the
sublime contempt so common in his class on all who
are not of the elect, and a very strange-looking young
man who might possibly be meant to represent the
prince.   There are also hatchments and memorials of
the Corbets of Sundorne, their family badge being the
raven, which is called Corbeau in Norman, and even
to-day in parts of England a " corbie" means any of the
crow tribe.   Their motto is " In coelo quies," signifying
that even crows are quiet in heaven, but folk-lore
teaches us that crows belong to the other place.   There
is much humour in the family mottoes of our aristocracy
if we regard them properly, and some of the Corbets
have improved theirs, and now have " Deus pascit
corvos" (God feeds the crows), which may be true in
a sense, but when I see a lot of rooks waiting for my
ducks to lay, and as soon as an egg is laid pouncing on
it and eating it, shell and all, I agree with the folk-lore
as to the black thieves, and wish their black patron
would take them all.

The grass in the churchyard is uncommonly rank,
for it was up to my middle as I waded through it to
look at two old yew trees.   The pits and trenches that
were there at the time of the battle are still surrounding
the churchyard, and under the sod are the bones of
thousands.   Hotspur's body is said to have been
reverently treated and buried at Whitchurch, but when
the King heard of that he had it dug up again, ex-
hibited between millstones at Shrewsbury, and cut into
bits, as a warning not to rebel against the anointed of
the Lord.   Hotspur had slept the preceding night at
a neighbouring hall named Berwick, and tradition says
he came away in haste in the morning with the wrong
sword, and it had been prophesied that Berwick (presumably Berwick-upon-Tweed) should be the death of
him.   It is evident Shakspere never heard of this

A PIETA OR IMAGE OF PIETY OR PITY

Images of the dead Christ in His mother's lap were resorted to for the saying of prayers. Very few indeed of the old ones are now left. This one of oak is weather-worn and worm-eaten; it may have been coeval with the church. The top of the head is fairly perfect in the original, but as X had to photograph it without a tripod and give a time exposure in the church, it was difficult to adjust the camera properly.

little legend.   He had to be somewhat of a partisan
of the Lancastrians, and to spoil his battle scene for
stage purposes, but to Hotspur he has given deathless
fame, and here are descriptions of the great warrior by
the prince and by the widow.   The prince's is—

"His wife says to him, 'Oh my sweet Harry, how many Scots hast
thou killed to-day?' 'Give my roan horse a drench,' says he; and
answers, 'Some fourteen'—an hour after, 'a trifle, a trifle.'"

The widow says—

> " By his light,
> Did all the chivalry of England move
> To do brave acts : he was, indeed, the glass
> Wherein the noble youth did dress themselves.
> He had no legs, that practis'd not his gait ;
> And speaking thick, which nature made his blemish,
> Became the accents of the valiant."

Here also, at Battlefield, Shrewsbury, Falstaff's soliloquy
on honour with other remarks are supposed to have
been made.   "What is honour?   A word.   Who hath
it?   He that died o' Wednesday?"   And bearing in
mind the fact that the battle was three miles from
Shrewsbury : "Lord! Lord!   How this world is given
to lying!   I grant you I was down and out of breath,
and so was he, but we rose both at an instant, and
fought a long hour by Shrewsbury clock."

And the clock is there to this day to testify to it.

From Battlefield we should have kept on our way
due north, but the day was very fine; we lingered
and were lost.   The neighbouring ruins of Haughmond
Abbey tempted us and women misdirected us.   The
woman at the church said she could walk to the ruins in
a few minutes, and told us to take the first turning off
the high-road when she meant the second turning.
When we had gone a mile or two and were evidently
going astray, without meeting any one, we overtook a
female higgler who was lying at full length on the top
of rabbits and onions on a little flat cart.   Being on the

bicycle I could not properly see her face, which possibly was half divine, but I was afraid she skenned, and she certainly had frowsy hair and a Welsh accent.   X says that I am too particular and sceptical.   He has faith and will always give any one the benefit of any doubt. We presently found ourselves pushing our machines up a steep sandy hill, and after wandering many miles more than we need have done, we found ourselves at the gates of Haughmond, and on them was a notice— " No bicycles admitted."

What was to be done ?   The gates were locked, and there was no one about ; so we promptly decided to lift our machines over the gate, take them to some oaks in the park, and there leave them.   We found the ruined abbey deserted by all, save pigs and fowls.   There certainly was a cottage and garden.   The former contained an echo and the latter potatoes.   The ruins are beautiful and the situation, as usual, most beautiful. The name is doubtless Haut Mont, the Norman for High Mount, and it is " the busky hill," that is bosky or wooded hill, of Shakspere's battle-scene.   King Henry the Fourth, speaking in the camp near Shrewsbury, says :—

> " How bloodily the sun begins to peer
> Above yon busky hill !   The day looks pale
> At his distemperature."

We noted the ornate carving of the triple-arched entrance to the chapter-house, and climbing a little up the hill amid the ruins we sat down to rest and lunch. Before us for miles and miles was one of the most lovely English scenes, the fertile fields stretching down to the Severn and rising again to the mountains of Wales ; the conical peak of Caradoc and the Longmynd by Church Stretton, other hills that we knew not, the spires and towers of the ancient city hazy in their smoke, and farther round the wooded height of the Wrekin.   The

white-faced Hereford cattle were knee-deep in the grass,
the wandering voice of the cuckoo was on the breeze,
and all the air was balmy and fragrant with the breath
of early June.

Haughmond, once unknown, even unnamed, "unvisited by the traveller, the hunter, or the forester,
untenanted save by the robber or the hermit," became a
Norman Abbey and grew rich.   It added field to field

HAUGHMOND ABBEY

whose fruits were for charity; the whole income and
produce of the demesne lands were for the hospice or
the guest-room.   Think of that, you ratepayers who
have to pay poor-rates, subscribe to hospitals, and pay
your own hotel bills.   Those lands were never sold.
They have been stolen from the poor and the public.

It chanced that by our feet were certain stones which
marked a Norman grave six centuries old.   On them
were ancient crosses and archaic letters.   Here is part

of what they tell, and its translation : " Wous Ki Passez
Par Ici Priez Pur L'Alme Johan Fis Aleine Ki Git Ici.
Deu De Sa Alme Eit Merci.   Amen."   (You who pass
by here pray for the soul of John Fitz Alan [or the son
of Alan] who lies here.   God on his soul have mercy.
Amen.)   Amen, but if our poor prayers are of any use,
anywhere or for anything, surely they could be put to
better use.   Is this an order of the conquerors ?   It is
in the language of the conquerors, not in that of the
people, nor even in the dead language of the priests.
Its very existence is probably owing to its not being
understood.   Who was he whose request has weathered
all these ages of sun and storm ?   He was one of that
proud hard-bitten Norman breed who held England in
their grip for centuries, John Fitz Alan, Lord of Clun,
the great grandson of the founder of the Abbey, who is
said to be a great-grandson of Banquo, the celebrated
ghost in " Macbeth."   When Banquo was stabbed in the
dark his son Fleance escaped to Wales and got into the
usual trouble about a princess.   Their progeny were the
ill-fated Stewart race, and this man Alan, a mongrel
mixture of Norman pirate and Scotch outlaw, with a
cross of Welsh and bastardy—a mixture that would take
a lot of praying for.

X says that he also is descended from Banquo, and
can prove every link of the pedigree.   Therefore he must
be some relation to the party who wants praying for.
That is awkward for me.   The pigs that were rooting
about in the Abbey grounds are coming nearer, and I sug-
gest to X that he should take a snapshot of them while
I sit upon his ancestors, for if they got the chance they
would grub up the old Norman and eat him, body, soul,
pedigree, and all, and be hungry when they had done.
Why shouldn't they ?   Am not I eating part of the fat
chops of one of their kindred for my lunch ?   Why
should we eat them and they not eat us ?   Yet it would
have been more seemly if the owners of this Abbey,

who probably are professing Christians, did not allow the ancient sanctuary to be rooted up by swine. My thoughts wander on to the herd of swine into which the devils entered, and the modern farmer's natural query as to "who peid for them there pigs." We might dream away the long summer's day in bliss, for all around us is perfection, but we are sixty miles from home and it is one o'clock.

Being a mile or two to the east of Battlefield and the road to Chester, I thought it better to make for Market Drayton, and shortly we came to some staring new cottages with acres of glass, which we were told were owned by the Wholesale Co-operative Society of Manchester, who had bought the estate of Roden or Rodenhurst, about seven hundred acres, for about £30,000. The best security our prosperous co-operative societies can have for their surplus funds is undoubtedly land, as it is with all others, but whether the growing of tomatoes will pay is quite another thing. Farming seems to pay hereabouts, for there are plenty of stacks in the country. I notice five corn-stacks in one farm-yard, although it is the month of June, and the wonder is how the farmer dare let them be seen.

Suddenly we come upon a large farmyard with a stone gable to the shippons and an ancient decorated window. The farmhouse is most picturesque, of many styles and gables. The cowhouse was a chapel, and the place is Poynton Hall. It also is photographed, and we roll on until we come to another ancient place named Shawbury. Parts of the church, like the name, are Saxon. The south doorway is very noteworthy and so is the immense font. There was once a Lord of Shaw-bury, who was waylaid and murdered in the forest of Haughmond, and because one of his men who saw the deed done accused a Husee of Hussee, or Hussey, of the murder, the court adjudged that the accuser and the accused should have trial by battle; that is, they should fight to decide if it were true or not, and then if Hussey could kill the accuser, who was the chief witness against him, it would prove he had not killed the other man.

In the church porch is a notice from which it seems that prayers for the dead are becoming fashionable again. On the village inn, the Elephant and Castle, is an immense magnolia and also a vine. The wooded heights of Hawkstone come nearer to our left front, and

HODNET: A DUSTY DAY

somewhere on the left are the ruins of Moreton Corbet, but we have no time to stay. The weather is perfection, but Hodnet is some miles in front, and there we mean to have our tea and rest. We get both at the Bear. X unconsciously falls asleep, though he vigorously protests that he was only dozing. Some men go to sleep and even snore, and then calmly tell us they were very nearly asleep. Washed and refreshed we sallied out to see the church of Bishop Heber. It was open to all comers, and through a door that was new in 1705 we came to a large font, possibly Saxon, certainly very ancient, with strange beasts carved about it enough to frighten those who had to be immersed. There was a church at Odenet in the days of the Saxons, and the present building seems to have been built at many times. The tower is octagonal, and the church is in two halves, two aisles without a nave. Aloft in the chancel are the weapons of war, the spurs and sword, "the bruised arms hung up for monuments" when the owner could

THE FONT, HODNET

wield them no longer. The powerful family of Vernons owned Hodnet and bequeathed it to the Hebers, who owned it for fifteen generations. Their name is spread abroad—

> "From Greenland's icy mountains,
>   To India's coral strand,"

by the hymn of Reginald Heber. We could see very little of his rectory, but the whole village is picturesque and well cared for. The trees are big, the roads are good, and the scenery over and beyond the black and white houses is fine.

Time flew swiftly by, and we had to cease photographing and inspecting, and to fly northward again. At Market Drayton we had over forty miles to go, and

dawdling
train

there was a train for Manchester, so we availed ourselves
of it, but it dawdled away its time with milk-cans and
yokels until it lost its connection at Crewe, where we
had to wait an hour for another train.   Like many more
idle folks we were tempted to drink, and we comforted
ourselves with another good tea.

HODNET

WICKET GATE TO BAGULEY HALL

OAKEN ROOF OF BAGULEY HALL

THE HALLS OF BAGULEY, HAWTHORNE, CHORLEY, SOSS MOSS, AND PEOVER

AS the lovely weather of early June became more hot and sultry we one fine day set forth from Didsbury to cycle calmly along, and photograph more of the picturesque halls in the neighbourhood.

Baguley Hall, in its central part, is a grand specimen of the great halls of our forefathers. The oak trees, or sections of them, which frame it are of enormous size, some of them being reversed and five or six feet in diameter. Only earthquakes or explosions can damage these, for fire, storm, and tempest have long been tried. In the hall rests the effigy of Sir William de Baguley, with his Baguley shield of arms. It was in Bowdon Church for centuries, and then desecrated and stolen to deck a churchwarden's garden, but is now returned to the hall where

> "At Bagily that bearne
> His biding place had,
> And his ancestors of olde time
> Have yearded there longe.
> Before William Conquerour
> This country did inhabitt.
> Jesus bringe them to blisse
> That broughte us forth of bale."

Poetic licence does not trouble about truth. It makes assertions with more or less truth, and calmly defies contradiction. The knightly family of Baguley seem to have enjoyed the manor from whence they took their name for only a short time. Some of them may have bided or herded or yarded there long, but the name and

family did not flourish, and in America, where the
"Biglow Papers" are well known, the Bigelows or Big-
lows claim to be the Baguleys of Baguley, for they,
having piled up their wealth, have naturally sought after
their ancestors and arms, and we with resigned amazement learn that the Baguleys of Baguley emigrated to
America long years before that great continent was discovered, and in the New World restored the fallen for-
tunes of their famous house.

From the hall we went by Longhurst Knowl or
Knoll—the rounded hill from which the valley of the
Mersey may be seen from its source to the sea—to
Baguley Lodge, a thatched house built on part of the
ancient waste or moor of Baguley, where the new Sana-
torium for the Withington district is to be built. It was
time to photograph the old house ere it fell or its beauty
was destroyed, for its thatch was perishing, its floors
were rotting, and over the portals where Ichabod should
be written was a mouldering shield of arms. Memories
of my childhood bring up vividly the remembrance of
a gross, fat man, a dentist named Helsby, whom we
thought delighted to eat children or pull out their teeth,
and when that ogre got too fat he retired to this house,
and I looked to see if the arms were those of the Hel-
lesbys of Hellesby, but they were not, neither would they
be his, for he should have borne a forceps and molar
gules and guttée.

As we wander past the asylum at Cheadle it seems
to us that the business of caring for lunatics is always
flourishing, as if it were far more remunerative to keep
an asylum than to keep an hotel. But why do not the
authorities provide these rough-haired patients plenty of
room to play golf? It would seem to be such a suitable
game for them.

At Wilmslow we turn aside to photograph Hawthorne or Harethorne Hall, now being hemmed in by
the builders on all sides. On a heap of builders' refuse
the camera was set up, and over the garden fence X took

BAGULEY HALL: SIR WILLIAM DE BAGULEGH ON THE RIGHT

HAWTHORNE HALL

a good picture of the many-gabled quaint old house that was rebuilt within its pleasant park and gardens just two hundred years ago. There used to be a beautifully blood-curdling ghost story about the place, but as new people are living there it might bring trouble to repeat it. My informant told me that Ephraim and Abraham Birtles had taken "twiggen wiskets to hould the goulden guineas of some treasure trove, an Ephraim wer a crumnibbler 'e couldner see th' guineas would slippen through the twigs for one lawyer Page had gotten hoult of th' estate some road, lawyer like, an when 'e deed foure osses could ardly drag 'im to th' church. They were as wet as if pumpt on, an folk said th' devil had fot im, for e'd us't to come again, an men set up aw neet to lay im sayin they'd fettle im, an then they dug im up agen, an when th' coffin were opent there 'e were as fresh as need be, aw comfortable like, wi' is 'ed packt up wi' common Lindow black turves."

By Th' Ryleys Lane we went to Chorley Hall, a still more quaint and curious home. Within a stone-bridged moat is half a stone-built house, with pointed Gothic doorways, dim religious light, and windows with mullions of stone. The front is to the bridge, to the left, in the accompanying picture. At right angles to it the other half of the house is timber and daub, adorned with quatre-foils, and mellowed with age. This contains an oaken panelled room with grotesque mysterious carvings, and here it is said the great Oliver once came for consultation.

Then, as the day kept fine and hot, we decided to go for Soss Moss Hall and on to Peover, but as luncheon had not been brought we must lay in supplies while they could be had. Therefore, at Alderley, we purchased apples, eightpence a pound, or sixpence for a large apple. Is not this rather dear in the midst of Cheshire? Oh yes, certainly; but then the apples come from the other end of the earth, and shopkeepers say they have to live. Under the fir-trees at Soss Moss we ate apples and sought for the black and white hall which stands close by the railway between Alderley and Chelford, of which several beautiful photographs were made. Its huge stone lichen-clothed chimney is signed and dated " T. Wyche, 1583."

Onwards again, by many winding and devious ways, we come to the thatched lodge at Higher Peover Hall. By the gates is the now common notice-board, " No bicycles admitted," and the lodge itself is locked with no one left to guard the roses. The chapel and the hall stand side by side. Parts of both are very ancient, curious, and beautiful ; parts of both are modern, common. and ugly. Mainwarings or Manarings, for the name is spelt in a score of ways, have lived there since about the time of Magna Charta. The line has been broken, but the name of Norman origin retained. The squire's widow married a parson ; she may have been a rare worrit, while he doubtless looked after the loaves and fishes ; and their progeny got the estates, assuming therewith the family name and arms, with all their ancestors, and all their virtues. It is these same ancestors as represented in the effigies on their tombs, their " counterfeit presentments," that we wish to see and photograph ; for X says they are his ancestors, and Lady Mainwaring takes care of them, and is jealous of letting common cyclists, all dust and dirt, into the church where these ancient Mainwarings, the assumed ancestors of the present ones, lie. The monuments certainly are very fine. If they are nothing else they are beautiful works of art. The earliest is said to be of Randle and Margery in 1456, he being in plate armour with collar of SS and " Jesu the Nazarene " on his helmet. The second is of John and Joan, about 1480, he also being in plate armour, with camaille, collar, and motto or dedication as on his father. His head rests on the family crest, his armour and studded sword-belt being richly ornamented, and his lady rests with lapdogs at her feet and angels at her pillow. Her headdress alone is a work of art, but the beauties and mysteries of woman's

CHORLEY HALL

SOSS MOSS HALL

dress passeth the comprehension and wit of man, and beggars all description. The armour on the knights is more than I can understand, for the more recent of the two seems to me to be the older. Incised slabs of the next century give elaborate pictures of the families of John in 1515, and in 1573 of his seventh son, "Phillip Meynwaringe, esquier, lord of Pever and Baddiley," with long lists of children and other virtues. It seems strange what became of all these children, for, not counting girls, there were in three generations thirteen, seven, and eight sons, legitimate, in addition to many recorded in the histories who were not legitimate, though they took their father's name. No one has troubled to count those who took their mother's name.

In 1586 another Randle rebuilt the Hall, and left that as his monument. Parts of his building, and some little of the one still older, remain. His great grandson Philip, who fought for the Commonwealth, is shown by a noble effigy on an altar-tomb, with actual armour on the chapel walls. The accompanying photograph shows not only him and his inscription, but an incised pictorial tablet on the wall behind, with encircling record full of detail. A microscope is needed to read it in the photograph, where the lady's cuffs are the most prominent feature. All around are shields of arms on wood, and stone, and glass. The family crest and motto are, of course, conspicuous, they being the same as given on page 13. The ass's head was taken as the family badge, and the halter was a sign of humility. But in later generations, as wealth increased, the halter was dropped, and the ass's head issued from a coronet, for the coronet could not rest on a head with such enormous ears.

The long hot day, with the load of camera and extra slides, has made us long for rest and tea. We find them both at Nether Peover, where is St. Oswald's church, timber built, with oaken columns, oaken arches, and oak carved and plain, in profusion everywhere. The inn also is one of the few inns where we can get good milk,

G

that is, milk not watered nor skimmed nor separated, but good and cool from some old-fashioned cellar or dairy. Even X had to admit that to drink a cup of that on a burning day was a foretaste of the joys of Paradise. And the inn has the sign of the Tabley Arms, with the Tabley motto, " Tenebo " (" I will hold," or " I'll stick "). How dreadfully sarcastic and yet how funny these aristocratic family mottoes are! The Mainwarings', " Devant si je puis " (" Forward if I can," or " I'll get on if I can "), is like the homely Quaker's advice to his son, " Make money honestly if thou canst " ; and the Tableys say, " I'll stick," like the Traffords when they can get their claws on anything, " Gripe Griffin holdfast." Translate these mottoes to the natives, and speaking from experience and the fulness of their heart they usually say, " They will so."

THE GOOSE CREW

The one to the right is the father gander Adam. He is a pure-bred wild grey-lag, one of three hatched from eggs found in Caithness in 1891. He has had full use of his wings for many years. He is wed to his grand-daughter, that being allowed with geese.

WHERE THE MAINWARINGS LIE

ST. OSWALD'S, NETHER PEOVER

Cockades, Pedigrees, and Esquires

About the time of the first appearance of the last paragraph I wrote as follows in answer to public queries as to the right to wear cockades, or to bear arms, or even to be termed Esquire, and although the subject has very little in common with pilgrimages its insertion here may be permitted, as it is interesting to many of the public as well as to the antiquary and to the historian.

The cockade is essentially a fighting emblem, a modification of the serrated comb of a cock, and it should show that the wearer of it is ready to fight for his master. When the retainers of kings, nobles, or chiefs were ready to fight about anything or nothing, they needed some distinguishing badge for their servants or followers, otherwise they might be belabouring their own side ; and although Irishmen might go into a row ready and willing, that whenever and wherever they saw a head they should hit it, that would not suit the more phlegmatic Anglo - Saxon. Consequently some badge should be worn to distinguish the parties, and in our last little Civil War the then High Church and Tory adherents of Prince Charlie adopted the white cockade as being very different from the black cockade, which was the badge of the German house of Hanover, whose descendants now occupy the English throne.

Therefore any one who holds a commission from the Sovereign as an officer in the army or navy is entitled to put a black cockade in the headgear of his male servants, as the master, and therefore by old custom his servants, may be called upon to fight at any time. Members of Parliament and Justices of the Peace are not entitled to the distinction, and it is doubtful if an officer in the Volunteers is at all times. When on military duty it would seem right that a Volunteer officer should be entitled to sport the cockade in his servant's hat if he wishes to do so, but then he may be a grocer, and sell treacle and other things when he is at his ordinary vocation, and it would scarcely seem right that any distinguishing badge should be on the servant who drives him to and from the toffy-shop.

There is probably no penalty attached to the infringement of this unwritten law or custom, any more than there is for any one claiming to be an Esquire when he is not one, or for any one who adopts crests or coats of arms when he has no right to them. Any man may change his name to Lord Tomnoddy, or anything else he pleases, and quarter the arms of all the aristocracy if he wishes, and probably no one will take any notice of it, though in olden times many a man was quartered himself, and his quarters stuck up on bridges and gateways, for quartering or taking the royal arms, and thereby inferring that he was of the blood royal. Nowadays the right to bear arms (or crests) may be purchased. It is called a "grant of arms," and the price, I understand, is £72, 6s. 4½d., off which there is no discount, not even the coppers. If a man is wealthy and willing he may also buy a pedigree. Of course the longer it is the more costly it is. I have lately seen one showing the descent of a newly rich man, who is well known in Manchester, from one of the Evangelists, although it was not an Apostolic injunction to make money. The pedigree itself shows how great and sublime is the faith of the present day. The commoner aristocratic ones begin with the rolls of Battle Abbey and the Norman pirates of William the Bastard, though none of them can truthfully continue long in legitimate male descent.

There are, in fact, two ways of getting a pedigree. One is to buy it, beginning with Noah, or Charlemagne, or Charles the Second if it is only a cheap one, and working down to yourself. The other and proper way is to begin with yourself, and work upward or backward in the male line. Some men who try this tell me they cannot get further back than their grandmother.

Another well-known Manchester man, who was of

ST. OSWALD'S, NETHER PEOVER

Scotch descent, found that his grandfather had been hanged at Newcastle-on-Tyne, *probably for sheep-stealing*. He gave up pedigree-hunting. Another one, for Manchester has produced some very great men, was made a Baronet and M.P. He treasured the skull and thighbone of the founder of his family, until, as he told me himself, some rude doctor showed him they were the remains of a woman.

At election times all our coachmen and servants become Esquires, and when butter is booming there is a crop of big signet-rings among the grocers. An Esquire was originally a scutifer or shield-bearer, a gentleman of landed estate, next in rank to the Knight, and who wished to be made a Knight. The title was gradually given to any gentleman of landed estate, the value of that estate being very indefinite, though until lately a Justice of the Peace for a county must hold landed estate to the clear value of £100 a year. When the Esquire was made a Knight, and girt with the much-coveted golden spurs, he was with semi-religious ceremony adopted, or "dubbed," a word derived from the Norman French word *adoubé;* and to this day, when we cut off our gamecocks' combs or cockades, a little art into the mysteries of which I was initiated fifty years ago, and have with each recurring season practised it again, we are still said to "dub" the cock.

GAMECOCK

THE ROYAL OAK—TONG

MY first real pilgrimage on a bicycle to a place of historical interest was to Boscobel and the Royal Oak, but as a full account of them with large photographs has already been published in my book on Folk-lore, I merely refer to them here to say, that then I left Standon Hall, where my uncle Woolf had lived his long life, and which had always been a second home to me, to find in the little-known border-land between Staffordshire and Shropshire not only the Royal Oak so famous in song and story, but the Royal Barn where the Mr. Woolf of that day hid the fugitive King Charles before he was in the oak.

In a glorious long summer's day I found the tree, or rather its successor, at Boscobel, but not the barn, which was miles away, or the ruins of the convent of Whiteladies which are near by. Again I went, this time with X by train to Penkridge, spending another glorious day, the pilgrimage of which I write. Another journey was taken with larger camera, and yet another long hard day was needed to find the barn from the Shropshire side of the county.

As numerous inquiries have come to me about the way to Boscobel, let me say, firstly, that the place is not open on Sundays, and I think it is not open in the evenings. The best train from Manchester is the 8.30 from London Road, by Stoke to Penkridge or Gailey. For drivers or cyclists the way is about sixty-one miles down the great south road through Didsbury, Congleton, Newcastle, Stoke, and Stafford, to where that road

is bisected by Watling Street, a few miles beyond
Penkridge.   Where these main roads cross one another
is an open space with an inn of the well-known sign of
the Spread Eagle.   Gailey station is close to and was
formerly called Spread Eagle.   There is a great signpost, the north arm of which gives Manchester 61 miles,
Liverpool 81.   To the south, Wolverhampton 8, Worcester 35.   To the
west, Salop 27, Chester
53.   To the east, Lich-
field 15, Birmingham
20, London 128.   That
big crossing of roads
must be about the
middle of England,
and Boscobel is pro-
bably five or six miles
from there.

ROYAL OAK

Under the majestic
oaks, by the spacious
farmyard or courtyard
of Boscobel, we entered
the old-fashioned gar-
den where the sum-
mer-house, raised aloft
on the mound like a
watch-tower, is so con-
spicuous, and in the adjoining field we lay in the shade
of the Royal Oak to rest and lunch.   The original
Royal Oak, that is, the tree that the King was actually
in, was long since made into snuff-boxes and keepsakes,
but this, its offspring and successor on the same spot,
is now a fine tree.   As there are so many photographs
of this journey, and the oak and the house were shown
before, I can only spare the space for a small picture
of the tree with the house beyond it.   All around was
calm and quiet, with sweet and pure air.   The remnants

of our lunch with the paper we stuffed down rabbit-
holes, to the consternation of the bunnies who im-
patiently stamped below, and X succumbed to smoke,
that idle habit which so deprives men of their energy
and alertness.   He would do nothing but lie on the
grass and smoke, murmuring something about *dolce
far niente*, which has been translated into "something
to drink," until he suddenly bethought him that he
ought to buy the place and live there.   What bliss to
be far away from noise!   Here are no telephones,
barrel organs, beggars, messengers, or callers.   An
historical yet peaceful air seems to pervade the place,
and a wonderfully romantic past to brood over it.
A comfortable home, with secret chambers for the
children, a tiny chapel to hold six or seven people,
secluded in the woods, with glimpses of miles of
open country.   I should have wondered if X had not
wanted to buy it, but for myself I was like Mahomet
when he said, "There is but one Paradise, and mine is
elsewhere."

Much there was to see in the neighbourhood, with
little time to see it in, and few to ask about it.   The big
barn at Madeley was too far away.   The ruined convent
of Whiteladies, the first house the King went into after
his flight, I expected to see on our way to Tong, but
we missed it, though we probably saw Blackladies and
the thatched cottage where the six Pendrill brothers
were born.   There was no one to ask, nobody bothered,
and nobody cared.   On our next visit we found Whiteladies, a walled-in ruin still used as a graveyard, in the
middle of a big field where the cattle graze.   Here as
the day dawned came the majesty of England after the
fierce fight in the faithful city.   Horse and all, covered
with blood and foam and dirt, must shelter in the house.
All men doff before the King, but here they strip him of
his royal clothes and give him hempen shirt and leathern
doublet.   Lord Wilmot's dagger cuts away his cavalier's

WHITELADIES

locks, those locks the ladies loved, and Giffard trusts him with his faithful serfs the Pendrills, for the Earl of Derby and the other lords must leave him to his fate while they each meet their own.

From Boscobel we found our way along a lane which was a stately avenue with beautiful scenery to an inn called the Bell, after the great bell of Tong, and, turning at the cross-roads, there we saw one of the most charming rural villages it has been our lot to see where'er we have roamed.

My remembrance of it is of a broad road winding up a wide valley of park-like character, with luxuriant trees and long stretches of ornamental water. In the distance is a too florid castle, with minarets, rather incongruous, but that is far away. Nearer by the water-side there is a decorated church, with octagonal tower and spire, and with a few houses of various styles and shapes around it. A great stone bridge carries the road to it over the water, and all about are ample evidences that Nature has been helped by art and wealth. As every one who writes of Tong quotes Eyton's description of it from the "Antiquities of Shropshire," I had better give at least the opening lines. "If there be a place in Shropshire calculated alike to impress the Moralist, instruct the Antiquary, and interest the Historian, that place is Tong. It was for centuries the abode or heritage of men great either for their wisdom or their virtues, eminent either for their station or their misfortunes. The retrospect of their annals alternates between the Palace and the Feudal Castle, between the Halls of Westminster and the Council Chamber of Princes, between the battlefield, the dungeon, and the grave."

At the grave we end, and my quotation ends, and by the graves of the bygone lords and ladies of Tong the moralist or the student may spend hours over their pictures in paint and alabaster, the men and women as they were, the great ones of the earth with all the poor remnants of their glory on them. Their gorgeous monuments have wonderfully escaped the ravages of time and churchmen. They are so numerous and elaborate that I will only mention those of which the photographs are given, and they were chosen because the light and space enabled us to take them better than the others.

The splendid altar-tomb where saints and angels stand all round in canopied niches with shields to guard the treasured dust within, while above them lie the beautifully chiselled effigies of the bygone lord and lady, is very fine. The knight who looks so calm and handsome in the repose of death is said to be Sir Richard Vernon, who died in 1451. He had been the Treasurer of Calais, and may have seen the burning of the saintly Joan of Arc. His father was beheaded after the battle of Shrewsbury. His wife Benedicta lies beside him, beautiful in feature and wonderful in dress. Few could look upon those charming counterfeits unmoved. Let us hope they are fairly truthful.

In the second picture of the same tomb there are two live boys who were tolling the passing bell, for even here people sometimes die. They promised to miss one toll and neither wriggle nor wink while I timed them for two minutes. All was satisfactorily accomplished, though X greatly feared his exposure would not be enough.

Our third picture is of the grandson of the above Sir Richard. Sir Harry Vernon, lord of Haddon and of Tong, who died in 1515, and his wife Anne, the grand-daughter of Talbot, Earl of Shrewsbury, Shakspere's "scourge of France." How comfortable they also seem to lie in death, with their infant by their side! All around the monument, above it and below, the sculpture is very fine. The near side is open to the Golden Chapel, a gem of the highest art. On its western end is the son, Sir Arthur Vernon, preaching in the midst of what once must have been a blaze of colour, for traces

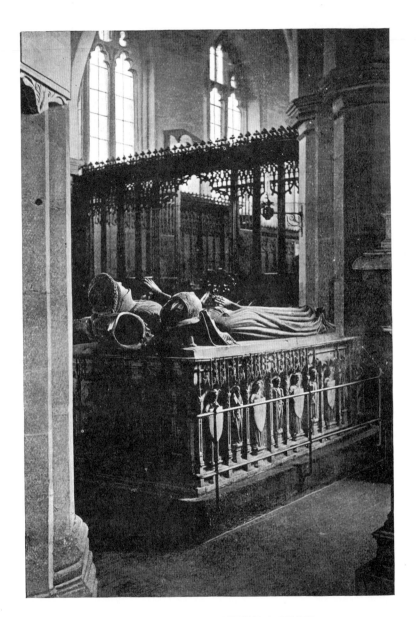

SIR RICHARD AND LADY BENEDICTA VERNON

of the gold, and the vermilion, and the azure blue may still be seen.

Lord (or Sir) Arthur Vernon, in his will, dated 1517, says he is a " prest hole of mynde and of bodye in clene lyfe," and he wants "a stone with his picture drawen thereupon, and a trentall songe for his soule and for his

SIR ARTHUR VERNON PREACHING IN THE GOLDEN CHAPEL

fadre's and his moder's and all xpen soules, and ev'y pore man that cometh to his burying is to have a peny and a loffe to pray for his soule, and yf not at that tyme to tarye unto the tyme convenient. Item his brother John is to have his napyre ware and all his beddinge, boks, chests, and coffers, but his skarlet gowne and murrey gowne with velvet Jaket to pay dettes to the church . . ." and so good bye Sir Arthur.

Beyond the tombs in the front of the second and third of these pictures may be seen a double-decker, a magnificent stately monument of the Stanleys, on which are their gorgeously ornamented effigies, evidently intended to be likenesses of them in life. At each corner is a tapering column of black marble, two of which show rather prominently in the photographs, though the richest work is not shown, and some of it is lost.

On the upper part lie Sir Thomas Stanley, second son of Edward the third Earl of Derby, in plate armour richly ornamented, and his wife, who had been Margaret Vernon, co-heir and sister of Dorothy Vernon of Haddon, whose romantic elopement on the night of her sister's wedding every one has heard of. On the lower part is Sir Edward Stanley, their son, in plate armour, polished, gilded, and coloured, with angels and roses and weapons and shields innumerable. The epitaph is believed to be by Shakspere :—

> " The memory of him for whom this stands
> Shall outlyve marbl and defacers' hands ;
> When all to Tyme's consomption shall be geaven,
> Standly, for whom this stands, shall stand in heaven."

Another splendid altar-tomb became famous, because on it during many centuries there were yearly hung chaplets or wreaths of roses, the tribute paid to Roger la Zouche and his heirs for yardlands, fishing, pannage, and nutting, in the pools and woods of Tong. When the La Zouches ceased to be on this earth, the prudent grantees brought their suit and service of wreaths of roses to the grave where their lordships lay. Below the floor of the Golden Chapel were lately found large quantities of ancient stained glass which had doubtless once been in the windows of the church, and a generous donor gave a thousand pounds to have them patched and matched and restored again.

SIR RICHARD AND LADY BENEDICTA VERNON
BEYOND THEM ARE SIR THOMAS AND LADY STANLEY

A brass to Ralph Elcock may be mentioned because he was born at Stopford, meaning Stockport, and is described as "celre cofrat istis coligii," which is translated as "cellarer and co-brother of this college." A tablet to a steward says, "Few so honest, none more so." By the altar is a door, sometimes called a leper's door, with three holes through which the poor outcast lepers might watch the celebration of the sacrament, a forcible reminder of other times and other manners. The choir stalls are wonderfully fine and elaborately carved, but we have no space or time for half the wonders of this remote country church, and I cannot do better than continue the stately words of the quotation from the "Antiquities of Shropshire": "These are the great names and reminiscences with which the place is associated! The Saxon Earls of Mercia, brave, patient, and most unfortunate victims of inexorable progress; then their three Norman successors, one wise and politic, another chivalrous and benevolent, the last madly ambitious and monstrously cruel; then the Majesty of England represented by Henry the First, a prince who in ability for ruling almost equalled his father, and has been surpassed by none of his successors; then the sumptuous and vice-regal pride of De Belmeis, bishop, general, statesman, and withal very priest, his heirs dim in the distance of time, and the adventurous genius and loyal faith of Brittany represented in La Zouche; tales of the oscillating favouritism and murderous treachery of King John; overweening ambition and saddest misfortune chronicled in the name of De Braose, a Harcourt miscalculating the signs of his time and ruined by the error; a race of Pembruges, whose rapid succession tells of youth and hope and the early grave; then the open-handed and magnificent Vernons; lastly, Stanley, a name truly English and honourable in English ears."

Here were heaps of ancestors for X, he never had

such a find in his life, and he worked hard at photographing.   I also thought I had found a long-lost
ancestor, for there was a college founded at Tong in
1410, and one of the three founders was William Mosse,
clerk, the same name as that of my great-grandfather,
who was baptized at Standon, which is not many miles
from there, in 1702 : therefore they were probably of the
same family.   As I was leaving the churchyard some
country-folk drove up, possibly in search of a grave, and
the leader asked me if I was the sexton.   I replied am-
biguously, like the Irish echo, " Do I look like a sexton ? "
We were certainly thirsty, but it was not gravediggers'
drink we wanted, and we must hurry for home.   We
were then considerably surprised to find that no one
could tell us our way.   No one in the village seemed to
have ever heard of Crewe, Stockport, or Manchester.
Belle Vue seemed to recall something vague to them.
No one had a railway guide ; even in the inn there was
not one.   No one knew which was the nearest or the
best station, and no one cared.   There was a constable
some miles off, they said, and he ought to know.   They
ought to do many things.   What a comfort it would be
to stay about here ; near to that exquisite church, a
miniature Westminster Abbey with its statesmen, and
warriors, and nobles, all silently preaching sermons
from stones.   If it could be kept as it is now, for
ever, as a temple of peace for friends, with no parson
to make a noise, with the sounds of country life
around, and the birds for choir, what a haven of rest
it would be !

But our restless natures say we must sleep at home,
and I advise to fly for Stafford, where there should be
many trains, as it is on the main North-Western line.
For fully two miles we cycled alongside or partly in
Weston Park, the seat of the Earl of Bradford, under
what is probably one of the finest avenues of gigantic
beech-trees in this or any other country.   Then we

SIR HENRY VERNON AND LADY ANNE TALBOT HIS WIFE
WITH THEIR INFANT CHILD

The part of the inscription shown in the photograph is
"Anno domini millesimo quingentesimo xv° Et dicta dne Anna obiit xvii die mens."

Translation: A.D. 1515 And the said Lady Anne died the 17th day of the month.

struck into the old Roman Watling Street, and turning
to the right along it we still skirted Weston Park for
miles along a road that all cyclists ought to traverse. It
was magnificent for scenery and shade or anything that
we could wish. After eight or ten miles we came to the
big cross-roads before described, and I going slowly
and reading the many names on the signpost, for most
of the chief towns of England seemed to be mentioned,
wobbled about, and called to X who was in front, when
suddenly my machine went straight into a great boulder-
stone by the footpath and reared up like a horse about
to jump a fence, and then lay down with me in the dust.
X was in great trouble and sorrow ; not at my accident,
which he plainly saw, as I had just shouted to him, but
because he could not get his camera out to snap-shoot
me as I flew through the air and then lay in the dust.
Two young ladies gazed in pity, and butchers driving
by laughed immensely, but there was no great harm
done, though the machine had to be doctored at Penkridge, which caused delay, while my little bruises had to
wear themselves out.

We became more anxious about getting home as
the evening was far spent and we had no lamps, but the
good day had put us in rare spirits, the homeward road
was all that could be wished, the south wind helped us
on. There were the milestones plain enough. Every
mile must be done under five minutes.

> Come labour on.
> Away with gloomy doubts and faithless fear,
> The toil is pleasant, the reward is sure.
> Come labour on.
> No time to rest, still glows the Western sky
> And o'er our path the lengthening shadows lie.
> Come labour on.

Never mind referring to the original version. If
Peter had prayed by the book he would have been drowned
before he had found the place. We got to Stafford in

the dark. Twenty miles done under two hours including an accident, and we caught a stuffy express
from London, full of men in cuffs and gaiters, who
were choked with dust, and yearning for drinks, or
snoring.

train descrptn

DOOR AT TONG WITH THREE ROUND HOLES

THE BARN WHERE KING CHARLES WAS HIDDEN — ATCHAM — URICONIUM — WROXETER—MADELEY-ON-SEVERN

3rd pilgrimage

THIS long day's pilgrimage was my third attempt to find the barn in which King Charles the Second was hidden after the battle of Worcester, and before he was in the Royal Oak. I was told it was still in existence, though some miles from Boscobel, being at Madeley on the Severn, or Madeley in Salop, not the village of that name in Staffordshire. As the Boscobel country is so sparsely populated and difficult of access, we made this attempt from the Shropshire side, and found the barn which gave shelter in its straw to the Majesty of England for a day and a night.

Having read all the contemporary tracts and diaries relating to the wonderful disappearance of the young King in 1651, let me give a short summary of them in my own words, for the original language is somewhat inflated. For instance, one author writes that when this "inestimable jewel" was hidden in the woods on his way to the barn, "the heavens wept bitterly at the calamity," or, in other words, it rained; and another man wrote, "The ashamed sun blushed in his setting, and plunged his affrighted head into the depth of luckless Severn, and the night, ready to stain and spot her guilty sables with loyal blood, was attiring herself for the tragedy." Therefore I will (like another writer) "humbly kiss the pen and paper which have the honour to write about His Sacred Majesty."

When the armies of the King and the Commonwealth met in their final struggle, the stern and stubborn
fighting of the Puritans gradually drove before them all
the gallant chivalry of the Cavaliers, and the young
King was hunted like a rat through the houses and
streets of Worcester, "The Faithful City." Cromwell's
"crowning mercy" had come, the anniversary of his
great victory at Dunbar, when, in their haste to hem
him in, he cried, "The Lord hath delivered them into
our hand!" This time also he did all that man could
do to make his victory complete, but the King had fled
and gat him out. Through the dark and wet night
Charles fled northwards with a faithful few, until, as
the day was dawning, Giffard took them to his lonely
house of Whiteladies, where, with Charles's horse in
the hall, a hasty anxious council was held. The Pendrill brothers, who were woodmen on the estate, were
summoned, and to their care the King was confided
by the Earl of Derby and the rest, who again fled
northwards, but were captured, though Giffard again
escaped at Bunbury. The woodmen took the King
to the woods, clothed him in their clothes, and hid
him.

Then one of the most romantic bits in history was
gradually unrolled, for though it is not two hundred and
fifty years since, the King of England suddenly disappeared in the midst of England—disappeared for six
weeks as completely as if the earth had swallowed him.
Not more than half-a-dozen persons ever knew where
he was. He was left with peasants in a wood. Kings
have often been left, "disowned, deserted, and distrest,"
but this King was a worthless one, with no resource
or character, devoid of truth or honour ; of an unlucky,
faithless race, few of whose forefathers had died the
common death of men ; a thing incapable of love or
hate, whose chief legacies were debts and bastard
dukes, who even to our own time have yearly taxed

DOORWAY OF WHITELADIES

the country; whilst those who saved him were plain
countrymen, whose simple faith was "Feare God and
honor ye King"; who knew him not, and had never
seen him; who risked their lives and all that they had,
for to harbour him was "death without mercy," and all
that a man hath will he give for his life. These are
well-proved facts that must rivet the attention of the
historian, the moralist, or the cynic.

When the night was drawing in, Dick Pendrill took
the King across country to a Mr. Woolf, whom he

THE ROYAL BARN

evidently knew personally. Now the King's troubles
increased. Many a time on the journey he threw himself on the ground and wished for death. He had to
wade through brooks and mire in ill-fitting boots and
clothes, wet to the skin, blistered, weary, and wretched.
It rained all day and all night, and was so dark that,
as the King said in after years, the only thing that
guided him was the rustling of "trusty Dick's" calf-
skin breeches. After nine miles of a most wearisome
journey they got to Madeley in Salop, and Charles was

left sitting under a hedge in the wet, while Dick went in to see Mr. Woolf. When the old man was asked if he "would harbour a gentleman of quality," he promptly said "No." He was known to be a staunch Royalist and Catholic, of shrewd, honest character, but the Royalist cause was ruined. Woolf was a suspected man; his house had been searched, and his son was in prison. Why should he, an old man of threescore years and ten, be hanged? Then the simple, honest woodman was further troubled, for what must he do, and to his friend and superior he confided all, and said, "It is the King." Like Isaac of old, in his perplexity Woolf may have "trembled very exceedingly," and said, "Who?" but of hesitation there was none. Fears of the hangman, risks, and doubts were cast to the winds, and for a day and night he laboured to save him, and did save him, for the hunted King lay in the straw of the barn for a day and night, while Woolf tried to get him down the Severn or across it. But it was all so carefully guarded that they durst not do anything, and so ended that day, Friday, the 5th of September 1651. In the night they returned, and the next day Charles spent in the famous Royal Oak at Boscobel.

The barn which was for one brief day the centre of English history I wished to see with its house and surroundings, for I was told they were in existence still, and we found them. The barn has not received a tithe or a hundredth part of the notice that has been given to the oak, for to lie like a mouse in the straw is not so romantic as to be like a bird in a tree and hear "the Roundhead hum a surly hymn." To me there is greatly additional interest, because the Woolf of that day is doubtless of the same family as my relatives of the same name to-day, within perhaps thirty miles of the place. The character of that Woolf as given in the contemporary pamphlets curiously corresponds with that of my late uncle, and, as I was making a feeble attempt to trace the connecting links in the pedigree, I was pleased to find a tablet in Audley church, Staffordshire, in memory of my uncle's grandfather, and the inscription on it would well apply to all or any of the three men. The tablet on the church wall says of Sam Woolf, of the Town House, Audley, who died 1797 :—

> "In friendship steady, in his dealings just,
> His greatest pleasure to discharge his trust ;
> He lived respected, and lamented died,
> Punctuality was his only pride."

The house and barn are much larger than I expected to find, and they illustrate and bear testimony to the truth of the histories which describe the man as " Mr. Woolf," and the barn as a big one. Was this Mr. Woolf a small squire, or large yeoman, or tenant farmer? He was evidently of some position, and well known. In the paltry gift of an Augmentation of Arms given to him at the Restoration he is described as Gent., and his crest is stated to be a demy wolf sable holding a crown imperial or. His house is a good large one to-day, with a fine old stone chimney and mullioned windows, and with the remains of a secret chamber that is now a cupboard.

We were courteously shown round and inside the house. The barn is immense, so big that I at once thought it must have been originally a tithe barn or grange for some rich abbey. Fifty or a hundred men might easily be hidden in it in passages and holes about the straw. It is by the side of the lane close to the church, and is now used as a malthouse. Its enormous oaken timbers are well preserved, and the interstices have been recently bricked up. In the history of Shropshire antiquities I find that Madeley Church and therefore the tithes were given to the church of Stoke St. Milburgh, and afterwards both churches were appropriated to the Priory of Wenlock. It is therefore probable that this great barn was originally built by the monks of Wenlock.

It was here that Mrs. Woolf dyed the fair skin of the King with what the histories call walnut leaves, the dye being most probably the juice of the green fruit, which, when being pickled, turns an intense brown colour that will dye any shade of brown, and the time of year was the season for the pickling of walnuts. The Mrs. Woolf to whose house I returned after my first attempt to find this barn is as hearty as ever, and as intensely Tory. She would do anything for a king, but as for that old Gladstone and Free-Traders, who ruin

MR. WOOLF'S HOUSE, MADELEY, SALOP
Taken from the yard of the Royal Barn

the country with education, foreign corn, foreign butter, or any other foreign rubbish, she would have them all well flogged. She blew me up for being tired and wanting a second quart of new milk after I had gone fifty-five miles with a bicycle on steep and stony roads in a hot day, saying that if I wanted to be a strong man like my fathers were I should have raw onions with toasted cheese and ale for supper, or beans and bacon, and then go to bed early and get up early, and work, as she had done for nearly ninety years.

As the advice is so good, I repeat it for the benefit of the rising generation.

The best way of getting on the Shropshire side of the country is to take the morning express to Shrewsbury, where we stroll through the quaint old city's hilly streets, which are gradually becoming familiar to us. X has never seen the Abbey Church, which lies outside the city across the English bridge, and in it is the tomb and effigy, or what remains thereof, of a pet ancestor of his, one Roger de Montgomery, of whom he is very proud, for Roger was a famous man, rich and respectable, the founder of many churches and abbeys, plentifully endowed, so that priests could sing for the repose of his soul for ever and ever without ceasing.

According to a local and contemporary historian, to whom I must refer again, Roger was left in charge of Normandy when William and his pirate band set out for the plunder of England; and though Roger only stayed at home and minded the women and children, he did it so well that he was rewarded with the earldom of Shrewsbury and 157 manors in England, and as many more as he could wrest from the Welsh. His manors were mostly in the debatable border district, where no one properly knew which was England and which was Wales. But what cared he whether they were Saxon or Welsh if he could get hold and stick? He is the only Norman who left his name on a county, for possibly the original name, if ever there were one, was quite unpronounceable, and his name was a semi-religious one, for Gomer was the son of Japhet, and Gomer's Mount, or Montgomery, is famous evermore. His castle certainly was burned as soon as he was dead, but the share of the plunder that he gave to the Church, the Church stuck to, with a tenacity as great as that of any Norman. In fact, all through the Norman Conquest, which was backed and helped by the Pope, the Church went shares at all the plunder, the robbers paid for their passage to heaven, and new churches went up as they do now when brewers have been having a good time.

X was anxious to photograph his great ancestor's tomb, so I introduced him to the effigy, which had long since lost his head. His hands also were missing, and his feet, with part of his legs, but they are merely details, the loss of which is insignificant to the eye of faith, though rather disappointing to the benevolent friend who is hopeful of seeing a family likeness. With great care and pains the mutilated Roger is photographed, and we go across the road to a coal-yard where, amid the coals and dirt and lumber, is a most beautiful carved stone pulpit, said to be one of the best monumental relics of its kind to be found anywhere. If it were a painting that a rich man could put in his house and say, " I gave a thousand guineas for that," it would be treasured, but as it is, it is of stone, a rare and costly sculptured work of art left in a coal-yard, with drain-pipes against it. Let us go hence.

Along the Abbey Foregate, a broad boulevard with rows of trees, we roll. Somewhere to the left is an old hall in which they treasure a pair of baby's gloves, said to have been made by Queen Elizabeth herself, who knew as much about babies as any old bachelor. Consequently the gloves are too small for any respectable baby of the present day, and therefore each succeeding generation, when the christening comes, has to have the gloves tied on the hands of the little dears when they are operated on.

By the road to London we soon reach open country on one of the most perfect days for cycling. The weather, which had been very hot, had been cooled in the night by heavy rain. The air was fresh, the roads good, and all about was something different to the Cheshire country to which we are accustomed. Barley was in the fields, a crop we seldom or never see in Cheshire. Orange-coloured roses in profusion were in the cottage gardens. A strange bird flew from the road which I judged to be a turtle-dove, and elm-trees became more frequent.

Presently we came to Atcham, and there can be few grander lonely country churches than that. It is on the Severn's steep and sedgy bank, embosomed in lofty trees, alone in a flower garden, with a broad and high bridge crossing the shining water. Unfortunately, it is one of the few churches we find locked, and we cannot find any one to give us the key, for we knocked in vain at the door of the neighbouring house. There are many objects of interest, and the church has one of the longest histories of any in England. From this little village there went forth a boy who was sent abroad to be educated for the Church, and who subsequently became one of our very earliest historians. "Ordericus, that simple, truthful, and earnest monk, to whose labours we owe so much," writing in his old age in Normandy, said that on Easter day, April 5, 1075 (that was ten years before Domesday was written, and yet the Church is not there mentioned), "I was baptized at Ettingesham, in the church of St. Etta the Confessor, which is seated on the bank of the river Severn, that great river of Severn. . . . A weeping father delivered his weeping child, and I left behind my native country, and my parents, and all my kin, and they, weeping and bidding me farewell, with loving prayers commended me to Thee, O most High Lord God."

This little notice shows the curious changes of a place name. Ettingsham is evidently the ham or home of the Ettings, the tribe or children of St. Eatta. Then it became Attingham, and was finally shortened to Atcham. It is very similar to our local name Altringham, which has only had one letter altered, though the natives still pronounce it Otricham. If they had persevered a little more, or been more lucky, we might have had it Otcham or Atcham, and saved ourselves unnecessary trouble. Nearly seven centuries since there was a great lawsuit about tolls at Attingham. It seems the monks used to ferry across the river and charge tolls. Then they built a bridge to save themselves the constant trouble of ferrying. Wayfarers objected to paying tolls for the use of the bridge when it was made, but the Abbot won his case, as they always did in those days, and was authorised to get "a penny for a cart of Salop and half a penny for any other cart."

Journeying on, we come to the long-buried Roman city of Uriconium, and here is another interesting place-name that has gone through strange mutations. It seems the great isolated hill, the landmark of fifty miles round, has kept (like so many other mountains and rivers) its Celtic or British name, Wrekin or Vrekin, for there was an attempt to call it Mount St. Gilbert by the Normans, and at its base was the Roman city Uriconium or Vriconium, a name very similar to Wrekinium. Then the Anglo-Saxons added *chester* to the name, as they did to the names of the Roman camps and cities, and it became Wrekinchester, or Wrochechester, spelt in various ways, and gradually shortened into Wrocheter or Wroxeter, as our own Mancunium *chester* became Manchester.

One of the many wonderful things which we may see to-day, and near to our homes, is a bit of a city of the dead, with the bones of the dead lying there, and the rooms, or part of them, in which they lived—a city which Ptolemy wrote about, and which seems to have been twice the size of the London of that day, flourishing at a time which to most of us appears as the beginning of the world, before Christianity was heard of, or the very name of England invented. The traveller or pilgrim, as he nears Uriconium, sees little difference in the fertile fields of Shropshire till he comes to an immense fragment of peculiar wall. This is all that remains above ground of the Roman Basilica, the town hall, public hall, and law courts of the ancient city. Near to it are the remains of the baths and hot-air flues which warmed them. Most striking of all is a pile of bones, human bones, bleached and dried up till no dog would touch them so long as he could get modern bones with marrow and gristle on them.

They are a powerful reminder of the legends of the sack of the city, when men, women, and children were butchered, and everything set on fire. The Welsh bard

URICONIUM

Llywarch Hen is supposed to have written of this, "the white town in the woodland," a heap of blackened ruins which he had known in happier days, "without fire, without light, without song, the stillness broken only by the eagle's scream, the eagle 'who has swallowed fresh drink, the heart's blood of Kyndylan the Fair.'" Skeletons are still found even in the hollow floors and flues of the baths. One of an old man was found still grasping at his horde of gold, 132 gold coins. How lucky he was to save them all—for some one else

fifteen hundred years after, when they had become
scarce and valuable. "Poison," said Romeo to the
apothecary as he gave him gold for the poison, "I sell
thee poison : thou hast sold me none." And the modern
farmer as he drives his plough over the city of the
vanished legions, what does he say ? "Them old
Romans, they makes rare muck. Best thing to do
wi' 'em and this ere land is to 'tater it ; 'taters pey
and folk liken 'em."

Lingering over the relics of the buried city of Uriconium, and listening to the nice old dame who proudly
pointed out the most curious mementoes of the past, we
found time fly far too quickly. Here was a tile with the
mark of the bare foot and rugged skin of the Roman
slave who trod on it nearly two thousand years ago ;
human teeth sounder and whiter than those of this
generation, though we did not see any three or four
inches long, as gravely written about by a parson. Cooking utensils, and the bones of the cooked food, and many
objects used in daily life are there. Nearly all the great
city is buried deep under the accumulated growth of
vegetation and mould, as completely as Herculaneum
and Pompeii are buried under lava and ashes, and on
the fields above the harvests come and go, enriched by
the blood and fire which the great harvest of death once
garnered there.

Where the southern gate of the city once stood,
where Watling Street went through the Severn, are a
few picturesque cottages and the grand old church of
Wroxeter. Ages after the sack of the city the Anglo-
Saxons became Christians, and built a church from the
ruins of the camp or chester, the Wrekinchester or
Wroxeter, and part of their church is now visible. In
the adjoining vicarage garden is a summer-house, an
amateur's attempt to rebuild a Roman temple. The
churchyard gate-posts are Roman columns, the tower
is immense, as if there had been no lack of stone or

land on which to build, and within the church are several well-preserved tombs with effigies illustrating most vividly the fashions of bygone ages. These monuments and the church itself may not be so highly ornamented as those at Tong, which is like a little Westminster Abbey lost and forgotten in the country; they are of later date, not being ancient enough to be mentioned by the author of "Antiquities of Shropshire." The church is dark, and I had difficulty in deciphering what was written, but here are a few of the inscriptions :—

> " Heare Lye the Bodyes of John Barker of Haughmond Squir and Margaret his wife . . . 1618, she being then thirty-three years, and the said John Barker being in good and perfect health at the decease of the said Margaret, fell sick the next day following and deceased the xvii day after. He being then forty yeeres and they leaving no issue of their bodies behind them."

These effigies are dressed and coloured to represent them faithfully, and on the hands of Squire Barker are the actual iron gauntlets he may have worn in life. Another remarkable tomb has cock pheasants as large as life about the recumbent effigies, and round the edges in Old English letters cut in relief something like the following :—

> " Hic jacet Thomas Bromley Knyght beying Lord Chyffe Justice, also beying one of the executors to the Kyng of most humane memory, Henry the eyght the whyche desesed . . . 1555."

This "king of most humane memory" was the spoiler of the hospitals, the robber of the charities, murderer, adulterer, thief, Defender of the Faith, and Supreme Head on earth of the Church of England. What things these Churchmen ask us to believe! The "humane memory" is chiselled in marble in high relief on the altar-tomb in the church, and the Lord Chief Justice—with his pheasants beside him—is said to have been "a Papist at heart," and yet kept his place under Henry the Eighth, Edward, and Mary, with all their changes of faith. His effigy shows him in a biretta or flat cap, which is said to be the original of the "mortar board" or college cap that some of us were once proud to wear.

Another effigy is that of a lady in stiff red dress, the circumference of which equals her height or length, and as she is lying flat on the tomb the dress stands up like a barrel. There is no dog or lamb at her feet. Cats were never allowed, for they savoured of witchcraft. It became fashionable at that period to have nothing commoner than angels, but as there was absolutely nothing on the effigy I wondered how the end of the lady could be arranged, though I felt frightened of looking too closely, for it is not becoming of a bachelor to pry into such matters. X said it was all right; there was a beautiful arrangement of "petticoats" I think he called them. Then I saw the end of this barrel-like structure had been worked by the artist-sculptor into circles of flounces, and frills, and finery, with two tiny feet in the midst of this whirl of bewitching drapery. The feet were not ordinary "beetle-crushers" that one would expect to carry such a weight, but ideal feet grown for show, and shod in black and red to match the dress, only they stood out stiff in the midst of the barrel. Methought the fashion changeth, but as it was in the beginning, so it ever shall be, for here was the pointed shoe of the exquisite, the square toes of the solemn and precise, the armed heel of the warrior, the high heel of the fool, and the footgear of the native before heels were known. Over and under and round about were literally scores of the quarterings of family arms, the impalements and emblazonments of the Newports, and they looked like the hieroglyphics on the cartouche of an Egyptian Pharaoh.

It is an oft-told tale to say the day was far too short

to see all that we ought to have seen, and many books could not contain the account thereof. There was a very ancient and noteworthy oaken chest for parish documents, and an enormous font made out of a Roman column, which had been rolled into the Severn and there preserved. We tear ourselves away, and make for the high-road to journey towards London again. The Severn is still to our right hand, and the Wrekin to the left. Off the road, on some high ground to the left, are black and white houses, in one of which the guide-books say there lived one Richard Baxter, who wrote innumerable books, " The Saints' Everlasting Rest " being one. We should like to rest, though we are not saints, and we like to roll along the lovely country also. A hare lobs along the road before us that seems inclined to have a little racing or hunting. We come to Leighton, where the village inn stands by the mill-pool under a spreading chestnut-tree, with seats around the bole, where children play and birds do sing, and care or trouble seems unknown. Is this the land where it is always afternoon? Even the postman rests. The ale bench tempts us, and the pigeons softly coo, but we are wandering pilgrims who must travel, travel on. We come to Buildwas, a ruined abbey, a building by the wash, for the land on which it stands is washed by the Severn where the great river turns southwards as it meets the hills.

No men who ever lived on this earth seem to have chosen fairer scenes in which to live and die than those Cistercian brothers who built their nests in the solitude of the woods by the fertilising rivers and meres of our matchless bits of English land. Here we do rest, for the ruins are free to all. On three sides of them is an amphitheatre of the everlasting hills, and across the base there runs the river. Here Roger de Clinton, the crusader, Bishop of Chester, who was lauded and execrated in turn, built one of the first Norman abbeys on the site of a hermitage where centuries before a Bishop of Lincoln had retired from the world.   These abbots were very grand men, and even Fair Rosamond worked them a cope.   One of them had some of the wisdom of the serpent left in him even after he had taken holy orders, for the King wanted money from him, and he answered they gave prayers.   The King reiterated he wanted both money and prayers, but the abbot showed him how he could not possibly have both.   History does not say how that abbot dealt with his flock, but I ween

BUILDWAS ABBEY

he wanted both money and prayers, and if he could not get them both he would take the money and chance the prayers.

The ruin and desolation that have come upon these once splendid abbeys is sad to see, though all may be for the best.   The greed of the priesthood doubtless caused their ruin, and the founders of Buildwas might almost have foreseen it, for in their charter of gift they expressly enjoin their *fratres carissimi*, their most beloved brethren,

BUILDWAS ABBEY

to "treasure up their treasure in heaven, where neither rust nor bookworm eat away, and thieves do not dig out nor steal."

We leave the pleasant valley of the river and turn up-hill, little recking what there was in store for us. We were entire strangers in the land. A fine and lofty iron bridge of 130 feet span, erected by Telford, took us over the river to Ironbridge, and we begin the ascent of Coal-brookdale. Far on the right is Broseley, known all over the kingdom for its long pipes so beloved by church-wardens when they can rest from their labours; for any pipe may give a solace, but these confer a grandeur and dignity also even to the least exalted churchwarden. We have to cease cycling to trudge and trundle, the country becomes more hilly, smoky, black, and nasty. The weather is hot and the day Monday. At most of the doorways and on the road lie and sit men and boys more or less dirty and undressed. Plenty of dogs also, which are better dressed than the men. Beerhouses are common. Tips of rubbish from coalpits or ironworks or foundries are all about. The road gets steeper and more toilsome, and for fully two miles we trudge and shove. Gradually we get over the top, and slightly descend to Madeley, which seems a curious mixture of remote village and coalpits or "works" of some kind. Here our first care was to get tea, for our throats were like lime-kilns or chimney-flues, and there seemed to be nowhere likely, so we asked and were told, "Oh, at Mrs. Onions's." There were plenty of public-houses, but they could not bother with tea. Their business was to sell beer. There were no country cottages with gardens, or indeed few or any houses that looked clean; so at the church we asked again, and were again told, "Oh, at Mrs. Onions's," and to the lady's house and shop we were directed. There we had some tea, but we could not have eggs, and we could not have mar-

I

malade or anything else, so we had to find a shop and buy a pot of something.

The euphonious name of Onions had taken my fancy and brought up memories of childhood, for my father used to tell us that when he was a lad at his father's they had a labouring man named Billy Onions, who had been kept up all night with a sick horse or cow, and who asked for a good breakfast in the morning.   He wanted "a peilful o' buttermilk, well stodged wi' 'taties."   That was the ordinary labourer's breakfast in that country then ; but he also wanted "after that a jorum o' black pudding or a rasher o' bacon wi' a quart o' strong ale on th' top."   So Billy Onions had a good breakfast, and pronounced the word "quart" long and deep, as if he enjoyed it, and with an accent on the *a* as it is in the word "far."

After tea we sallied out and found and photographed the barn in which the Woolfs hid the King as above described.   We also found the grave of Fletcher, the celebrated Vicar, but not the ancient church in which he used to preach.   That has been "restored" away, and a building put in its place hideous enough to make any vicar turn Methodist and preach in the woods or the neighbouring barn.   Madeley-in-Salop should be a place for pilgrims of the Wesleyan persuasion to visit, if any of that devout body do not deem it too superstitious to go and see and feel that which deeds and legend have rendered more or less holy.   John Wesley wrote and spoke of Fletcher as the most holy man he had ever seen, and his testimony is supported by others.   He laboured in his ministry sixteen hours a day, and starved himself on a shilling's worth of bread and cheese a week.

Our long hard day's pilgrimage is done; a day of much pleasure and instruction ; and it seems our best way home is to cycle about seven miles to Wellington, a dreadful road part of the way, though another part is

by the base of the picturesque Wrekin, which we finally
encompass, having in the course of the day travelled all
round it. When the "proud Salopians" indulge in feasting and revelry they drain deep draughts of barley
wine, the öel of their forefathers, and one of their
time-honoured and all-embracing toasts is

"Here's to all round the Wrekin."

CHURCH FONT MADE FROM ROMAN COLUMN,
WROXETER

THE BIRTHPLACE OF THE PROPHET

IT is written, "A prophet hath no honour in his own country," but the proverb refers mainly to the honour a prophet hath or hath not in his lifetime, amid local jealousies, and prophecies gone wrong. When he is safely dead and buried we can begin to praise him and make him famous. If there be any one in these days of secondary and other sorts of education who does not know who is the great prophet of Cheshire, let me say that his name is Nixon, a contraction of Nick's-son, and that the name of Nixon is a name to conjure with in Cheshire. The country folk there look upon him as being quite as inspired as if he had come from Palestine, and rather more trustworthy, and they like him all the more because he prophesied of local things and places, and is dead.

Amid the conflicting accounts of Nixon's life or lives, for he seems to have lived at different times, there is little or no doubt that he was born in the parish of Over, probably on a little farm held by his father under the Abbey of Vale Royal, and possibly at the one named Bridge House. He seems to have been a "softy," with cunning enough to know that if he could get his "dark sayings" to be considered as prophecies he would be treated respectfully as a prophet, that is, something more than a common preacher, and would live free from care or trouble.

Nixon became so famous that he was sent to Court to prophesy before the King. Some accounts say this happened in the reign of Henry the Seventh, others that it was in the time of James the First. The former is probably correct, for the prophecy that brought him into fame had reference to the battle of Bosworth Field. All the records agree in saying that he was "clammed" to death at Court, which probably served him right, for it was said in Cheshire that he would quickly eat a shoulder of mutton, and then ask for bread and cheese to fill up with. There have been Cheshire men who have eaten a calf at a sitting, but they have done something more than preach and idle. It is worth noting that the two kings mentioned are perhaps the two most likely of the English monarchs to have clemmed their servants and retainers, and what was the good of keeping a drivelling simpleton with goggle eyes who ate more than he was worth?

As my childhood was versed in the folk-lore and dark sayings of the country folks' witches and wizards or prophets, I soon learnt some of Nixon's prophecies, especially those interesting to children. There was one about a boy who should have two thumbs on one hand, and another about a miller who should have two heels on one foot. We could believe anything about a miller until the honest one with the tuft of hair on the palm of his hand was found, but for a boy to have two thumbs on one hand was rather perturbing. Any of us might have that, and a dreadful rumour once got spread abroad that a boy had put his thumb out and a new thumb was growing at the joint. We watched ours carefully every morning, but nothing wonderful occurred, and we could only repeat the doggerel :—

> "Then shall great confu-si-on
> Come to this realm of Albion."

To go and see Over, the headless cross, and the grey forest so often spoken of by the prophet, we got on the train at Cheadle Hulme and off it at Church Hulme, or Holmes Chapel, as it is now called, cycling from thence westward through Middlewich, which is a most awkward town for cyclists, the streets being narrow, steep, and winding. We are told to go past the church, but the church seems to be upstairs with several ways past it. There was a stout party idling by, one of a type often seen in similar places, but this one was stouter and more conservative than usual. For it was plainly evident that he was slow to get out of bed, to wash himself, or even to dress himself, for he had not buttoned his waistcoat—perhaps he could not button it. He had not gone with the times and got new clothes as he became stouter. In the intervals of coughs and grunts, and in a voice that seemed to come out of an empty beer-barrel, he tells us, " Go on yon and yo'll see th' Whoite Bur, then th' Bu's Yed, and then th' Red Cou : then there's th' Whoite Lion, an' th' Red un, an' th' Gouden, and then yo'll be at th' Cemetairy." I did not wait for more, for it seemed we might all get to the cemetery and stop there. How could thirsty cyclists get safely past all those public-houses in one short street, besides a few more not mentioned where the liquor was perhaps not so good? for, as some one said, they had never known any " drink that would make drunk come " that was really bad, though some was better than others. However, we get safely past them all, out into the country and up a hill, where roads diverge, and there is a seat where we eat our lunch so as to save carrying it any farther.

Middlewich

As we journey on, the sights, sounds, and smells of the country become worse and worse, until we are in one of the vilest holes, the chief place of the slink trade of Cheshire. " Slink " is a slang term for meat whose history is doubtful, the word being expressive of the way the dealers in it slink past the local authorities. In the large dairying district of Cheshire there are great numbers of old cows and other beasts which are " killed to save their lives," as the country folk say ; and calves which no one has seen alive, which have never heard

Slink meat

the sound of the church bells, as church-goers poetically describe them. These are transformed at Winsford, and thereabouts, the meat being consumed wherever it can be passed off. Our great city has a full share. Councillors may take counsel together, and their officials may blandly affirm that no trade in unsound meat can possibly exist under their excellent supervision, for their inspectors are everywhere; but the slink butcher slinks past them all, the buyer of that which is cheap and toothsome buys, and the butcher waxes fat, while the piemen and the sausage-makers flourish.

In my wanderings about Cheshire and dealings with the dairy-farmers I have often come across these slink butchers, and a curious tribe they are. They have always a "tit" that can "fly." It may be a really good and showy pony, or a poor old slave, without one sound leg, possibly with one eye, or none, long yellow teeth, spavined, galled, and with splints innumerable. It will stand for hours in the cold, and wet, and darkness, often outside a public-house door whilst its master is "boozing"; but if he should stamp on the floor of the trap, or whistle sharply, off goes the pony like the wind, and is soon out of sight. Every by-lane, or field track, or back street, is known to them, and seldom indeed is "the slinker copt on the job."

Up the long hill from Winsford to Over we trundle our bicycles amid perfumes indescribable. What hath Araby the Blest to offer in comparison with these? It would be a relief to have a few whiffs from the Ship Canal. The boiled bones, the hides, and the chemicals are so different from the cherry bloom and sweet-scented clover that we expect to smell in Cheshire. The steep hill and the filth remind one of Talk-o'-th'-Hill or Coalbrookdale, but here the stinks are worse than there. In his deepest dreams Bunyan never dreamt of such as these, or the trials of his Christian pilgrim might have been as ours.

For the last two or three miles we have at intervals seen a church with a fine old tower on the hillside to our left, apparently away from everywhere. It is the old church of Over, the one spoken of by the prophet, where the raven should build in the lion's mouth beside the grey forest, thereby clearly showing and foretelling that the King of England should be driven from his throne and return again no more. All which duly came to pass, for there was a stone lion on the church tower, probably a gargoyle, and ravens being common birds then, built their nest in the lion's mouth, and the black marauders stopped the kingly jaw. *Q.E.D.*

Tradition says that this church was to have been built on the top of the hill, but the devil would interfere and roll the stones downhill every night, until the lazy monks and builders let him have his own way. It was all a tale invented by them, for if they had sprinkled the stones with holy water he durst not have touched them, or he would have been scalded. Or if they had had a modern hymn-book they might have known that

> "Satan trembles when he sees
> The weakest saint upon his knees."

Over has a long history. If the prophet could have foreseen what the place was coming to he might have prophesied terribly against it. As it is, he may turn in his grave and be thankful he was clemmed. When the great King Edward fulfilled the vow which he made in the storm and fear of shipwreck, and founded his abbey in the lovely solitudes of Cheshire, he gave to Over a market and a fair at the Feast of the Exaltation of the Cross. Centuries afterwards we find it written in "The Vale Royall," "Ouver is but a small thing, yet I put it in here because of the great prerogative that it hath. For it hath a maior, . . . and the church is lawless." These "prerogatives" were considered to be grand things, for mayors were scarce, and there was not the

corresponding disadvantage of rates. Over and Altringham had mayors for ages before less aristocratic towns
like Manchester could have them, and a local poet
bubbled over with the couplet—

> " Th' Mayor of Autrincham an' th' Mayor of Ouver,
> The one's a thatcher, the other a dauber."

This is interesting to the student of history and of local
government, for it shows that both these men were in
the building business, and to this day wherever there is
much building being done, the builders strive to get on
the local councils, for it pays them well to do so. They
tell the voters it is for their (the voters') interests they
should be elected, for they understand the business and
know all about jerry-work. The simple believe them
and have their reward. The man of the world tells
them that councillors are not chosen for mere goodness
alone, but they must also belong to some political side.
The builder's politics are in his pocket, but when he has
to choose sides he naturally distrusts that one where the
voters think for themselves, and gravitates to the one
where they follow their leaders and do as they are told.
    "The Church is lawless." This probably meant that
the Church was regarded as a sanctuary long after the
Reformation, and it probably accounts for the lawless
population that throng the neighbourhood even now.
For, as in other places, sanctuaries were found to attract
bad characters and to be a nuisance. Manchester was
once specially made into one, but the townsmen soon
petitioned against it. They said, "their lynen yarne
had to lie out in the night for half a yeare to be whyted,
and wollen clothes to hang upon the taynter," that they
had thieves enough already, and objected to outsiders
coming, and the privilege was abolished. Prior to the
Reformation all churches were sanctuaries, and any
criminal fleeing to them was safe from any vengeance
but the vengeance of the church, for none knew better

than the clergy how to twist all things to their own aggrandisement. As a relic of the old times the space in a church which is enclosed by the rails round the altar or communion table is still called the sanctuary. History seems to shudder at any violation of that. The murder of Becket caused the subsequent exaltation of the Church above the King. The desecration of Tewkesbury Abbey with the murder of the princes of the House of Lancaster, and the sacrilege of Bruce, the hero of Scotland, when he stabbed the Red Comyn who had laid hold of the cross, horrified the country.

> " ' Talk not to me,' fierce Lorn replied,
> ' Of odds or match—when Comyn died
> Three daggers clashed within his side!
> Talk not to me of shelt'ring hall,
> The Church of God saw Comyn fall!
> On God's own altar streamed his blood.' "

There is nothing particular to see in the old church at Over. Like many others it has unfortunately been "restored." It was rebuilt about 1543, and under a canopied tomb in the chancel lies the founder or re-builder with the inscription in old lettering : "Of your charite pray for the soule of Hugh Starky of Olton esquier * * * On his soule Jhu have mcy." His arms, a stork, are inscribed in many places, and there is little else to tell the tale. The church is curiously situated, for, though it is near to a densely populated unsavoury town, it is three fields from anywhere, with only one small public-house, a cosy old-fashioned thatched cottage called the Bell, if I remember rightly, nestling by its lych-gate. This large open space round the church may have been the curtilage of the ancient sanctuary, which must have extended beyond the bounds of the ancient churchyard or church, or there would have been no room for the refugees. They would have been crowded out, perhaps starved out, or even shot at.

There are other curious facts about our ancient

churches which have long since been forgotten. The Rev. S. Baring Gould, who probably knows as much as any man about churches and saints, was lately shown by an observant old parish clerk of a church that had for- tunately escaped "restoration," how the small gates in the rood-screen were purposely made that they should not fasten or shut, thereby signifying that the gate or way from death to life is never closed, for the nave of a church is for laymen, and is typical of this life; the chancel is for the clergy, and is typical of the life to come; and through the rood-screen we dimly see our superiors, the choir boys and the clergy, in the higher regions where even the churchwardens only go when they take up the collection.

The ramblings of my tale have not yet touched upon the rambling prophecies, for they are many, and nearly every Cheshire cat has its own version. A man complained rather sorely that I had written of a boy who should have two thumbs on one hand and a miller who should have two heels on one foot; but the real prophecy, he said, was that a miller should have two thumbs on one hand, and that had come to pass, for he had seen him at Nogginshire Mill, and shaken hands with him, and that I might do the same. He added, this proves that Nixon was a true prophet, and every- thing he had foretold had come to pass, or would do some day. Nogginshire Mill is near Little Budworth. It was to be turned with blood and water for three days when something else happened. The three-thumbed miller was there a few years since, my informant says, and would shake hands with any one for a trifle, but the shaker had better beware of the extra thumb.

Nixon being an illiterate man, his prophecies were not committed to writing until a century or more after his death, and that was a great advantage to them, as they could be varied to suit the narrator or the course of events. I was giving them traditionally, but in a pamphlet dated as long since as 1740 I find there are variants as to whether the miller or the boy was to have three thumbs. So we had better give both of them the benefit of the doubt. I will merely mention a few proverbs and then go on with our journey. " With our own money and our own men shall a dreadful war begin." Fancy any prophet of evil prophesying such foolishness, and yet it has been fulfilled many times. Since his day we have made war upon every nation on the earth, and if a few Dutch Boers (a boor being a country term for a primitive uneducated man) track out into the solitudes of Africa, we are soon after them. Another saying was :—

> " Landlords shall stand
> With hat in their hand
> Begging the tenants to keep on the land."

When he thought or prophesied that, the wish was father to the thought in the poor husbandman or tenant farmer, but it has not come true in Cheshire yet, and never will; the soil is too rich. Let us try others. " There shall be wars and troubles, and men shall be so scarce that the child shall say, Mother, mother, here's a man." " The crow shall sit on the headless cross in the forest so grey and drink of the noble's blood so free." The headless cross is often mentioned; there are still one or two about Over. " Five wicked priests' heads shall be sold for a penny," or priest's heads a farthing each. These seem to refer to the Reformation and the hanging of the abbots, or riots against the priests which took place at various times. A case is recorded where the parishioners were punished for playing football with the head of a monk. A prophecy about the joining together of the Abbey of Vale Royal and the Priory of Norton is said to be fulfilled by the stones being taken from their ruins to build Acton Bridge.

> " In the forest at oaks three,
> A well of blood shall run and ree."

Many of these prophecies are as "bloody" as the talk of an ordinary betting-man. One account of the three-thumbed miller says he is to hold the bridles of three king's horses up to the knees in blood. It reminds me of a "fire-eating" Tory who boasted he could fight up to his knees in blood. They brought him some good

GYPSY CARAVAN IN THE FOREST

old Cheshire cheese for supper, rare old stingo that was with difficulty kept on a deep dish. He turned pale and retreated, for all the fight oozed out of him at the sight and smell of the luscious cheese.

One of the best-known prophecies relates to an eagle which is said to perch on Vale Royal House when an heir to the house is born. This prophecy has all the advantages which wealth and rank can give to it, for the eagles are kept in readiness; in fact, I saw them last year—they were ready even before the marriage took place. With a piece of advice that may be useful to every one, let us take our leave of the great prophet of Cheshire. "In the days of trouble it is well for a man to sell his goods and keep close at home."

If all the Jeremiahs that ever were had come and prophesied against this land as we saw it up that long and filthy hill to Over, or the prophets of evil had cursed it, it could hardly have been worse than it is: the light of the sun is darkened by the smoke; the stench is horrible; what should be fields are tracts of blackened slime, where the skeletons of the trees stand gaunt, and withered, and blasted, as if the destroying angel had swept over all, smearing all things with the abomination of desolation.

From this filthy land we gladly hasted to the forest where on good roads, mid blazing bracken and purple heather, with grand old trees overhead, we rolled along peacefully and contentedly. The wild forest country is as beautiful as when the raving prophet saw it, wonderfully beautiful, but my pilgrim's fancies take me round to another church in the neighbourhood, one that was said of old time to be "the very middest of all Cheshire, though it may peradventure lack an inch or more of so being." At Davenham there is little left that is old but the steeple tower. Across the lane from the church is another old parsonage, the home of the Stipendiary who at the County Police Court in Manchester deals out justice tempered with mercy. In the churchyard is the grave of Stephen Chesters Thompson, sometime alderman of Manchester. It is but a short time since I sat at table with him one day, and in less than a week after stood by his body in its coffin listening to the deep tones of a woman's voice singing, "Rest in the Lord. Wait patiently upon Him and He shall give thee thy heart's desire." Is this the heart's desire? The long rest in the home of his youth? After life's fitful fever with its too exuberant prosperity, the bursting of the bubble, the brave struggle for recovery, there cometh rest, the long rest amid the kindred in the scenes of early youth and love.

A CHESHIRE BARN—PRIMITIVE THRESHING

ERBISTOCK

ERBISTOCK is one of the most charming spots in the country, a *terra incognita* to the great majority of readers, a pleasant day's journey from our great city, unknown to the tourist, unvisited by the cyclist, unspoilt by the tripper, standing in a narrow gorge where, 'twixt its lovely wooded hills, the once sacred Dee rushes to the sea as it did one thousand or ten thousand years ago. Americans may boast of their cities which are only ten years old and have ten thousand inhabitants; X and I prefer those which are ten thousand years old with only ten inhabitants. Erbistock is qualifying to be one of the latter. Its name is said to have been St. Erbyn's stoke or stock, a stock being a place stockaded or fortified with wooden palings, and Erbyn or Erbin lived in the land before the heaven-born Arthur and his Round Table were heard of.

The ancient church has, as usual, been unfortunately destroyed, or what its custodians would call restored. Why cannot they let the old churches alone and build their new ones somewhere else, as has been so well done at Warburton in Cheshire? They say the old ones are damp, and dry rot gets in, affecting even the pulpit and the preaching, while others say the chief thing of all is to have sound doctrine preached from the pulpit. The remedy, of course, is to have plenty of fresh air, and there is room enough out of doors for the preaching, though there might be few to listen, and more soothing than it is the calm of some ancient house of prayer

where, in the dim, religious light, there are sermons on
the stones beneath us and around us, the memorials of
those who are gone before.   At Erbistock the venerable yews that girdled round the church remain most
beautiful and picturesque.   Some are stately and erect,
others almost prostrate and propped up, all of them
flinging their long arms far and wide over church and

ERBISTOCK

road and river, the toughest of all wood, the emblem of
immortality.

   To journey thither we went by the Shrewsbury
express to Whitchurch, to find our way from thence by
the aid of maps and cycles to the goal of our pilgrimage.
We had gone by the same train to Whitchurch when
we went on the voyage of discovery to find the lonely
church of Shocklach and the old home of the Egertons,
and we had then noted the inscribed gravestone of

K

the first Talbot, Earl of Shrewsbury, at the door of
Whitchurch Church. The inscription had puzzled us,
for it is in Old English letters, worn away in places, and
in abbreviated Latin. The stone is shamefully neglected,
for it is worn by countless footsteps, when it might so
easily be covered with mats. The inscription on the
stone begins differently from the one on the monument
in the church. Perhaps the old request for prayers was
deemed too heretical to be allowed in the new and reformed church. The one says, "Orate pro anima"
(Pray for the soul); the other, "Hic jacent ossa" (Here
lie the bones). The fourth word we puzzled at for some
time, and had to give it up, although we had the benefit
of the advice and company of a newly fledged M.A. of
the seat and heart of learning, Oxford, for, as an Oxford
man said—

> "All that can be known I know it.
> What I know not is not knowledge."

From books we find the mysterious word was an
abbreviation of *prænobilis*, or most noble, and amid the
many titles of the great Earl who died in battle was that
of Marshal of France. His sword (long since stolen)
was said to have had bad Latin on it but good steel in
it, and to have struck fire from the helm of the Dauphin
of France. The first part of Shakspere's "Henry the
Sixth" is full of allusions to this "man whose glory fills
the world," "the warlike Talbot, a fiend of hell," "the
terror of the French, the scarecrow that affrights our
children," and then he is said by an eye-witness to be
"a weak and writhled shrimp."

> "Is this the scourge of France?
> Is this the Talbot so much feared abroad
> That with his name the mothers still their babes?
>
> .   .   .   .   .   .
>
> Ten thousand French have ta'en the sacrament
> To rive their dangerous artillery
> Upon no Christian soul but English Talbot."

The old man died as he had lived—in battle—and his
son also, and all the fruits of a hundred years of war
were waste.

From Whitchurch we asked our way to Hanmer, a
quaint old-fashioned village with irregular houses, lofty
church tower, and open grounds stretching in long slope
down to the mere, beyond which are wooded hills and
country halls. The body of the church was burnt down
a few years since, the blackened chancel being still in

HANMER CHURCHYARD

ruins, but the rest has been well rebuilt without pews
or benches, and the effect on entering is striking and
pleasing. The scorching of the fire is still shown on
some ancient yews, beneath whose shade we ate our
simple lunch and enjoyed the prospect and the pure air.
The Oxford man could not understand a lunch without
beer, bitter beer, lager beer, ginger beer, or some sort of
beer. He could not call us "miserable cold-water
devils," for we did not even have cold water, though
we had some gooseberries, which are not very classical
food. The sublime contempt that some people have for

gooseberries is amusing.   It is only when the juice is
sold as champagne that it is appreciated.

From Hanmer we roll away about six miles to
Overton-on-Dee, a small country town with broad streets
and ancient church, of which the graveyard is circled
round with magnificent yews.   On every side these
trees stand erect and well preserved, a continuous circle
of them, beneath whose pillared shade

"The rude forefathers of the hamlet sleep."

The Welsh preserve and protect their yew-trees better
than we do.   They had laws for the maintenance and
preservation of their consecrated trees and saints' yews,
which were highly valued and are still taken care of.
But there seems to be a lack of local or county histories
of the Welsh borderland, while in the neighbouring
counties of Cheshire and Shropshire every parish is
noted in the excellent county histories.

Of the places I am now writing about it is difficult to
find any mention or historical fact.   From a scrap in
Archæologia Cambrensis, Erbistock is said to have been
founded by Erbin or Erbyn, who was a prince of the
Damnonii and father of Geraint, one of the knights of
Arthur's Round Table, but what do we really know of
any or all of that lot?   The scraps of history are scarcely
fit for publication.   A princess of Wales was sent as
hostage to London, and the King treated her right
royally, and made their son a duke.   Many of our ducal
families have their proud origin in a similar way, but
this Duke of Gloucester wanted a pedigree and descent
from the gods, just as in our day an ex-mayor of Manchester traces his descent from an Evangelist and Saint,
one of the glorious company of Apostles.   Therefore
one Geoffrey of Monmouth was set to blend history,
tradition, legend, and myth into a deification of the
British chiefs, the term British including the Welsh of
the west coast generally, Cornwall, and Brittany in

France. Following that, Tennyson wrote his " Idylls
of the King," "the blameless King," King Arthur, in
twelve books, dedicated to " Albert the Good," as some
image of himself: and therein we may read of the
wonderful Arthur—

> " The shining dragon and the naked child
>   Descending in the glory of the seas ";

of ladies " clothed in white samite, mystic, wonderful,"
with incense curling round them, and their voice as the

OVERTON-ON-DEE. CHURCH AND YEWS

sound of many waters, in a blaze of light, flame-colour,
vert, and azure. Where every one is so supernaturally
grand and so superfluously good, it all seems too good
for this world, and yet even here there are wonderful
transformations, for from my office in the busy street
called Hanging Ditch, I see lorries laden with sections
and pieces of dead pigs, and men excitedly handling and
talking about the ghastly, slimy, flabby flesh, and from
the names on the lorries I see it is going to be smoked
and cured, and will come again e'er another market-day
transformed as Arthur was, clothed in white wrappers,
mystic, wonderful, of many-tinted lovely golden brown

in colour, the finest smoked Wiltshire bacon, warranted to keep good two or three weeks.

My earliest knowledge of King Arthur was derived from one of the songs which used to be sung at the harvest-home at Standon Hall. They were all ancient, old-fashioned songs, and probably had as much truth in them as the more aristocratic versions :—

> " King Arthur had three sons,
>   Big knaves as e'er did swing ;
>   He kicked them all three out of doors
>   Because they would not sing.
>   *Chorus*—Because they wouldn't sing,
>   He kicked them all three out of doors
>   Because they wouldn't sing."

As Erbin founded Erbistock it is possible his son Geraint, who became one of the knights of the Round Table, was born there. He became Pendragon, or chief King of the British, and fell in battle "against the heathen of the northern sea." Tradition says he was buried in a golden boat with silver oars, but some one stole them long ago. What could they expect? The Welsh borderland teems with romantic history. Is there none to write it? An old historian complained that if he wrote the truth he offended men, but if he wrote untruth he offended God. That is true to-day, and an historian must also possess ample means if not wealth and leisure. Is there any wealthy Welshman in Manchester who would find some poor Welsh scholars the means for works of patriotism, writing the histories of their parishes and counties, which, for the good of the greater number, should be written in the language of the English?

At Overton-on-Dee the thirst of the Oxford man became acute. X offered him a peach. Trifles like peaches would never assuage that thirst. He wanted something wet in a big can or bucket, and went to find what he termed a coffee-shop, being absent for a long time. When we met again we rolled off along a beautiful country, that became more hilly and wooded as we approached a fine stone bridge that, at an immense height, spanned the foaming river Dee. Here another halt had to be made, for the scenery up and down the river is beautiful, with overhanging woods and a little inn, upon whose signboard are two nondescript beasts embracing one another, which may be heraldic monsters or only cross foxes, though why foxes should be cross, unless they want their supper, we do not know. On the parapet of the bridge is a young swallow that has possibly tackled a wasp, for its eye is bunged up, its bill distended, and will not shut, and it pants in agony ; but we can do nothing for it, and, as often happens, must shut our eyes to the misery around us, and look on its fellows rejoicing in their life.

THE DEE AT CROSS FOXES

We now turn to the left, upstream of the river, up the Vale of Erbine, along a country lane in the woods, and hear the river rushing far below us. The trees and foliage are grand, but the work becomes harder, and there is no one from whom to ask the way. At roadside cottages there is no one in, but from a brick building like a school there is a sound of much cackling, and several women, who seem to be preparing for a festival, are so overpoweringly polite that we think men must be scarce about here, and we fly. After many ups and downs we find ourselves descending a rather dangerous

hill towards the river, and suddenly we pass under
the long arms of the spreading yews, with the little
church on our right hand, and the river far below
on our left. Whither we are going looks doubtful, for
we seem to be in private grounds. But all is well, for
just beyond the tiny church (I wish I could write ancient
church, but that is gone) is a little old public-house, with
ropes stretching across the river at a good height from
it, and this is the ferry, the centre of Erbistock, the goal
of our pilgrimage, and a delightful little place it is.

The beauties of the scenery do not for a moment
deter us from asking about tea, and we are told that
we can have it at once, with milk and eggs and all that
we can wish for, and we may sit in an arbour among
the flowers on a rock over the brink of the river, and
the kettle will boil directly, and meantime we may fish,
or boat, or play, or idle. When we express surprise
at the absence of visitors, our young hostess says that
on fine holidays there are as many as thirty to forty
persons there at once, and then she is busy. We think
of the thirty or forty 'bus-loads which would pour down
like a torrent of suffocating lava if the place were in
Lancashire, but we hold our peace, and under a canopy
of fir boughs and heather propped up by poles, round
which the flowers twine in this garden in the woods,
we enjoy our tea. Many feet below us rushes the
sparkling river, so near that if we get a black crust
or some butter which might be fresher we throw it to
the fishes or the waterfowl. A hen comes to look at
us, and reproachfully says something in Welsh. I
understand enough of the language to feel she is telling us to be careful of the eggs, for if we only knew
the trouble she had to lay them we would not gobble
them up so hastily. I give her an empty shell and ask
her to fill it again, and she eats it greedily, and is grateful. What a lesson for all of us!

There is a Welsh proverb about Erbin, so I ask

the Oxford man if they teach Welsh at Oxford, and he tells me not to "talk shop." He says he knows a man who knows Sanskrit, if that will do, but as for Welsh—why, goats talk Welsh. The fact of being in Wales, and having recently discovered a Welsh version of the well-known motto of the Prince of Wales, made me wish to find some one who knew something of the language and history of the country. All schoolboys are supposed to know that the crest and motto of the Prince of Wales were the badges of the blind King of Bohemia, who was taken prisoner by the Black Prince at the battle of Crécy, and that they were inherited by all the Princes of Wales who came after him. The crest is the well-known ostrich feathers, and the motto is " Ich Dien," meaning " I serve."

From a note of unknown origin which is in my possession I find that the only signature of the Black Prince is in the Record Office, where he signed " Homuth Ich dene," meaning " With (or in) high courage I serve." It is not improbable that he changed the motto which he had inherited from his grandfather to the one something like it, which he had acquired by right of conquest from a king in battle, for the latter was of grander origin than the former.

The Welsh legend is that the Prince's motto should be " Eich dyn," it having been used at the birth and proclamation of the first English Prince of Wales, the grandfather of the Black Prince. When the great King Edward conquered the country he built Carnarvon Castle and sent his wife there, with orders to bring forth a son, who should at once be proclaimed to be the Prince of Wales. The son came, and the father, who prided himself on religiously keeping his promises, held forth the newly born babe on the ramparts of the castle to the crowd of Welshmen below, saying in their language, "Eich dyn," that is, "Ecce homo," or "Here's your man." Thenceforth "Eich dyn" was to be the motto of the

Princes of Wales, and Merlin had long previously prophesied that they should be crowned Kings of England
when money should be round.

Who was to enlighten me about this? I remembered Shakspere had many allusions to the Welsh
language, showing that it was fairly common in his day
and place, though he never wrote any of it, but he said
the devil understood it. It was not likely the devil
would come to the Old Parsonage, and when he is in
Hanging Ditch he is too busy to be bothered with
trifles. Therefore I thought the best thing for me to
do would be to see one of "his own," and consult a
respectable solicitor. The first I saw was a perfect gem
of politeness, skilled in the wisdom of the Egyptians,
learned in all kinds of lore (I nearly spelt that word
l-a-w), who knew how to be silent in all the languages
of Europe, and was conversant even with the dialects
from Cymric and Romany down to that of Stretford,
where the pork butchers are famed for their oaths and
their pies and black puddings. The legend that was
new to me was old to him, and when I asked if he
believed it, he smiled at my simplicity, and without
further answer calmly resumed his legal studies.

Then I sought another, and found a cold-blooded
common lawyer with the air of an oracle, who grimly
answered, "Your pronunciation of Welsh makes my
belly ache." There may be some who object to the last
two words, for a friend of mine, who is a county magistrate, and of sublime respectability, told me that if I
used such words he should complain to the editor, or
discontinue reading my writings, for he disapproved of
his daughters seeing objectionable words; and therefore
not to shock these superior children, who are above the
pains and aches of common folks, let us substitute the
more familiar "tummy-ache." I wrote the Welsh motto
on paper for my legal friend, and he at once said the
spelling was bad. I offered to spell the words any way

he liked, but he replied it was not a question of what he liked or disliked, but of right and wrong. To that excellent moral precept I said I was a member of the Church of England, and publicly confessed every week that we do those things which we ought not to do, and we leave undone those things which we ought to do. This mollified him, for he is a somewhat rabid Dissenter,

ERBISTOCK

and the oracle gave me a guarded confirmation or confession of belief in the legend. He even condescended to show me how to pronounce the words, the first being like a sneeze and the second as if it were *ddthyyn*.

There was only one person in Manchester, he informed me, who thoroughly understood Welsh, and the name was Jones. I used to visit a lady of that name, but they are so common now—there are more than a hundred Joneses in Didsbury alone. He said this was

a doctor, and I ought to see him, though he knew I was
as shy of doctors as of parsons.   He might have added
lawyers, for lawyers, doctors, and parsons generally hang
together, or ought to hang together, although there are
differences of degree and opinion as to their usefulness.
This legal luminary began to smoke, so I asked him if
he had heard the new version of the old tale of swal-
lowing a half-sovereign.   A certain lawyer by some
wonderful mischance swallowed a half-sovereign, emetics
were given to him at once without result, then a stomach-
pump was strongly worked, but all it could bring up was
forty pennorth of gold, two-thirds of the half-sovereign,
to the value of six and eightpence, having been absorbed
into the lawyer's system almost immediately.   Fearing
an action of ejectment, and remembering Shakspere's
words on the breath of the unfeed lawyer, I thanked
him in haste to depart.

Tea in the garden, tattle and tea, with the woods
above us and the river below.   The dragon-flies and
swallows dart past, and in the drowsy afternoon the
butterflies flutter by and all nature seems content and
happy.   Then from the woods on the farther shore
there come cries of women who wish to be ferried
across the river, and the Oxford man says, "What a
lark!   Beauteous maidens in distress!   I will row them
o'er the ferry."   But the elders stop that rash youth,
"None of your playing Ulysses to those blooming
syrens : you would upset the boat among you, and they
would clasp you in their arms and dive into the foaming
flood, and who would there be to take home your
bicycle?   Besides that, they might be frights.   The
distance lends enchantment to the view, and their voices
certainly sound sweeter across the water."   Therefore
we left the beckoning syrens to their fate, and when a
country gorby wound up a windlass and hauled them
across the water, romance and enchantment vanished
into air.   Neither X nor Ulysses offered them any tea,

for we had drunk it all even to the dregs, and two quart jugs of milk also. Then a bright idea came to me, and the Oxford man took the camera to a ledge of rock, and X and I got into the ferry-boat—two men in a boat— to be photographed as if we were crossing that dark river poets write of, from whose further shore no voyager returns. In the gorge the light was some- what dim, but for the first time we were taken

ERBISTOCK FERRY

together, and a pleasant memorial of a very pleasant day and place was secured.

Then we had a wonderful journey home. Ruabon was said to be the nearest station, but the roads thither were steep and bad, and we were advised to make for Wrexham, which would be about six miles off. No one knew anything about trains—it was something for them to know towns—but a penny pocket guide showed that we might catch an express to Chester if we hasted to

Wrexham.   The station was beyond the town and the train was in the station when we got there, but we caught it and were soon at Chester.   Then our further route was again doubtful.   There was an express to Manchester, which only stopped at Warrington, but we do not like going to Manchester.   Could we get from Warrington to Broadheath?   We could try, and the railway officials wired to the low-level station at Warrington for a train which we might possibly catch.   Our express was in to the minute.   We rushed below and again caught our train and landed at Broadheath.   There another express came almost immediately and was at Cheadle in about five minutes.   Therefore we had travelled from Wrexham to Cheadle in four different expresses, and in little over two hours—a remarkably good journey home from a very satisfactory pilgrimage.

DECREPIT YEW AT ERBISTOCK

"Thy fibres net the dreamless head."

PEELS

WITHIN two miles of this old Parsonage at
Didsbury there are two spots which still
bear their ancient British name of Peel. As
we wander farther afield we often come
upon other peels, with or without their once familiar
name. The word, though short, is spelt in so many
different ways that it may be as well to give an account
of it and its meaning before mentioning the many peels
there still are around us.

Some of the variations in spelling are as follows :—
Pale, Peel, Peele, Peal, Pele, Piel, Pile, Pyll, Pylle. The
last but one is probably the nearest to the ancient
British or Celtic word meaning defence or fortification,
and the pronunciation of it would be as usual peel.
A Cheshire farmer would still talk of putting a pele or
peling round his orchard if he wanted an unclimbable
fence to keep out the boys, though the local schoolmaster might tell him he should pronounce the word
paling, and possibly advise him to buy barbed wire.
Some people who do not consider themselves outside
the pale of civilisation cause others to stumble grievously
because they throw their orange-peel, the outer defence
and covering of the orange, on to the footpaths instead
of giving it to the horses, who are as fond of it as the
children are of the fruit.

A wooden pile is a long piece of wood stronger than
a pale or pole, and buildings are still built on piles in
certain cases to make them more secure. A tower is
a pile of building, and if it be surrounded with a moat

or deep ditch of water it is then a typical pele.   The
word has many forms through which one meaning runs,
that of being a safeguard, and it is probable that our
earliest church towers were orginally built for peles or
towers of refuge.

Assuming the modern word peel or pele to be the
same in pronunciation and meaning as the ancient
British pyll, it is not correct to speak of Peel Hall or
Peel Moat.   The correct term is The Peel, just as in
country parishes the Church, the Hall, or the Court are
spoken of ; and when it became customary to have two
names, some John or Robert living in a peel would have
it for his surname.

In the ancient parish of Didsbury, in the township
of Heaton, and on the border of Burnage, there is the
rectangular moat or fosse that formed and guarded the
ancient peel plainly visible.   It is now commonly known
as Peel Moat.   Large trees grow on the mound inside,
but there is not one stone left upon another above
ground, neither is there tradition or legend to tell its
tale.   Church registers show that it was inhabited in
comparatively modern times, but of other records there
are none, unless they are buried with the owner's deeds.
A silver cup was found in the adjacent soil that would
doubtless have a curious history if there were any one
to tell it.

Two miles south of Didsbury, there is a much better
preserved and more interesting peel in Northen-Etchells.
There the moat is perfect, with water in it, and a beautiful old stone bridge with angular buttresses and recesses
over it.   The house is mostly modern, though there are
some parts of much greater age.   The stairs are solid
logs of oak a yard wide, stretching from wall to wall,
and at every few steps there is a right-angled turn, the
whole being a strongly fortified stairway, and at the top
there is a room still bearing the ancient name of the
chapel.   There are many records of this place, one of

THE ANCIENT BRIDGE TO THE PEEL IN NORTHEN-ETCHELLS

the earliest being that in 1360, Thomas de Arden, or
Arderne, got a license for an oratory in Echeles, that
being doubtless the original of the room now called the
chapel.   In 1527 Robert de Honford (Handforth) of
Etchels, who bequeathed xxxiijs. iiijd. to the rebuilding
of Chedle Church, and his body to St. Wylfryd's,
Northenden, is described as of The Peele.   In 1578
the old house was apparently being rebuilt, for Robert
Tatton of Wythenshawe in his will mentions the manor
house of the Peele "as not sufficiently builded for my
wiffe to dwell in."   In 1633 Richard Bulkeley of Chedle
died at the Peele, and at the beginning of this century
it was modernised into a farmhouse, and the oaken
carved work taken to Wythenshawe.   Twice has the
crown seized and confiscated it, or, in other words,
robbed the owners of it—once when Henry the Seventh
coveted the vast possessions of Sir William Stanley of
Holt, one of those to whom he owed his crown and
kingdom, and whom he judicially murdered, and once
again when his bloated son got jealous of the wife for
whom he had sacrificed a better one and chopped off
her head and the heads of her courtiers, Sir William
Brereton of Cheshire being one.   Philip and Mary of
bloody memory sold the confiscated manors of Echells,
Alderley, and Aldford for £2600 to Robert Tatton of
Wythenshawe, and the Fittons of Gawsworth.   The
Peele then became the dower house of the Tattons,
the last stage of its strange, eventful history being a
farmhouse, but as it lies in the fields away from everywhere, it might again be made a beautiful place if some
one with taste and money restored it somewhat in its
former fashion.

On the west to north-west side of Manchester there
are several peels, two of them in one township, which
is very uncommon.   They are Kenyon Peel and Yates
Peel in Little Hulton; Astley Peel; the remains of
moat and well of one at Houghton in Winwick; and

L

another moated one at Farnworth, Widnes. At Stretford there is a place where the name alone survives. There is also the well-known Pile or Pyll of Fouldrey, off the coast of North Lancashire. That is a most picturesque ruin, having been built as a strong tower of refuge by the monks of Furness, and after centuries of neglect and decay it still rises over the waters in solitary, desolate grandeur.

There were not only two peels in Little Hulton in the last century, but each of them was inhabited by a judge. One of them took its additional name from Sir Joseph Yates, who was a Justice of the Court of King's Bench. He appears to have been the son of a woollen-draper of the same name in Manchester, and to have transmitted his legal knowledge to the family he founded, several of them having inherited the qualifications of a judge, and a great-grandson being at the present time the stipendiary for this division of the county. One of the numerous tribe of Fletchers bought the old peel, and having more brass than brains, he one day told Barry, the architect, to build a house like Worsley Hall on it. A large and handsome house was built on the site in which Mr. S. F. Armitage now lives, but all that is left of the old peel is part of the moat, and a mulberry-tree that is eloquent of bygone days.

The other judge at the other peel was Lord Kenyon, whose descendants of the same name still own it and occasionally live in it. It is a charming old place—a quaint, old, black and white house in a little courtyard, with an imposing gatehouse, on which are the motto, "Peace be within these walls," and the initials of George Rigby, the Clerk of the Peace for Lancaster, and Colonel in the Parliamentary Army, and his wife Beatrix, of the Hulton family. The date is 1637. Twenty years after, their daughter Alice took it as her dower when married to Roger Kenyon. There are barns and stables, with coats of arms all worn with age upon them, stone seats,

and a summer-house, from which a shocking Cupid, an
Italian work of art, spouts water on the unwary.   There
is an old-world air about the place, an air of periwigs
and patches, of panelled rooms and ghosts, of elaborate
mantels with gorgeous coats of arms, of stiff brocade and
deadly rapier, that involuntarily carries one's mind back
to the centuries which are gone, and contrasts most
vividly with the miserable Little Hulton of to-day.

There are many deeds and documents of the time of
Queen Elizabeth which are still in existence relating to
"the Peles of Hylton"; they show such curious customs
that a few extracts from them may be interesting.   A
word frequently used was "colemynes."   It looks a
peculiar word, but is quite harmless, being another form
of the familiar coal-pit.   The leases bound the lessee to
grind his corn at ye pele myll, to cause what money he
or his company had to spend, to spend it at ye publick
house, to do blacksmith's work at ye smithy, to buy
coals at ye pitts; though in an older one, dated 1575,
the lessee "may dygg and carrye awaye all such coles
as shall be founde growing within and uppon ye lande
. . . without any fraude or guyle."   He is also to keep
watch and ward when required, which seems even then
to have been a very ancient service.   Other leases are
for "ffoure score and nynteene yeares yelding twenty
shillings upon ye ffeast of Pentecoste or White Sondaye
and ye ffeaste of Sct Marten ye Byschoppe in wynter
(November 11) by eaven porcons and two good and
sufficient capons at Easter and two good and sufficient
hennes at ye ffeaste of Sct Thomas ye Apostle yearly."
There has also to be done "heyring (harrowing), plow-
ing, soweing, shearing, bynding, and settinge up, leading,
filling of mucke or dounge, and carting of tenn good
cartlodes of turves from the mosse to the mancon house
called ye Peele of Hulton or Hall of Wich Eaves."   The
"boon" work must be well and sufficiently done, it
being evident that if the tenant is to do anything for

his own harvest he must do it at overtime. The "boon"
"hennes" at Christenmas must also be presentable, and
of the value of eightpence each, as if any one would
make Christmas presents of tough old scraggy hens, and
keep the pullets for himself.

A document dated 1584, between Edmonde ffleete-
woodd of ye Peele in Little Hylton, Esquyer, and
another, recites "in settlement of differences which they
may might should or ought to have for any matter
cause or color whatsoever from the beginning of the
world until the day of the date hereof except. . . ."
There were evidently some of the Devil's Own walking
about the earth even then, for after such comprehensive,
all-embracing terms as the deed begins with, when
differences which the parties might have had, or ought
to have had, or have had, from the beginning of the
world, are going to be settled, there comes " Except—"

On the westerly side of Cheshire, beyond or on the
edge of the great forest, there are places where the
name of Peel still clings to what are now farmhouses,
and in some cases the encircling moat, part of the
ancient defences, still exists. On a fine autumnal day
we ventured forth to find them, and to save time and
labour we go by train to Latchford, where the Ship
Canal has transformed the country with broad roads and
bridges. From thence we cycle towards Chester, turning
aside to inspect the church at Daresbury, a fine old
church, renovated and restored, yet not spoilt. There
is a spreading yew-tree, and as we linger by the gate,
two smart grooms ride past leading other horses with
side-saddles, and from them we learn the hounds are in
the neighbourhood, the meet being at Daresbury Hall.
Of course we must go, though bicycles are not adapted
for hunting, and the morning is so misty that the show
and pageantry are somewhat spoilt, though the many
varied sights of the meet revive some happy memories.

From Daresbury we sojourn on by the Chester Road

KENYON PEEL

to Frodsham, one of the oldest towns in the country, for
Frodsham must have been a thriving place a thousand
years ago.   The great Norman survey describes it as
having a priest, a church, two and a half fisheries, a mill,
and salt wich, with other wealth.   Even in this short
record we may note how those clerical clerks mention
one of their brethren, the priest, first, as if he were of
more importance than church, corn-mill, or salt-works.

Le Hegh Strete, that is, the High Street, was, and
still is, a mile long, and the church is up a steep hill
away from the town, by one of the many Overtons which
there are in Cheshire.   Thither we wended our pilgrim's
way up the strait and toilsome path, where by the roadside sat a blind man begging.   That may be a quotation,
but history repeats itself, and the poor are always with
us.   In a grand situation is this grand old church of
Frodsham, though modern buildings are springing up all
round, where even of late were fern-clad hills sloping to
the rich meadows below.   Its massive rounded pillars
may be relics of the Saxon's church, and fragments of a
large stone coffin are lying in ruin, which might be
better taken care of.   The sexton tells us this coffin was
recently found at the base of a pillar in the church, and
I think he said that he had measured the skeleton within
to be seven feet six inches in length, but perhaps he
stretched a little.   Its contents are dispersed and gone,
and they who should have treasured what was laid
within their consecrated walls, leave it outside, broken
and desolate.

On a painted board, of the date of 1661, which
records a benefaction of "tenn poundes to ye poore of
ffroddesham," there is mention of "the new Pale";
therefore the neighbouring peel may have been rebuilt
at that time.   Another tablet on the church wall has a
more unusual inscription, for it recites how one Peter
Banner, a carpenter of Frodsham, was troubled, at the
age of fifty, with a dropsy, and was "tapp'd" fifty-eight

times, having had 1032 quarts of water taken from him. That was more fluid than there is in seven barrels of beer. How much must he have drunk? And then to be "tapp'd" in his turn! What a writing on the wall for the would-be worshipper when the parson is prosy or triumphantly refuting some heresy or ism for which no one cares a jot, to read the fate of poor Peter Banner a hundred and fifty years ago.

The Normans built their castle of Frodsham where invading armies would pass between the marshes and the hills. The rocks rise steeply from miles of estuary, swamp, and marsh. Very different types of country here meet together, and the river gives access to the sea. Castle and manor were granted by the great King Edward to David, the brother of Llewelyn, who was soon afterwards accused of treachery, tortured, and dismembered. Other lords arose, and lived and died, leaving behind them little that is worth recording, until one dark night, when John, Earl Rivers, lay dead in his castle, some wronged and desperate wretch set the place with all its contents on fire, and the neighbours gazed with horror on this untimely burning of the body of their lord. Doubtless some would shuddering say, "T'owd un's fot un"; but time softens all things, and manners change, and things called railways spread over the land like spiders' webs, and just as the pass between the hills and the marsh was suited for the Norman Castle, it was also suited for the iron road, and therefore castle and jail and mills and ancient greatness were swept away for the exigencies of modern travel.

Round the beacon hill and in the outskirts of the forest we have a most pleasant ride to Alvanley, though we miss the peel at Kingsley; but as my remembrance of it was that it was merely a modern farmhouse, though surrounded with a rectangular stone-lined moat, we did not go back to it. The hall at Alvanley is one of the numerous places where X's ancestors lived, therefore it must be found, and it is easy to see that it is a farm-house, built with stone from an older building on the same site. It stands on a hill at the end of a straight drive, with remains of what was probably a moat, and with roomy barns and stables down below.

Through bits of the most lovely wild forest scenery we make our way for the other peel, which is in Moulds-worth, and a very important-looking place, quite a palace. For here stayed William of Orange, that wary, silent schemer with a bad cough, when he was on his way to the battle of the Boyne. There is a large and lofty stone house, with perhaps an acre or two of orchard and yard, surrounded with remains of moat and fortifications or walls of brick arranged in semicircles or escallops, with big stone balls on all the gates and coigns of vantage. Black pigs are a striking feature of the place. Everywhere they lie about like great, fat, black sausages, or grunt and grub with lesser sausages, every black pig having four white feet and a white face Many of them are blessed with names ; for instance, Peel Daisy or Peel Jessy, instead of Daisy Peel or Jessy Peel. They are Berkshires, noted in the showyards of many countries. X has half a mind to buy some, but they would be awkward things to take on a bicycle. So we travel on amid devious winding roads, and soon come to a well-built little house of stone, with projecting windows, and inscription reciting that it was "repeared by me John Davies of Mandalay, A.D. 1674." The name of the place is now contracted to Manley, and the cottage, once so carefully and ornamentally built, has well withstood its centuries of changing weather.

Our journey takes us through varied country—from the Ship Canal by the railways and works of Frodsham, through the rich farming lands of Cheshire, noted here-abouts for early potatoes and early gooseberries, and in the midst of the forest primeval. Here the bracken glows below the white-stemmed birch-trees and the

stately oaks and firs.   The edible chestnut flourishes,
for the road below it is often strewn with its fruits,
which may be bad for our tires, and we wonder where
the boys can have come from to destroy all this ripening
fruit, forgetting there may be squirrels until the sight
and sound of many jays remind me of them.   Some of
the lanes are sandy, and experience has taught us how
suddenly deep sand stops our career.   At one point X
was going ahead, exulting in his youth, perhaps a dozen
yards in front of me, when suddenly he stopped "dead,"
and just as it seemed impossible for me to stop or avoid
running into him, I also was blocked with sand.   Then
he walked a bit until his eagerness overcame him, and
I followed, determining to keep twenty or thirty yards
behind.

Suddenly he disappeared, and just as I was wondering whether he was going to heaven in a whirlwind, my
machine lay down and upset me in the sand.   I jumped
up immediately and ran to see what had become of him,
for he and his belongings had disappeared as completely
as if the earth had swallowed them.   It had nearly, for
he was at the bottom of a deep ditch with his bicycle on
top of him.   I called, "Are you there?   Are you there?"
as men vainly cry to the telephone, and a faint answer
came back, "I'm all right; go away."   I tried to pull at
his bicycle, which was fast tied up with briers, but he
kept murmuring, "Oh, go away and let me collect my
thoughts."   So I went to collect my own machine, with
any coins or unconsidered trifles that might be lying
about.   When I returned and asked if his collection
was finished, he said, "Can you see the hole my head
made?"   There were some rabbit-holes about, but
nothing to show where he had fallen, and the wonder
was how he, like the apple, got into the dumpling, for
he lay comfortably on his back at the bottom of a deep
ditch all overgrown with ferns and briers, which covered
him as completely as the leaves hid the babes in the

wood.   I doubt if he could have got up by himself, for
the bicycle was above him, also in the ditch and en-
tangled in the briers.   It was a difficult job to get everything disentangled, and as both of us were upset and
lost and one buried, we did very well for babes in the
wood, the wicked uncles being three men hoeing turnips
in an adjoining field, who left us to our fate.   They would
probably have jeo-
pardised   their
bodies and souls for
a pint of beer, but
as for crazy cyclists.
why leave the hoe-
ing of turnips for
that rubbish ?

After that we
went wandering on
to find Plemondstall
or Plemstall church,
a lonely church in
the low fields by the
little river Gowy.
It   is   surrounded
by fir-trees, quaint
and   ancient.   At
the east end is a big
tomb with skeletons
"as large as life,"

LECTERN AT PLEMONDSTALL

sculptured on the stone, and there are some remains of
old oak in the church.   Tradition says the place was
originally consecrated by an eremite or hermit named
Plegmund or St. Pleymonde, who had been tutor to
King Alfred, and consecrated seven bishops in one day.
Perhaps all that responsibility caused him to retire to
this out-of-the-world place, where no one could find
him, here to end his days by a well of water, which,
of course, became holier and more useful than ever.

CHEADLE AND PRESTBURY, WITH THE HALLS BY THE WAY

L O! the winter is past, the rain is over and gone, the flowers appear on the earth, and the time of the singing of birds is come." Let us leave the loneliness of the crowded city with its stifling breath and dull, monotonous roar, our varied cares and troubles, the heaping up of riches or the labours in which there is no profit, and off to the fields and woods where "the heaven's breath smells wooingly" and the glad earth is offering all her best. For the sweet influences of spring come upon us all, even upon those who in lifelong sorrow mourn for others who have gone the way of all the earth, and whose great pilgrimage is ended. In the gleaming springtide even moping and depression lighten, and sadness tends to flee away. Therefore we also wish to breathe the pure fresh country air, to see the woodlands carpeted with acres of hyacinthine blue, to listen to the lark's ecstatic hymn, and to smell "the smell of a field which the Lord hath blessed." Whither can we better go for all these pleasures than southwards, amid the old familiar scenes in Cheshire? Where, on some breezy hill o'erlooking miles of fertile fields, or on some buttressed bridge o'erspanning sweet and clear water, or in some quiet country churchyard amid the tombs and yews, we can, like "Old Mortality," eat our simple lunch and moralise on things in general.

By the Cheadle village green I meet with X, who, like a good workman, is always prompt to time. Our

journeying to-day must be sedate and slow, for the
bicycles have had their winter's rest, and another
year has told its tale on them and on us, whose old
joints are not so easy to oil as are theirs. "Chi va
piano va sano, e chi va sano va lontano" (He who goes
softly goes safely, and he who goes safely goes far). We

CHEADLE CHURCH

may learn wisdom even from the foreigners, who say we
take our pleasures sadly, but we do take them, and softly
and safely we roll along.

The ancient church of Cheadle stands where it did.
The natives call it Chedle, a name which sounds like
Chedil, the hill of "good St. Chad," the Chedde or
Cedde of Saxon and Domesday times. Some stirring
scenes have taken place in that old fane. The Te Deum

for Flodden, and the lament for the young squire fallen in the battle. The outcast last Abbess of Godstow, driven from her nunnery on the banks of the pleasant Isis, coming here to end her days, and build the chancel of the church to be her own memorial. The fiery sermon in the time of the Civil War : " You must not only pray, but pay, and fight also." Then, after civil turmoil, came the dark ages and the slumber and dust of two hundred years. Now there has been restoration, and the last addition is a new wire-guard put to preserve a bit of old glass in an eastern window. The guard has been put there by a dissenter, for those who should take care of the ancient things neglect them. " Vanity of vanities," saith the Preacher, and also saith the glass, " All is vanity !"

Truth is stranger than fiction, and what does this bit of old glass say to those who can read the hand-writing on the wall? It is the cognizance of Sir John Stanley, a noteworthy man, warrior, and saint. Space forbids a record of his life, but here are a few of the facts of it. He was a chance child of a bishop. The illegitimate are often said to be the ablest men. At seventeen years of age he won his spurs in the thrice famous fight on Flodden Field. Then he married a girl of twelve whose father had fallen in the battle, and whose effigy rests beside his. There may have been vows or promises as the dying father bequeathed the care of his only child to his comrade in arms. Young Stanley certainly married the girl and got the estates of the Honfords of Honford, or Handforth, as it is now called. The united ages of the newly married couple amounted to thirty years. Then he built the Stanley Chapel in the Cathedral of Manchester, where his arms are still over the portal, though the requests for prayers for the souls of him and his wife and their parents are gone.

Then he quarrelled with the all-powerful Cardinal Wolsey, and got locked up in prison. His fate was probably an unjust one, for it seems to have soured him and proved to him that "all is vanity." True Christianity, or Communism as it is now called (the holding of all things in common), took hold of him. He renounced the pomps and glories of the world. He gave up all he had for charity. He took religious vows of poverty, chastity, and obedience. His wife did the same just to keep him company, but it is evident she backed out of the vows as soon as he was safe, for she married again and became the mother of another family. Let us not judge her. She only followed her nature, and obeyed the oldest commandment. Their renunciation of one another and the world was "in the face of the Church," before the magnates thereof, in the sacristy of St. Paul's, London, on the 25th of June 1528, and emblazoned vellum still records that his name was enrolled in the martyrology of Westminster Abbey, and in the old churches of Manchester and Cheadle his cognizance, or what remains thereof, may still be seen.

THE STANLEY ARMS

Lands and funds he had already given for pious uses, penny doles to poor widows and poor maidens, wages to priests or poor who would pray for him, with many elaborate safeguards and quaint old terms long since forgotten, for all has passed into oblivion, and in our time who fingers the money or who does the praying no man knoweth.

A few years since I went into the Cathedral of Manchester to see if the arms of Sir John Stanley were the
same as those in the church of Cheadle, and if any of
the requests for prayers were left.   As I passed up the
aisle several people were quietly praying, and, to my
astonishment, one of them was a man whom I had
known to be selling flour about Hanging Ditch for
thirty years.   It was on a Thursday morning, the day
of the weekly corn-market, and about ten o'clock, before
the market had begun.   Was this man praying for a
good day, or giving thanks, or, like the historic publican,
asking for mercy?   The prayer for mercy would seem
to be more fitting when the day's work is done.   Un-
observed I passed on quietly and quickly, wondering
whether I was awake or dreaming.   In all our ancient
towns and cities the corn-market is held close to the
oldest church ; it may be for obvious reasons, and the
fact may have given rise to proverbs, but few are the
corn-dealers and small their credit who avail themselves
of their advantages.   Even exceptions may show how
much better it is to leave the churches open all the day
than to lock them up all days but Sunday.

There are other little bits of this old broken glass,
remnants of that which once gave glory to the light in
Cheadle Church, and scattered mingled colours o'er the
darkened oak—tiny bits of faded dirty glass, which tell
their own romantic tale.   For here are three bucks'
heads "cabossed," a well-known badge of the Stanleys :
and the crest is an eagle's head with something in its
bill, another difference from the eagle and child, or " brid
an' babby " of our Lancashire folk.   Old records tell
that in the third quarter of the shield and in the eagle's
mouth were eagle's feet, the badge the Stanley men
wore on their cap and breast broidered in gold, their
cognizance in the day of battle.   On the sinister side of
the shield is the impalement of the Honfords, the scythe,
an emblem of several old Cheshire families, whose long-

forgotten forefather was probably some furious yeoman,
who rushed into the fight mowing down his enemies with
his scythe, his only weapon, which he justly took to be
his badge when granted the right to bear arms. In the
last quarter there is a star. Can the romance of history
further go than to say that the star which the Honfords
bore was that which fell from heaven in the Holy Land
before the armies of Saladin and his Saracens, and in
defiance of them was then and there seized by a Honford
and fixed upon his shield? Others of the family bore
it through the famous wars in France, until it paled
before the saintly Joan of Arc, and flickered out with
the last male heir of the race on " Flodden's fatal field."

Encircling all are remnants of the mournful motto,
" Vanitas vanitatum, omnia vanitas " (Vanity of vanities, all is vanity). The dead knights' marble effigies lie
calm and still—

> " Soldier, rest! Thy warfare o'er,
> Sleep the sleep that knows not waking ;
> Dream of battlefields no more ! "

The many Cheshire men who fell in that stern fight on
Flodden are worthy of a better record, and it has long
been my wish to write one. " Ars longa, vita brevis "
(Life is short, though art be long).

Cyclists may do worse than rest awhile within the
church at Cheadle. It is not always locked like that at
Didsbury. The doors are usually wide open. Any one
may " go to scoff and stay to pray "; they may stare
and gape about, that will do no one any harm. Let
them look at the grand old roof with its carved oak,
or the artistic ancient screens with the symbols of the
vanished families, or the sermons in stones—they are
often better than the sermons which are shouted at
you. There is some interest in our forefathers, even
the heathen feels that. The crowds go hurrying past.
Catch some of them, and ask whose image and super-

scription is this, where the stained glass gleams o'er the sculptured stone, and the latest heir of all the ages will probably stare in dazed astonishment, or with sublime contempt turn from what to him are merely bits of rubbish, to ask, "What's won?" or to buy the last edition.

What care the hurrying crowds for the mournful motto when the blood is hot in their veins? Sir John Stanley had no time to think of vanity when he charged like a whirlwind into the Scottish hosts, who vainly fought and died around their king. His strange eventful history changed when the proud cardinal, who had "sounded all the depths and shoals of honour," and whose last vain regret was that he had not served his God as he had served his king, had injured him; and now that he and his are fast sinking into mere oblivion, his legacies perverted, his gifts forgotten, his cognizance nearly destroyed, we may still read the odd words of his motto on the vanity that is the emptiness or the nothingness of life—"Vanitas vanitatum!"

There are many halls in the once great parish of Cheadle, the most conspicuous of them being Cheadle Bulkeley Hall—the house of X. It stands by or on the remnants of the village green, and is noteworthy for its ghosts and mulberry-tree. The ghosts are well known and well authenticated by many persons who are still living. One is of a fascinating lady in a mob cap, who smiles and sighs and sighs and smiles even at a bachelor. Cheadle is a great place for spirits. Even the rectory is not free from them, though why a ghost should stop about a rectory is one of those things which no one can understand. Old parsonages are not uncommonly haunted by them, as is the house from which I write and another to which I shall refer; but in these cases the ghosts have driven the parsons out, and the latter have had to seek for peace elsewhere.

CHEADLE VILLAGE, FROM THE GREEN TO THE CHURCH

Dame Katheryn Bulkley, the last abbess of Godstow, who was buried at Cheadle in 1559, is still said to haunt the rectory where she died, bewailing and bemoaning her cruel fate and the calumnies on her nuns and sisters.

Another old hall with a shrinking sad sort of a female ghost (the injured lady having been poor Fanny Fowden) is Adswood Hall, a lonely house which stands near to the bridle road, which was long preserved by

CHEADLE MOSELEY HALL

farmers to drive their cattle to ley in Derbyshire, and now is chiefly used by cyclists. This house has still its cockloft or priest's hole, as the once common secret chamber was termed, and a good oaken door three to four inches thick, with a "squint" or tiny door, part of the bigger door, through which the inmates could safely shoot at unwelcome visitors. I wish our front door was like it.

Cheadle Moseley Hall is the ancient timber building

M

in a field to the left of the road to Stockport, and its predecessor, or Cheadle Savage Hall, when the Savages owned their share of the manor, was possibly part of the old fold-like-looking black and white house to the right of the road to Wilmslow.   There are other interesting halls, too numerous to mention here.   Their records may be found in the book of the Chronicles of Cheadle.

> "Somewhat back from the village street
> Stands the old-fashioned country seat.
>
> *   *   *   *   *
>
> In that mansion used to be
> Free-hearted hospitality.
> There groups of merry children played,
> There youths and maidens dreaming strayed.
>
> *   *   *   *   *
>
> All are scattered now and fled,
> Some are married, some are dead."

As we journey southward we come to a lane on the left called Stanley Lane.   There was a toll-bar there called Hurlbote, and the inn was once called Stanley Fold.   Down the lane is a picturesque black and white house called Stanley Hall, which is owned and well preserved by the Society of Friends.   All these names of Stanley are reminiscent of the Sir John Stanley before mentioned, though there is nothing to connect him with them.

Farther on is the village of Handforth or Hondford, and on turning to the left over the station there is the finest timber-built hall of any in the parish.   As there are several photographs of it in my book on Cheadle they are not reproduced here.   The porch is very like those of Dutton and Adlington that are in this book, and its deeply carved inscription tells us in Old English letters that "This haulle was buylded in the yeare of oure Lord God MCCCCCLXII by Vryan Breretonn Knight Whom maryed Margaret daughter and heyre of Wyllyam Handforth of Handforthe Esquyer and had

Issue vi. sonnes and ii. daughters." Nothing is said here about the lady's former marriage and family and divorce. The hall was supposed to be built—like so many others of the time—out of the spoils of the religious houses. It still has a handsome Jacobean staircase.

From the above-mentioned family descended Sir William Brereton, the Commander-in-Chief of the armies of the Parliament in this north-western part of England during the Civil War. Many were the battles and sieges he fought all over the country, and he was generally victorious, but when "the King enjoyed his own again" he died, and as his body was being brought from Croydon to be buried in the Handford chapel of Cheadle Church, it is said that a great flood suddenly arose and swept both coffin and body away, because he had fought against the King, the merry monarch who was Head of the Church, and it is inferred that the flood was one of water and somewhat supernatural. Perhaps some perfervid Royalist chucked him in the water, for even the buried Puritans were not then allowed to rest in peace.

Sir William Brereton left behind him a record of his travels, which is interesting reading even to-day. He reckoned that one acre of land in Handford was worth any two in Scotland, and not even Jane Kelsall's cot on Handford Green was as bad as where he lodged in Ireland. He also brought "coy" men from Holland, and made a coy or decoy for catching wild ducks, thirty roods broad, and its site may still be seen on the left of our road, where there is a wooded ravine with a streamlet winding through. Pellstart was his name for some water-fowl which is as extinct now as its name, and his "tharck" cakes were probably oat cakes or oaten bread, possibly with rye or barley mixed.

On our right hand, down a nice old-fashioned little avenue of sycamores, is another old parsonage. It was rebuilt a few years ago, but the ghosts were not laid, for

"the study" was left, a low old room with a trap-door
to a small cellar or dungeon below; and though carpets
may be thickly laid and no mention made of ghosts, yet,
when spirits are about, a creepy and peculiar sensation
comes, and—for the sake of women I had better say
no more.

Down the hill to the little river Dean the road is
steep and paved and bad, and on the other side of the
river it is steeper and worse. The cyclist, therefore,
had better trundle and shove up the long hill. Farther
on the ways are good. Soon we come to the old chapel
of Dean Row, which has weathered the storms and
schisms of two hundred years. It was probably built
out on the waste, five miles at least from any market
town, as were so many of the Dissenters' chapels, for
fear lest their unorthodox beliefs might sap the morals
and endanger the commercial honesty of their neighbours, the ordinary market folk, who, though quite
willing to believe everything they were told to believe
in religious matters, would, in the affairs of this world,
prefer to trust to their own senses, and even in open
market hold up an egg to try and see if it were full, or
what there was in it. The ownership of the chapel is
said to have passed in the whirligigs of time from the
Presbyterians to the Unitarians, and there be some men
who say of the latter body that they are fit to buy and
sell eggs in any market.

What a beautiful and interesting little place this
chapel-yard is. It is a well-kept burial-ground, radiant
with flowers and verdure. Although it may appear
incredible to ordinary Christians, or even to heathens,
I know well a place where the parson of the Established
Church, in his ill-will, lately pulled up and threw away
the flowers and plants which were planted on a venerable
old woman's grave. Here there is a lych-gate, with
swallows' nests under the eaves, the nests being plain to
be seen and unmolested. At the other place, the dear

DEANROW CHAPEL

little choir boys were allowed to take a bird's nest, unrebuked, excepting by the birds, as the congregation were leaving the church. In this old chapel-yard the first gravestone has on it a large incised cross, so some one must be getting more "high" as well as more "broad." There is another grave on which a big boulder-stone that was dug out of it has on its polished face its own memorial.

Here are the everlasting yews, and the sweet-brier and gillyflowers, and the old-world name of Dinah. There is a lofty sun-dial, with three squared faces to the sun. Money was evidently more plentiful when that was built than when the chapel was built. The latter is plain and cheap, made of brick, which it is hoped the ivy may soon cover. It is relieved with quaint old-fashioned outer staircases, stone mullioned windows, diamond panes, stone knobs, high-backed pews, and bits of time-worn oak. Over all there broods the air of hoar antiquity, the feeling of peace and rest. The perfume of the flowers floats o'er the graves of the dead, and as the daylight dies the birds quietly cease their song, for they, too, soon will be at rest.

Beyond the old chapel at Dean Row the road forks to the left and right fronts. The way to the left is a steep descent to the river and up again to Woodford's church and inn. This ancient name was Wydeford, but the native folk, with the tendency of their fathers to pronounce *d* as *t*, call it Wutfut. We take the way to the right, passing some pits by the roadside where the trunks of big trees seem to be always rotting in the stagnant water, and round us there unfolds a lovely panorama of country. To the right is Alderley Edge. Straight in front are the Lyme Hills, with the Cage, the keeper's house by the Bow Stones, and White Nancy, all backed by Derbyshire from Kinder Scout to Shutlings Low and the hills towards Leek, the whole plain being studded with ancient farmsteads, herds of cattle, luxuriant vegetation, and all the signs of rich fertility.

In the fields in front is a many-gabled house called Newton Hall, and round about is Newton heath. The name recalls the fact that the once new town has vanished. Even the church or chapel is gone. Musty records, written in clerkly Latin, still refer to it, but all that stands above the ground to mark its site is the sacred tree, the ancient yew, an uncared-for wreck. Through its hollow trunk the children creep and play. It might be burnt for firewood or used for a gate-post, but the labour of chopping at it would be much too great. The farmer knows that if his cattle nibbled it death would soon ensue, and therefore faith and superstition and its own imperishable toughness help the glum old tree.

Across the lane is another yew, clipped into formal shape or want of shape, an arbour below, an arm-chair above. Robust and tall, though not in its prime, its age may be taken to be a little over that of the adjoining house, a squarely, solidly built house, roofed with tons of massive stone, and dated 1702. One John Browne built himself an abode, signed and dated it in a proper manner. He made no boast of heraldry, and merely indulged in a useless *e* after his name. It reminds one of an old tale about rooks, who are such staunch Conservatives that they always make their nests and noise about the house of the richest man in the parish. They have been known to desert a rookery when some new-fledged Radical has come to inhabit the ancestral hall round which their nests were built. Once upon a time the old squire was dead, and a dreadful rumour got spread about that some people named Smith were coming to the hall. The rooks were greatly perturbed, not knowing whether to leave at once or not, but an old patriarch advised delay, and

BROWNE'S HOUSE

THE BENTS

kept close watch until he saw the luggage coming, and the amount of it showed there was wealth, and therefore the chance of getting some of it or its proceeds, and the labels showed that the name of the new family was spelt with a *y* and an *e* at the end—Smythe, not common Smith. Their dignity, therefore, was satisfied, and the sanctimonious gentry in black went on with their egg-sucking, potato-stealing, and other sins.

John Browne built his house well, with good oaken staircase and massive beams. Now there are holes in the roof and the tenant has notice to quit, though he was born there, and has lived there more than half a century. Some of us, even in these electric days, like to hear of any one living in one house, content, for fifty or more years. Behind this house is another one much older, with a most picturesque projecting dormer window. Wattle and daub protrudes between the massive oaken timbers—hazel rods and bents daubed with clay, impervious to any weather. This ancient cot is tumbling to decay, as it has been for centuries. Shepsters build in the roof, while swallows flit around, and the house seems made for the birds. A cheery, cherry-faced old woman shows us how clean it is inside, and all so charmingly artistic, as is the old name, The Bents.

Across the fields to the left, over the river by a wooden plat bridge and up the hill, is Woodford Old Hall, ornate with quatrefoils of black and white, and overhanging upper storeys on its northern side, but, like so many other ancient houses, perished and gone on its southern or weather-beaten side and rebuilt ugly and common. Its age can only be guessed, but it is very great, as the new hall to which we are going is dated 1630, and this one, as its name imports, must have been old before the new was built. The big barn has the initials " I. D." for John Davenport, and 1660. The guardian yew-tree is there. We walk through fields to find our way to Woodford New Hall. All around us is lovely country. It is difficult to imagine we are so near to Manchester. We see the rich grass of Cheshire stretching for miles to the neighbouring hills, the trees in the bright new foliage of May, and the apple orchards in bloom. The swallows flit and poise themselves around us, and the wandering voice of the cuckoo floats by. The cattle look sleek and contented. It is evident by many signs that the land is good, and also the landlord and tenants. The signs of poverty and neglect even on good land, as on the neighbouring estate, are not here. The gates swing on their hinges freely, and have good fastenings. There are actually little wicket-gates at the footpath, and a handrail to a footbridge, which is only a few inches wide, and evidently not intended for cyclists.

Woodford New Hall was built of stone and brick, for we are getting nearer to the stone country of the hills. Over its portal is the date with the initials and arms of the Davenports, members of the once all-powerful family in the Forest of Macclesfield who owned the estate then and own it now. One room is panelled in oak. The oaken beams are carved, and on the tiny panes of glass are relics of revelry where, it may be, the fear of the future haunted the feast even as a spectre. For, nearly two hundred years ago, the Davenports and their neighbours, the Leghs, of Adlington, scratched their names on the little diamond-shaped panes of glass in the window, and one wrote, " Long live good company !" and women wrote, " Heaven long preserve us both." Whether these women wished to be preserved in heaven or on the earth they did not say ; let them have the benefit of any doubt. They were here then, now they have gone hence, and other memory of them is forgotten. The times are changed, and the family. Buxom dairymaids show us round, who are justly house-proud of their furniture and produce, for their butter and cheese are good, their calves are sleek and dosome, and

WOODFORD OLD HALL

they have many goslings, all bespoken by men in Stock-port, who long to feast upon the gosling's tender skin, and eat their flesh with sage and stuffing.

Through the fields and by the woods where, in the damper spots, the marsh-mallows are a blaze of gold, and the lady's smocks and anemones are sheets of pearly grey, we wander on to regain the road we left, and visit Wyllot Hall, another many-gabled, rambling, picturesque old house. Here the front gates are tied up with string, and nobody is about but a noisy, angry dog. There seems a lack of everything but children, whose voices come from the back, and from whose mother I ask some of the usual questions—May we photograph? Is there a date on the house, inside or outside? Is there any old oak? I dare not ask about a ghost when I see the children and the scared look of the mother, but I do ask if there is any old furniture, and I am told there is none.

Then I say, "What about that cradle? It must be more than one hundred years old." It was the third I had seen that day, for some of these old farmhouses have very good ancient oaken furniture. This cradle seemed to be bigger than usual. It would have held two or three children and the cat if there had been a flood, and a small Noah's ark had been wanted in a hurry. These deep, old-fashioned cradles are interesting pieces of furniture in any house, and this one would have held a child of seven stone weight, but if either of us had bought it and taken it home, what would the neighbours say? X says he doesn't care what any one might say, but experience teaches us, among many other things, that those who are most valiant when abroad are meekest when at home.

I was brought up to regard signs and omens, and as the bicycle gives a rather bad side-slip, I see there is a magpie perched on a bough of a tree right across the road in front of us. Instantly I spit at the beast,

saying, " Devil, I defy thee ! " and the chattering fiend
flies off in search of further mischief.   A gentle whistle
completes our charm, and we have no more side-slips
nor talk of cradles.

Still travelling on our pilgrim's way to Prestbury,
every mile of this fertile country shows us some time-
worn, weather-beaten house, but few have their long
eventful history so graven on their many styles of building as the Hall of Adlington.   Over a steep little bridge
across a busy bustling river, we come to woods where,
in midsummer, is a grand display of snow-white flowers
several inches across and perfumed like orange blossom,
lofty waving bushes of the best variety of syringas.   A
muffled sleepy mill is there, with old millstones outside
the door, and a pool, a remnant it may be of the once
useful moat.   On its waters the waterhens and wild
ducks splash and play, and beyond is a many-gabled red-
brick house, its front to the park being built of stone,
with enormous columns and inscription, classical, grand,
and ugly.   Between these outer walls there is an inner
house with courtyard, a gem of black and white, signed
and dated, with lofty central hall, open to the heavy
beamed roof, gorgeous with emblazoned heraldry.
There are very few of the old English halls that
have so well escaped the ravages of time.   One was
built here in 1505, or, as the inscription said, "a do
MCCCCCVRRHVIIXX"—the latter part meaning in
the reign of King Henry the Seventh, the twentieth
year.   It was rebuilt or enlarged in 1581, as the inscription over the doorway still showeth, and the beautiful
central hall, with its hammer-beam roof, had then 181
shields of arms of the families related to the Leghs.
The display of heraldry is much less now than it was
then, but it is still large and interesting.   There is also
an organ, on which a doubtful tradition says Handel
first played " The Harmonious Blacksmith."

THE PORCH, ADLINGTON HALL

If half or a quarter of the family alliances of the
Leghs, as shown in this collection of arms, be true, then
every Cheshire cat should be related to them.   Proverbs say—

> " In Cheshire, Leghs are thick as fleas,
>   And there are Masseys like to asses."

Certainly the name is common, and it behoves every
one to be careful how they spell it, or there might be
bloodshed, for family pride and feuds are many.   The
oldest and properest way to spell it is Legh.   The
deviations of the careless and the sinner are many.
The family historians give a wonderful family descent
where there is a lack of evidence, but when they come
to something authentic flat contradictions arise.   For
instance, a connection of the family, though much interested in hospitals and charities, prides himself upon the
stern and unrelenting Protestantism of the family ancestor, who rabidly went about destroying hospitals and
charities at the great spoliation of the religious houses.
Then another learned historian shows that the Legh of
that time was an only child, nine years old, who was
almost certainly brought up a Catholic, for his father
had left a special request that " an honest priest should
sing mass for his soul in Prestbury Church."

Many of the facts related in the histories are certainly interesting alike to the cynic, to the student of
history, and to the folk-lorist.   There is a rare record
of some of them.   In the reign of Henry the Eighth the
squire of Adlington was a George Legh, who married a
woman with the appropriate name of Joan Lark, and as
she had had two children by the celebrated Cardinal
Wolsey, she brought some more easy virtue into the
breed, and is possibly the lady referred to by Shakspere
in the lines—

> " I'll startle you
> Worse than the sacrum bell, when the brown wench
> Lay kissing in your arms, Lord Cardinal."

This George Legh got a lease of the manor and advowson of Prestbury from the abbot of St. Werburgh's, Chester, which lease was probably obtained through the influence of Cardinal Wolsey, who, like his lord the king, would get his cast-off mistresses married if he could, even at some one else's expense. It was over this transaction that the Sir John Stanley previously mentioned incurred the wrath of the then all-powerful Cardinal. This lease was gotten in 1524–5, and the lessees were to farm the church and its belongings. In 1529 George Legh died in the Fleet Prison, leaving one son two years old. At the Reformation the manorial rights and advowson of Prestbury were transferred from the old abbey to the new bishopric of Chester, and then followed the grabbing by the landlords, on the trumped-up dispute as to title. This time the robbery was from the new or Reformed Church. Thomas Legh, who came of age in 1548, "bought" the manorial rights, and died the same year, so he does not seem to have enjoyed them very long. There are many time-worn proverbs about ill-gotten gains or what runs in the breed; here is an old-fashioned one, "What's got o'er the devil's back oft goes under his belly." This Thomas Legh left a newly born son, on whose behalf the manor and advowson of Prestbury had to be paid for again in 1580 and again in 1586, under the juggling of Queen Elizabeth, her favourite, and the land-grabbers.

In the Civil War the Thomas Legh of that time, with four sons and his brother Urian, fought for the King against their neighbours and relatives, the Breretons of Handford. The hall surrendered to the Parliament with one hundred and forty soldiers, seven hundred "armes," and fifteen barrels of powder. Thomas Legh died the same year. His descendant, Charles Legh, rebuilt the hall, or fortunately only part of it, the grand, classical, ugly part, in 1757; and as folk-lore tells us it often happens to those who build for themselves fine

THE COURTYARD, ADLINGTON HALL

houses, he soon died, and he was the last male of his family. For one hundred and twenty years the name and arms have been patched up three times by being what is called "assumed."

This last Charles Legh enlarged his park and gardens and planted the so-called "Wilderness," a maze of giant yews, most picturesque and interesting, for here in parts the brightest day is as the night, where the owl flaps about and shrieks at the intruder, and even until recent years herons built their nests and rare birds still had shelter. Beyond the marshy wilderness and nearer to Prestbury is a small peel where the moat is perfect though nearly dry, and an ancient cot is on the site of the manor-house of the Duncalfs, known by the picturesque name of The Fox Twist.

Farther on we come to a large and ancient farm-stead by the lane-side, which a countrywoman calls the Yewards, whatever that may mean. Of its history we can learn nothing, but presently we smell a smell, a many-mingled odour, reminding me of Chorlton or Davyhulme, or that last new thing in farming, a sewage farm. Beyond this filthy tract, where the omnivorous rooks seem in their glory, we see another ancient farm-stead far away in the fields, the name of which denotes its history. It is called the Spital House, as it is said to stand where once was the hospital of the monks of old. We should like to see what remains there may be of an infirmary that was built five or six hundred years ago, but between it and us is the river, and there is no road. So we keep to the beaten track, and winding up and round by Butley Hall, where the squire lies dead in the house, and in the churchyard the grave is being made ready for his burial, we glide downhill to the sleepy village of Prestbury.

At the quaint old vicarage X at once unlimbers his camera and prepares to photograph, but I have more urgent work to do, that is, to look after tea. " Tea

indeed!" says a woman; "no, that you carn't; I cann'r
be moidered wi yo." Why? "It's washing day. Yo
should come some other day." I meekly try to explain
that as I am not a churchwarden and do not turn a
mangle, I forget about washing days, and want some
tea every afternoon. This nymph of the soapsuds
merely reiterates, "I cann'r be moidered wi yo," and
as I was turned thirsty and empty away I learnt her
lovely name was Phœbe. However, there are other
inns, and we are not in such dire need as we were on
the long hot day over the Broxton Hills, when we got
to the Beeston Castle Hotel and were told we could not
have tea, because there was none ready, and we could
not have milk because the milk was sour. At the
Black Boy they take us in and do for us, homely and
comfortably.

What quaint old names these inns have! The
Black Boy reminds one of a time when it was fashionable for gentlefolk to have a black servant or slave, or
"coloured gentleman," as he would be termed now.
The ladies used to go to church with a black boy
walking behind them carrying a pile of family Bibles or
Church Services, for it made them feel so good to tell
their poorer neighbours how they had rescued the little
nigger from slavery or cannibalism, shown him the error
of his ways, and converted him to Christianity. The
nigger would grin and be happy so long as there was
plenty to eat, but if there was not, he would sooner
have eaten his missus than be converted. The Admiral Rodney is another inn whose sign shows its age,
for it is one hundred and twenty years since Admiral
Rodney blew up the fleets of France and Spain in
blazes and smoke, or sank them deep below the waves,
raising England's power at sea far above the combined
Powers of all her hereditary foes, and he was therefore
canonized by being placed on the signs of inns.

THE OLD VICARAGE, PRESTBURY

Prestbury, well fitted by nature and art and the long consecration of nigh upon a thousand years of history, still draws its pilgrims from far and wide, as it has done for many centuries, It stands, like one of the Cistercian abbeys of old, in a lovely valley on the banks of a sparkling river that once was sweet and pure, with fertile fields all round it, and girt about with the everlasting hills. Its origin is prehistoric, for none of its many historians essay to tell us how or why it got its name of the "priest's burg," or why its parish was forty miles in circumference even when many townships and lordly manors had been shorn away. The histories are so many, for five or six local men have written of it, that I shall merely take the reader as a modern pilgrim for a stroll in the churchyard, there to see for ourselves some of the history of the ages, and read in varied forms the many lessons of life.

Under a glass case are relics of the cross, from which the gospel was preached in Saxon times. The worn remnant was dug up at one of the recent alterations to the church, and its only history is written in its workmanship. Then there is a gem of time-worn Norman architecture, all that is left of "Our Ladye's Chapple," the parish church before the present one was built six hundred years ago, and probably preserved because the Davenports of Henbury long kept it for a family sepulchre. Over the beautiful round-arched doorway are seven figures, worn beyond recall, and over them is a Latin inscription of recent date too involved and turgid in its phrases to be translated by any ordinary learned society.

When doctors differ, who dare laugh? One of the historians describes one of the figures as a rampant wolf leaning against a pillar, while another says it seems to him to be the Holy Ghost descending as a dove. Let us be thankful that even this bit of Norman ornate work is left and cared for. Near to it in the church there is a little, ancient, well-proportioned Decorated window, and there are columns and arches and monuments and work of almost every style of architecture, with an original sanctus bell *in situ*.

For us, as common pilgrims of the day, let us sit about the tombs and learn what they tell us. Firstly, any one accustomed to churchyards would soon note the great quantity of gravestones with quaint and beautiful lettering, and sixteen hundred odd for date. These are rare anywhere, and very much rarer is a flag or stone of the previous century. We find one of 1599 where the five is like the letter S, a very old-fashioned form. Here is the name of a man who left some money to the parish, Ouffe. The modern slang for money is ouf. It is proudly inscribed above Paul Ashton that he was father and grandfather to ninety-four children, and was aged ninety-five. The number of children were evidently gaining on the number of his years as he got older, for he must have had a good start. At Cheadle churchyard old Randy Allcock honestly confessed that he did not know how many children he left. No wonder the Allcocks and Ashtons are numerous in the district.

> " This place we chose to be our bed,
>   Thou, man alive, do not dig up ye dead."

A great tomb with a long inscription tells how much money was raised for the widow and children of a quarryman named William Wyatt, who was shot dead, and whose brother was wounded by two highwaymen named Walmsley and Bate, who had tried to rob a man named Ernill. All happens in good order, for the robbers got hanged at last, and the epitaph ends, "As for man his days are as grass, as a flower of the field so he flourisheth; for the wind passeth over it and it is gone, and the place thereof shall know it no more."

Another nice little story of a freebooter is given in very original verse, which I copied most carefully; the

IN PRESTBURY CHURCHYARD

last two lines rhyme exactly when spoken by the vulgar
tongue :—

> " Beneath this stone lyes Edw'd. Green
> Who for cutting stone famous was seen,
> But he was sent to apprehend
> One Joseph Clark, of Kerridge End,
> For stealing deer of Esquire Downs,
> Where he was shott and dyd o' th' wounds."

This Joe Clark was said to be an outlaw who had killed
one of the followers of Prince Charlie in the '45, but
it is quite as likely he was one of them.   The borderland of counties, especially if in the hills, is always the
haunt of the lawless, and near here the hills of Cheshire,
Derbyshire, and Yorkshire join, with Staffordshire not
far away.   The names of two of the townships in Prestbury parish denote their wild character—Ravenowe or
Rainow, and Wildboarclough.   The living on those
wind-swept barren moors was so hard that only the
hard-bitten could thrive, and they are said to have
grown up so dour that they died standing up.   The
dead were brought over miles of these hills for burial at
Prestbury, but there are no records that they buried any
of them upright, as at Rosslyn they buried the Scottish
Earls of Orkney, the St. Clairs.   Only the horse-coper,
the shepherd, and the slink butcher could live on those
scanty hill pastures.   It is said that if you go at midnight to a cattle-dealer's grave and shake a horse's
bridle over it, telling where there is a horse that could
be fetched, there may be heard a rustling down below,
and a whiff of chill air passes, and when the day dawns
some one has lost a horse.   If a child be lost, they say
the angels have taken it to Abraham's bosom ; but if a
horse be gone, the likeliest place to find it is down a
coalpit ; though coalpits are uncanny places in which to
seek one's own.   Wild and strange are the tales told in
the lonely farms ; though the flesh grows creepy, one becomes enthralled, and the townsfolk wonder at the country

N

gorby's superstition, while the hill farmer wonders how those ignorant townsfolk can have delight in dull debates on the disposal of sewage, or get excited about the rival merits of the pail or closet systems.

Here is another epitaph. Sarah Pickford is described as a Bachelour. It reminds me of one of the City Fathers who took his relaxation and enjoyment as a tailor, and sometimes inflicted lugubrious speeches upon his colleagues; one of them, in Irish accents, muttered, "Whenever I hear that man spake he remoinds me of an epitaph in Dublin which says some one was born a man but died a tailor."

Some other original inscriptions are now missing, though records of them have been preserved.

"Those goods I had whilst I did live
Unto four monks I freely give,
To eate and drinke and make good cheere
And keep my Obit once a yeere."

In this case it would seem that some one must have swallowed the principal as well as the interest, and their principles also. A tablet to a lawyer said in learned Latin that he was "learned in the law, pious [Oh!], prudent, the delight of his comrades, the ornament of his family [very likely], a treasury of science, exemplary in temperance, patient in labour, of much virtue . . . and died young in a vehement fever." Fancy all that, and more beside, about a common lawyer! I should think the parson got jealous about any one being so uncommon good who was not in the Apostolic succession, and popped the tablet inside some grave.

There are several volumes of most interesting parish registers and accounts that must be mentioned, be it ever so slightly. In 1558—that is, after the dissolution or reformation—twenty-seven townships agreed to continue and apportion their "long tyme laudable custom" of collecting "serage silver on the feast daie of St. George the Martyr, for church expences." Serage or

cerage means wax, and the money was originally a payment, instead of providing wax candles for church uses.
It became practically a church rate, and paid for, among
many other things, " A poke for ye chalys, " Two
Shepeskynnes for ye byble," " a goose and drink for ye
Ryngers," " ye Whip-dog," " curfue rungen," and heads
of so-called vermin, the price of which altered in a very
interesting manner.   For instance, moles or waunts were
to be paid for at sixpence a dozen; but in 1732, 5480
had to be paid for, so the moles were sadly lessened and
the funds also.   Foxes were at one time valued at one
shilling, at another at five; urchin or hedgehogs at
twopence; otters at seven and sixpence, so that they
must have esteemed their fish highly.   There are many
other things to note, but we must travel home.   In the
churchyard, forest trees grow too big, making it dark
and damp and sometimes sticky with honey-dew.   Only
evergreens, emblems of immortality, should be there.

I had told X that I must find the " Spitalhouse," or
ancient hospital, even if I had to carry my bike and ford
the river.   The way to it was not as bad as we expected, and we were well repaid, for the farm buildings
are undoubtedly very ancient and probably were the
original hospital of the monks, cut into and altered,
more's the pity!   But still there are the split or adze-
worked oak-trees half a yard or two feet thick, from
floor to roof ridge.   This ancient hospital was probably built hundreds of years before one was heard
of in Manchester, and has been almost unnoticed by
historians.

Time flies, and the farmer sends us, by what he calls
a short cut, to our homeward road past the site of Gad-
hole, where he said there lately was one of the finest oak-
built houses in the country, but it was on the luckless
neglected estate of Adlington, gone to ruin and decay.
We walk up and down banks steeper than the roof of a
house, across potato-fields in ridges, up to the knees in

blue-bells, rose campion, and bracken, and over stiles to another lost house, which, its inscription tells us, was built by Hugh and Dorothy Mottram in 1714. We are now in Mottram, where other time-worn houses sheltered generations of Mottrams and Mottersheads; and then we find Mottram Old Hall, where the Calveleys lived and reigned for three hundred years. It is still a large, interesting, well-preserved house, encircled on three sides by the original moat, the first storey being strongly built of stone and evidently once fortified, the upper parts picturesque gables of black and white. This was the third moated house we had seen within a short distance of one another, and about twelve miles from Manchester.

Our long day's journey comes to an end as the day-light dies, and that sweet sleep is earned which nothing sooner brings than cycling; although our local Member, Sir John William, tells us, on his great authority, that sleep is best produced, even in the tumults of the House of Commons, by a good conscience and religion.

IN MUCH WENLOCK

WENLOCK PRIORY

WENLOCK—EASTHOPE—ACTON BURNELL

THE long days of midsummer and the express trains that run between Manchester and Shrewsbury enable us to have pilgrimages to scenes of historic interest and wondrous beauty in the fair county of Salop, and to return home, after nine hours of wandering there, by a train that does the sixty miles between Shrewsbury and Stockport in less than ninety minutes, and is always prompt to time.

Over the English bridge and by the Abbey Church we cycle south-east from Shrewsbury, keeping more to the right hand or south than we did when on our journey to find Woolf's house and barn, where Charles the Second sheltered after Worcester fight. Passing through Cressage, a village whose name is a contraction of Christ's oak, where there is a noted oak tree, we gradually mount the hills which seem to be a part of the backbone of England. High up in a hollow in the hills is Much Wenlock, the Wenloch of Domesday, where was the oldest, wealthiest, and most magnificent of the many religious houses in Shropshire. Eventful, indeed, has been its history. Three centuries seem a long time, but it is thirteen centuries since a damsel named Milburg founded there a house for the religious, which prospered and grew for nigh two hundred years, when the Danes sacked and burnt it. Then it lay waste and desolate for as long again, until the Lady Godiva of legend and her Earl rebuilt it, and again it was ruined. The Normans brought their Ciugniac monks from La Charité, in Burgundy, and the stately pile rose grander than ever. A Saxon saint was wanted to appease the Saxon folk, and balsamic exhalations—that is a polite term for smells—showed where the uncorrupted body of the saintly Milburg lay. Thither flocked the pilgrim, the devout, the sick ; and the priory flourished and prospered enormously for four hundred years, throwing off Clugniac offshoots under Benedictine rule.

Then came ruin again. It was robbed of all it had by the lust and greed of our own reformers, and now is beautiful even in its ruins. The remnants of gigantic walls and towers rise from a garden ablaze with poppies and roses. The fig, the peach, the magnolia flourish on the ancient stone-work ; up aloft grow snapdragon and valerian, pigeons and peafowl strut around, and the air seems steeped in peace and calm decay. Is it a wild dream to think that the glory which has departed may come again? It has revived from worse ruin than to-day's. There are no foreign fleets like those of the Danes dare sail up the Severn now. Kings and their courtiers dare not rob the charities now : and the power of the priest decreases as the people learn to read. When our English tongue was in its infancy a noted reformer wrote : " If hevene be on this erthe, it is in cloistre or in scole, where all is buxumnesse and bokes to rede and to lerne."

X says this is a glorified edition of an old parsonage garden, and just the place he should like to live and die at. Meantime he improves the shining hour and photographs diligently. We did not know until afterwards that the Prior's house is almost unique of its kind, the ancient house wherein live gentlefolk to-day ; stone built, with arches and cloisters two storeys high, rooms like chapels, and flags worn by the sandalled feet of the long-forgotten, whose presence still seems to brood over their former haunts, and, according to some, is actually seen.

THE PRIOR'S HOUSE, WENLOCK

MUCH WENLOCK

Beyond the church, with its spacious court or yard and most picturesque setting, is the black and white Guildhall built over the butter market. The Town Council and the magistrates meet above, and the stocks and pillory and rings in the whipping-post are all handy. Much Wenlock has not much of a market. Three women and a goose can make it, and if all four cackled together on their more or less imaginary wrongs, the noise would be dreadful. The goose may be the faithful wife of one gander for thirty years, rearing her family of hardy annuals every year only to see them torn from her and devoured; and some day women kill her, pluck her, dress her, fettle her up, and take her to market, calling her a nice plump young goose and themselves Christians. These little tricks must have been done a long time, and even in the shadow of holy church, for I read that fines and contributions were paid in geese, and that the King in 1224 issued a royal decree that Wenlock market should be held on a Monday, not on a Sunday as heretofore. Therefore let us hope that country folk and others also now think over their little sins before they commit them.

In the church registers is an entry worth noting, dated June 26, 1559: "Service celebrated firste in ye Englyshe tongue." Before that date all the muttering was done in Latin, which, being more unintelligible, was naturally more awe-inspiring. There is said to be an octagonal room in a house here of which six sides are owned by one lord and two by another. There certainly are some beautiful old houses, as may be seen in the accompanying pictures. We cannot see the holy wells, with the Boorish and Welsh names, St. Milburg's and St. Owen's, and many things besides, for time is short and we are far from home, with a journey through an unknown land before us; it being written that in the neighbouring hills there is a place called Easthope, where is a little ancient church with an iron-bound hour-glass over the pulpit, unbroken all these years, a sanctuary ring on the door, unrestored pews, and rood-screen. This wonder should be found and noted.

From Much Wenlock we steadily mounted again up the side of the Edge. Wonderful vistas gradually unfolded around us, the skies were bright and clear, and hills and mountains seemed to stretch on and on in endless array, farther than the keenest sight could follow. The air became keener, the rocks strange, the wayside vegetation changed. Young birds were numerous, a shrew-mouse ran across the road, a dead mole lay with strong fat white hands upturned, as some one had run over its snout. Turtle-doves seemed common, yew-trees grew wild, and the snails took their striped houses with them. I called at two cottages to ask the way, and in each of them I noticed the old-fashioned rack hung from the ceiling.

Down the hillside to the left we were told to go for Easthope, but the place is so small we nearly overran it. There are only two or three houses and a tiny church behind a farm. The church is smothered with big trees, and there is no way to it but through fields and over stiles. A colt comes to chew our tyres, and swine are evidently, as they were of old, the chief product of the land. They are in crowds or untended herds all over the place. X finds an answer to a conundrum that puzzled him in his youth, "What makes more noise than a pig under a gate?" Why, here there were several pigs under several gates, with "their sisters and their cousins that they reckon up by dozens and their aunts," all shrieking together in diabolical chorus louder than fifty barrel-organs on the spree. We could not find a man, and it was no use shouting. We wanted several things, chiefly tea. The cottage was locked, the church gates were locked, the farmyard was empty. At last I found a woman. Slowly we learned from her that we could get to the church by going to the rectory, but as for tea she merely glared at us and never answered. Perhaps she was trying to reckon up how much we should eat, and how much she could charge, and whether we would slope off without paying. So after a rather painful suspense I asked if the kettle boiled. She glared again, a nice-looking old woman in her way, but she leaned on her stick and at last said "No." Then I asked if the fire was lit, and again, after long consideration, the witch said "No." We turned and fled.

This seems indeed to be a place where it is always afternoon, where time stands still or nothing mars the even tenor of its flight. Perhaps the woman scorns the modern tea and loves the barley wine, the ale of her Saxon forefathers. She may be a descendant of Gurth or Wamba or the aborigines who fed their droves of swine on the pannage of the oaks before the Christians came. But where are the men? Are they off to the war? also as of old. Everything seems asleep—except those blessed pigs. Listen to their music. Scores of them, droves of them, all clamouring for food. So are we, but some one does care a bit for them, while we are pilgrims and vagrants far from our home and all who care for us, and have been eight hours on the job without a drink.

The geese and women were quiet, but would have nothing to do with us, and the nearest approach to a man was when we saw the parson down the lane. Of him I asked the way to Church Preen, where I had read there was the biggest yew-tree in England. He had never heard that, but he could tell us that the place was about a mile off, and that we should have to carry our bikes most of the way as the path went through thick woods, damp hollows, and over rocks. We certainly would not be able to get tea anywhere in that country, and if we wanted to go to Acton Burnell and on to Shrewsbury that night we had better set off at once. There was a chapel near by, he told us, at a

place called Langley, where they stabled their cattle in
the house of the Lord, and used the oaken pews for calf
cotes, but the Society for the Preservation of Ancient
Monuments were going to stop that—some day.

Wearily and thirstily we trudged up Wenlock Edge
by the way we had come, where we ate our last apple,
and then we dived down on the other side with brakes
hard on, for we could see the road, or bits of it as far as
the eye could reach, and a fairer land there could not be.
All around were halls and castles, ruins and churches,
not the wretched-looking modern churches, but venerable objects of beauty, with gigantic trees and much to
interest the historian, the architect, and the artist. Here
is one at Hughley, with rough-hewn oaken porch by the
roadside and elaborately carved rood-screen inside. We
just miss Kenley, where the tower is said to be Saxon
or Roman, and in whose parsonage Alison, the historian,
was born. We should take days instead of hours to see
all that we pass by, but time keeps flying, and we must
push on to Acton Burnell, where we know there is a
grocer's shop where we can have tea, for we paid a
flying visit last autumn, and in all this model country
we have come through there are no public-houses.

Few indeed are the places where the history of
England is illustrated so beautifully and so compactly
as at Acton Burnell. Here are the remains of the Parliament House, the meeting-place where King, Lords,
and Commons met, the second time they ever did meet
for the making of laws for England; and the stately
Baron's castle where the King and nobles lodged with
all the pomp of chivalry and clang of arms, while the
humble commoners were housed and met in an enormous barn. Of it the gable ends alone remain. The
castle walls and towers are still four-square, roofless, and
majestic, given over to the birds and bats. Far above
the highest towers wave the spreading branches of the
finest cedars of Lebanon I ever saw. From a photo-

CASTLE, CEDAR OF LEBANON, AND GABLE OF PARLIAMENT HOUSE,
ACTON BURNELL

GABLE OF OLD PARLIAMENT HOUSE, ACTON BURNELL

graph of one against whose bole I stood I estimate its height to be about a hundred feet. These cedars have probably been grown from seed sown here centuries ago, and that seed may have been brought from Lebanon or the Holy Land by Burnell, the Crusader. Other cedars and pines there are around the castle and the church of wondrous beauty, for on our hurried autumnal visit I had noticed cones or fruit high up some of the trees, and like to a turnip in size. The church is ancient, rather too much restored, and resplendent with marble monuments and famous brasses. Adjoining its yard is the cemetery for Roman Catholics, with a gigantic gorgeous crucifix, for they who own the place are of the old faith, and that may account for some of the care with which these antiquities are treasured. The hall is the ugliest house in the village, being what some would describe as a Georgian mansion ; others, a whitewashed factory.

These various buildings lie close together, and to photograph by the windows of the hall it was necessary to ask permission. I therefore went round to the front door while X went to hurry up the tea, and then he seemed surprised to hear that a smart footman had taken me for a gentleman, and we could go where we liked and do as we liked. We turned our backs upon the staring modern house (Why should men of wealth and taste live in the ugliest house in the parish?), and in an English park in the leafy month of June, in brilliant showery weather, mementoes were secured of scenes in themselves beautiful, and interesting to all who are interested in the history of free government.

Acton Burnell was one of the many Actons or Oaktowns of the Saxons. It took its second name from a wild lawless family named Burnill or Burnel, who got it by some means. One of them entered the service of Prince Edward, volunteering in fact for a crusade to the Holy Land. He returned before his master, who was long delayed and nearly lost. It may be remem-

bered that Vale Royal Abbey was founded by Edward
in fulfilment of a vow when in danger of shipwreck.
Robert Burnell rose to be Executor and Regent for the
King, Bishop of Bath and Wells, and Chancellor of
England.   Edward the First, or the Great, for he was
the first great Englishman to be King of England—and
probably he has had no equal, except Cromwell, among
her rulers in justice, policy, or war—summoned parliaments to aid him in the government of the realm, and
one of these parliaments, probably the second, met at
Acton Burnell in 1283.   It was specially noted for passing the Statute "De Mercatoribus," concerning merchants or traders, which enabled them to register and
recover debts owing to them, or to arrest the body of
the debtor and hold him, and after a quarter of a year
his lands and goods also until the debt was levied.

It seems a very startling thing to-day, when nearly
all of us are more or less traders, that at so recent a
period of English history there was no law for the
recovery of debts.   The king, lords, and clergy were
above the law, and the serfs and villeins below it.   The
middle-class traders or merchants were only struggling
into existence, and the statute of Acton Burnell first
protected them in giving them the assistance of the
law for the recovery of debts ; and yet very few indeed
of the traders of to-day ever heard of the place not
far from the centre of England where this great statute
was agreed to, and still fewer have been on pilgrimage
to see it.

There are many other things concerning the laws
and customs of our country to-day, in contrast to those
of years ago, which rise unbidden to our notice when
we wander as strangers and pilgrims through the land.
On this journey, after leaving Much Wenlock, we travelled nearly twenty miles without seeing a public-house.
The country, scenery, and roads were perfection, but
we wanted tea, and knew not where to get it.   We did

ACTON BURNELL CASTLE

have it in a little room about three yards square at the back of a grocer's shop in Acton Burnell, enjoyed it, paid for it, and started again refreshed for Shrewsbury. In olden times the inmates of these ruined cells and religious houses would have relieved wayfarers with or without payment.   Consider and contrast the custom of the country and the law of the land, as it was then and as it is to-day.

When a modern wayfarer or tramp asks at the casual ward of a workhouse for a night's lodging—and if he sleeps under a hedge or haystack or begs he is liable to be sent to prison—he is asked by a more or less pompous, arrogant, callous official, "What's your name?" "How old are you?"   "Do you ever work?"   "What at?"   "Where did you sleep last night?"   "Where are you going?"   "Are you married or single?"   "How many times have you been relieved before?"   "Turn out your pockets!"   With any other questions, including at times inquiries even as to the colour of the wayfarer's hair, if he happens to have any left.

In olden times the custom was for the monk who kept the door of a monastery where some wanderers asked for food and shelter, to fall on his knees and thank God that he was of some use and could minister to one in need, and then to conduct the tramp inside, give him food, drink, and lodging, and let him go as he liked, without asking a single question.   The monastic houses were hospitals and schools as well as casual wards, and the very word hospital has been gradually contracted into hostel or hotel.   All were free.   Those who bene-fited could pay if they wished, but they were not asked. The community of monks consisted of brethren of all sorts and conditions, living their lives for the common good.   Some of them worked on the land, and were gardeners and farmers, others on the roads or bridges, and at buildings.   There were schoolmasters and students, physicians, historians, philosophers, and idlers, but as a community there is no doubt they did an immense amount of public work, literary, scholastic, and charitable, that in our time has to be more or less managed or mismanaged by public officials and paid for out of the rates.

In those days the relief of the needy and the expense of it came from "free alms" and charitable work, and it does seem somewhat antiquated for the dispenser of the charity to fall on his knees and be thankful that he was given the opportunity of succouring the distressed or the hungry. But now that we have to pay for it all, and not always get it, it would be still more surprising and quite superfluous if similar thanks were given, with the gruff order, "Turn out your pockets!" of the modern poor-law official, who is often merely a converted Bobby.

Rest! weary pilgrim! Rest and stay
In ingle nook this thirsty day.

LUDLOW, STOKESAY

OFF we go by express train due south for ninety miles. Ludlow's lofty town and Stokesay's mediæval dream are the goals of our pilgrimage to-day. The very name of Ludlow sounds ancient, while that of Stokesay sounds aristocratic like unto decayed gentility. As low means high in Anglo-Saxon, or, more correctly, a hill tumulus, the former name means the lofty hill burying-place of the people, and the latter means the Stoke or stockaded fort of the Says. Until recently Stokesay was written as two words.

Ludlow's history is fine. It may be briefly condensed as follows : Under the early Saxon kings for many years money was coined at Ludlow. Then they found they could make it faster through a church. Edward the Confessor, who was described by an eminent historian as zealously pious but extremely injudicious, was one day accosted by a beggar. Having no money on him he gave his ring to the supplicant, which nowadays would be considered a foolish thing to do, for although I have often known men wear a big ring when they have no money in their pockets, yet it would not be right to give that ring to a beggar, for it might get him into trouble, and perhaps leave the giver without a copper. In this case the ring turned up again, though the beggar vanished, for two pilgrims from Ludlow to the Holy Land there met an old man, white and hoary, who gave them the ring, saying he was Saint John and would soon meet the King in Paradise.

Of course the King was glad to get his ring back, and would do anything to help the pilgrims of Ludlow to have a big church, which prospered amazingly, though the priests were not satisfied for long together. They always want something more ; in this case they wanted

THE FEATHERS INN, LUDLOW

more saints. So they dug about until they found the bodies of three, nicely labelled, Irish saints. They kept these in a box and waited for miracles and contributions. The church grew grander and grander, and is sometimes said to be the largest parish church in England, but still the mystery remains, Why did they get Irish saints?

They were probably cheap, for if there were no English ones there were always plenty in Wales—old-fashioned saints are quite common there—and the church stands just on the Welsh borders. The north transept of this grand church is called the Fletchers' Chapel, so I feel a family interest in the place. The other transept was the Cordwainers', but as service was being performed when we were there we could not see the many beautiful curiosities. The misereres or carved seats made to turn up for leaning upon are very fine, but how is it they were ever allowed to remain? for although one represents the devil carrying off the fat alewife to hell and conveys its own lesson, another represents a fox dressed like a bishop preaching to a lot of geese, which seems a shocking idea.

The castle of Ludlow is a grand ruin, with the oldest of the five round churches of England within its spacious walls. Its history is also far more than we can even refer to. Here Edward the Fifth was proclaimed King of England and then taken to London to be killed and buried in the Tower. Henry the Seventh kept his eldest son Arthur here at school also, and then married him to a woman older than himself, killing him in that manner. His poor heart was wrapped in lead and separately buried, and one day a plumber bought it for the sake of the lead. Milton's play of "Comus" was first acted here by the children of the Earl, who were lost in the neighbouring forest; here Samuel Butler wrote "Hudibras," and many other wonderful things happened. The Grammar School is said to be the oldest in England, and there are fine old buildings, for the Guild of Palmers built hospitals and sanctuaries and did many good and lasting works for the enrichment of their town.

Down the long steep hill we roll northwards while the thunder-clouds are gathering round. We haste while we can, and as the storm descends our sanctuary is gained at the pretty village of Bromfield, where there

o

is a big lych-gate to the churchyard, and a fine old
church with open doors and cards printed with description of the church and its antiquities for the use of all
comers.   Wherever we find an open church we find it
beautifully kept.   The dirty ones are only used on
Sundays.   Adjoining the church's lych-gate is the gatehouse of the ruined priory with the house over the gate.
The ruins and the church join together.   The river
encircles them, an avenue of Irish yews leads from
them, orchards are on the slope of the hill, the mill
hums below, and the bridge now spans the road.   The
lych-gate is a beautiful place to have our lunch as we
shelter for an hour, and we gather up the fragments and
the paper and leave all as neat as we find it.

The Domesday Book says Brunfeld has XII. neat
herds, XV. villeins, XII. boors, and VIII. teams.   How
the meaning of the words has altered.   The owner was
lost and the church grabbed the land, and with the land
would go the boors and the teams.   What did it all
matter to them?

The rain ceases.   On we go to Onibury on the Onny.
An ony on yo ony on yo sounds as if it came from
Lancashire.   A sleepy little hole, with a short squat
tower to a tiny church and rough-hewn oaken porch.
The country round is white with hawthorn, refreshed
with the rain and redolent of perfume.   Onward we
glide until there rise before us the embattled walls and
towers of Stokesay.   Are they real, or a painted canvas
like a Belle Vue show?   They seem to be solid, yet
they are deserted; substantial and in good repair, yet all
is silent.   There is no sound but the jackdaw's queru-
lous caw and the plaintive bleat of cade lambs.   The
winds toss about the trees and the clouds are chased
over the surrounding hills, while the charming buildings
seem to be a mansion of the dead.   Will they vanish
or crumble away if we touch them?   The whole thing
looks as if it might be some unsubstantial pageant, an

PRIORY GATEHOUSE, BROMFIELD

STOKESAY

illusion, or a vision. "The cloud-capp'd towers, the gorgeous palaces, the solemn temples" are not yet dissolved or passed away. They stand solid, very much as they stood six centuries ago. In the little church we sit in high-backed pews with oaken roofs and hat-pegs, sheltering from the rain and reading texts on the walls. We wished for milk, and here we read "As new-born

STOKESAY

Babes desire ye Sincere Milk of ye Word that ye may grow thereby."

When the rain is over we find in the churchyard by the castle's moat two gravediggers hilling some one up. They cut thick sods of turf and place them upright round the grave, making a grass mound shaped like a coffin. We talk about their work, and they ask me how we do in our country. I tell them we can seldom have grass or flowers on a grave. Some parsons object, and one

pulled the flowers up and threw them away. It has long
been the fashion to put a ton of stone on the grave to
keep all down, with prison bars around, but now they
burn the body. "What, burn the body?" gasped the
men, and they shrank from me with horror. After that
they kept their eye on me as if I had come from the
fiery pit, and when I asked the name of a flowering
plant like spurge, which grew on the rugged walls, they
said, "It's moss; ony foo knows that."

IN STOKESAY CHURCH

Access to the castle yard is through and under what
is probably the most beautiful gatehouse in the world,
all gables of carved oak, mellowed and worn by time.
Across the court is the grand hall of immense height,
whose open roof is blackened by the smoke from the
flueless fire which once burned in the centre of the room.
It is more than fifty feet long, with four lofty Early
Gothic windows overlooking the moat. To the left are
the many-sided irregular twin towers of the castle, and
on the right there project on brackets, far over at a
great height above the moat, timbered buildings most
singular and picturesque. Five generations of the

THE GATEHOUSE AND CHURCH, STOKESAY

THE COURTYARD, STOKESAY

Norman Says were Lords of Stoke. Then came ten generations of Ludlows, a Vernon of Haddon, wars and changes; and lastly, from the profit on gloves, these most interesting and beautiful buildings of many styles and ages are well preserved.

From the courtyard, up stairs of stone, we find an ornamented room with tea-table ready spread, the last thing wanted for the bewitching scene. But alas! alas! and lack-a-day! we are told the tea is private. A picnic party expected that afternoon has sent it on before them. Our hopes are shattered, but the old woman in the gate-house will make us tea in her own little parlour and give us some rhubarb jam of her own making, which she says is most excellent. While the tea is brewing we note the almanacs and photographs of gamekeepers, parsons, and police. The rhubarb jam is full of black things which X is eating rather recklessly. As he has doctors who may have to be consulted, I ask him if he knows what those hard black lumps are. He replies, " Dead flies," and goes on eating them. I remind him of the cade lambs in the courtyard, and the sheep or rabbits outside, but he says you cannot be too particular when you are hungry. He wants to please the old lady, who says they are only black currants she has put in for flavouring, and he repeatedly asks her about one of his neighbours, a very big pot in his village, who is said to have bought an estate near Stokesay. The old woman says she knows him well enough; he is only gardener at the Hall, but "he's a boomussin fellow; he's allus boomussin," and as the word was new to me I made a note of it. X might eat as many of the "black currants" as he liked, but the old woman stuck to her text that his friend was only the gardener. I looked for currant bushes in the garden but could not find any, though there was rhubarb, and the cade lambs followed us bleating plaintively, pictures of innocence.

Then X confided to me that that was just the place

he should like to live at. Having heard him say that
of other places, I interjected, "Where would you keep
the cow? There would be three acres of ghosts, but
the cow would have to live in the churchyard." He
photographed desperately. We had three hours in
which to cycle twenty-two miles to Shrewsbury. We
must tear ourselves away, for when we were at school
we learnt Latin, or thought we learnt it, and then forgot
it, but one time-worn proverb is not forgotten, *Tempus
fugit*.

BRIDGNORTH

BRIDGNORTH

BRIDGNORTH, "quaint old town of toil and traffic," a rare conglomeration of old and new dovetailed together. Here is the haughty Norman castle built to last for ever, to withstand all that men and time, wind and weather, could do against it, now actually leaning over as if by all the laws of gravitation it ought to fall, but it does not fall. Round it is the modern recreation ground, where the usual notices tell you to keep off the grass and ignore the overhanging pile which some day may crush both man and grass. Look over the castle ramparts, and far below, across the abyss, is the railway station, while down in deeper depths again is the river, the famous Severn, with red rocks beyond, and all around, at varied distances and varied heights and depths, are the everlasting hills.

The day is very hot. For our simple lunch we seek some quiet spot by Severn's sedgy brink where, in the shade, the children try to fish while real fish glide by like shadows, heeding neither us nor them. Beyond the many-arched and buttressed bridge, the brown-roofed houses of the town rise tier behind tier on the hill crowned by St. Leonard's Church like some old watch burg on the Rhine. All along the long bridge is a motley crowd of loiterers, workers, and idlers, who bask in the blazing sun and gossip through their midday hour of rest. There are groups of girls who would do for " Rhine daughters" in the Valkyrie, if they would only get in the river and dive and sing and swim—it

would seem so like an opera. X makes bold to ask
them what they work at. They answer sharply, "Carpets," and look as much as to say, "Is there anything
else you want?" I say, "We had better be going,"
but X says he wants a drink. Memories of old proverbs about women and wine and the root of all evil
flash across me, when a happy thought suggests itself,
"Let us have some cider, for we must be near the
cider country." We mount and away in search of cider,
and get it on draught, cool like nectar, while the ther-
mometer registers over 130 degrees in the sun, and we
had been in the sun.

Instead of resting in some church's quiet shade, we
rest to-day within a pub and drink. Good young men
may note the consequences. X wants more cider. So
our discussions on Shakspere's references to Bridgnorth are cut short, and he is coaxed away to photograph the many-gabled house wherein was born the
author of the "Reliques of Ancient English Poetry,"
whose ancestors were grocers in the town named Piercy,
evidently a form of Piers or Peter, a name which took
the aristocratic form of Percy as the bishop became a
famous author and collector. It is many years since I
read or heard any of those rare old ballads, but one
couplet relating to some doughty old warrior appealed
strongly to a boy's love of the heroic, and still comes
back to memory :

> "As one in doleful dumps,
> For when his legs were smitten off
> He fought upon his stumps."

The picturesque, irregularly timbered house, inscribed
with pious verse and dated, is photographed a second
time, for it had stood out in high relief beyond the
bridge in our first picture, just where the steep hill
comes down to the river. Beyond it is the street called
Cartway, apparently because no cart could use it, so

BISHOP PERCY'S HOUSE, BRIDGNORTH

BRIDGNORTH MARKET-PLACE

exceedingly steep, narrow, and tortuous it winds upwards. And yet we are told that it was up and down
here the London coaches and traffic were hauled in the
good old days when men and horses worked. We
could but wonder and struggle on in our upward climb,
like Falstaff "larding the lean earth." In the spacious
market-place above is a curious magpie market-house,
built on lofty arches, a quaint town-hall above, all
badged and dated, containing wondrous civic maces
with other treasures, and a shelter below for many carts
or market-folk from summer's heat or winter's rain.

Beyond is the last embattled gateway of the town,
where overhead there is a Blue-coat School, and near by,
in a verdant close, with Elizabethan houses around, is
the great church of St. Leonard's, mostly restored, but
well done and well kept. One timbered roof is old
and very fine. There are curious cast-iron monuments
and a sword, which looks more like a rapier, of the
Colonel Billingsley who was slain in the churchyard
during the Civil War. One of the church vessels is a
chalice said to have been taken from the bony fingers
of a skeleton when some graves were robbed. It may
have been the consecrated vessel treasured by some
priest in life and death, and other priests connive at
the robbery and have no shame in the sacrilege. The
churchyard is now grassed over and the dead buried
in some hills across the river. Round the close are
many styles of building, a timbered cottage, home of
the author of "The Saint's Everlasting Rest," a
grammar school with many gables, a solidly built old-
fashioned rambling place, with lots of lads about it,
and beyond it are some almshouses for poor widows,
built by one whose mother was buried near by, and as
some one else has dreamed of doing likewise they also
are photographed.

Nearly all the town, including church and schools
as well as castle and houses, was burnt or destroyed

during the Civil War, and therefore most of what we
see, old-fashioned though it looks and is, has risen
since then. The Percy house, which was built by a
Forster, escaped (because, as some may say) on it was
graven, " Except the Lord Build the Owse the Labourers
thereof avail nothing." From the church close on the
hill to the town by the river there is a terrible flight of
steps. Beyond the river is one of the oldest dwellings
in the land, a hermitage wherein a Saxon prince sought
for solitude and rest. This is no mere myth; the tale's
authenticity is well proved. Athelstan or Ethelward,
or whatever his name may have been, for he probably
was careless enough himself about the matter, did undoubtedly seek for peace and rest in this cave in the
rocks in the secluded forest of Morfe.

Under the gatehouse to the north we leave the
ancient burgh to find our way to Stanley Park, where
there is a lodge in the woods from whence old servants
came and where we have our tea. Then we cycle
through the park, through bracken and birch, with
noble trees of fir and copper beech around, past the
hall and out beyond. The place is the home of the
Tyrwhitts, and from their cognizance, a peewit, the name
is supposed to be an older form of the name of that
useful and beautiful bird. Their motto also is good.
It needs no translating, and there is no doubt as to
its meaning—" Time tryeth troth."

Past the park and by its flower-wreathed lodge we
soon come to the little village of Astley Abbots, whose
name denotes its antiquity, all beautifully kept, with
black and white houses of all sizes, noble trees, interesting church, with walled-up Saxon doorway, and near it
two deeply splayed tiny windows, more fitted for a castle
than a church. Here hangs an old-fashioned lover's
garland, hung up in memory of a maid who died on the
eve of her marriage; and among other noteworthy bits
is the grave of Colonel Billingsley (whose sword we saw

DUNVALL

in Bridgnorth Church), with four emblazoned shields
of arms and the motto, "Procul ingratitudo." Did he
also feel the ingratitude of the faithless Stuart race who
knew not gratitude or even thanks, for, relying on their
fancied Right Divine, they thought their subjects' lives
and lands and all were theirs, and why should men be
thanked for yielding to their King what was his own?

We are directed across a few fields to a fine old
house called Dunvall. It reminds me of Standon Hall,
but the inside seems to have been little changed since
the day it was built. The stairway is open with wicket
at the first step, gradually ascending as it winds round
the open hall, quaint and picturesque, of oak nearly black
with age.

On we go again through lovely country, which
gradually becomes more black and smoky and repulsive
as we near Broseley, famous for the long clay pipes
which add so much to the dignity of churchwardens.
Up and down, with jolts and bumps, we go through vile
and stinking holes until we cross the Ironbridge, which
gives its name to the dirty district, and turning to the
left we are on the Severn's other bank, with better
roads for Shrewsbury.

We shortly cross the river again, to rest awhile and
photograph the massive ruins of Buildwas. The long
hot day is drawing to its close, for it is now six o'clock,
and the western sun shines straight up the roofless
nave and chancel, gilding the ancient sanctuary with
glorious light.

> "When the dying flame of day
> Through the chancel shot its ray."

Around us is the peaceful calm of a lovely summer's
eve in a most romantic spot, and we long for rest and
peace, but there is none for the wicked, for our old com-
plaint comes back to us and we must hurry on. The
express leaves Shrewsbury at 7.30, and we have twelve

miles to go.   Hastily packing tripod and camera, weary
and thirsty we rush for home.   At the ninth milestone
from the city we find we have a full hour with a minute
or so to spare, and have little doubt of catching our
train.   Then comes a long steep hill.   The first mile
takes nine minutes, the next seven, the next six.   Six
miles to go and forty minutes to do them in.   We have

CHAPTER HOUSE, BUILDWAS ABBEY

not lost ground, but we are getting very worn and
weary.   The day is one of the hottest on record, with
a temperature of from eighty to ninety in the shade,
Another long hill comes, up which we cannot cycle.
Glorious views unroll themselves all around us lit up by
the sinking sun, but we have no time to gaze on them,
or to rest.   Thirst and fatigue become painful.   We roll

down hill again when suddenly there rises before us the
ghostly wall of the ruined basilica or Town Hall of
Roman Uriconium. By Atcham's Tower and classic
shore we see the fish jump and the water-fowl play as a
cool breeze sweeps down the river, and struggling desperately on we gain the city by the English bridge as
all the chimes and Falstaff's Shrewsbury clock proclaim
the time of half-past seven.

Up Wyle Cop, the Wylde Coppe of the " Ingoldsby
Legends," where Bloudie Jacke's head they hew and they
hack and they chop and they pop on the top, we toil.
Castle Street is all taken up for repairs. We rush on
regardless of tyres, and we get to the station seven
minutes late, to find the express gone and ourselves
utterly exhausted.

SHROPSHIRE

THE last chapter records the only pilgrimage in which we missed our train, in which we over-exerted ourselves, and from which we passed a sleepless night. The extraordinary heat was the cause, and one result was the following meditation on the journey through the land. Volumes have been written, and others time will bring, on this fair land of Salop, where, in a short day's ride, one may pass through scenes where all the stages of our English history rise before us, and where we may not only vividly see, but actually touch, the homes and hearths and bones of those who made the history before the names of England and the English themselves were made.

As we struggled, hot and weary, up the valley of the Severn towards Shrewsbury, in the gathering twilight, there suddenly loomed before us the ghostly grey wall of the ruined basilica of Uriconium. We were on bikes, things that Cæsar never knew, rolling along the Roman road, and there are the remains of the buried city, the Wrekin, or Vricon camp or chester, with the bones and weapons of those who perished with it. A big heap of human bones, all exposed to wind and weather, bleached, withered, and sapless, the very dogs sniff at them and treat them with contempt. Here are the Romans' teeth and their money. Any one may buy either for a trifle, quite irrespective of their original value. I wonder whether the haughty Roman would sooner have lost his money or his teeth. Through long ages the soil has absorbed their flesh and blood, and enriched thereby it grows fine barley, now ripening to the harvest, a lovely dazzling whiteness, destined to be made into pale ale, when the remnants of the Romans will be drunk by Englishmen.

> "Imperious Cæsar, dead and turn'd to clay,
> Might stop a hole to keep the wind away."

It is thirteen centuries since a British bard sang of the slaughter and destruction at Uriconium, the desolation of "the white town in the green woodland, their halls without fire, without song, the silence broken only by the eagle's scream, the eagle that has drunk the heart's blood of Kyndylan the fair." What has become of the Britons whom the Romans conquered and whom successive bands of savages drove ever farther to the west, and of the prehistoric people who were here before them, and whose hill forts are still around our way? Among those hills and mountains right before us, where "the weary sun" is setting in a blaze of gold and crimson, there dwell the remnants of the tribes—a race of men small in stature but fiery in spirit, with hair as black as their crows, but it soon turns grey, as well it may, for their pleasure is in economy and in psalm-singing their joy. Local proverbs say that pigs and parsons are the chief products of the land. Gloomy beliefs thrive on their stormy hills, where the great pride of the yeomen is to have a son in the ministry and plenty of pigs in the sty. Then if they can charge an English lodger twopence extra for the mustard he has eaten to his ham and sing a hymn, their little cup of happiness is full.

In their pedigrees they far surpass the English, who are but a modern mongrel nation to them. Three Saxons' heads are often borne by them as arms to show what they could take as one day's work, and whereas we in Manchester think it a wonderful thing to have had a Mayor who was a descendant of one of the Evan-

gelists, the Welsh have pedigrees going back to Noah
or the gods, with prophets and apostles half-way down
the list, and it is in print that on the Day of Judgment
their musical tongue will still be heard.

Up this river Severn, in whose valley we wander,
there came many a pirate band—Angles, Jutes, Saxons,
Danes.   Slowly and painfully came the Christian mis-
sionaries when the fair-haired "angel-faced" English
slaves were sold in Rome.   The savage religions of
Woden, the war god, and Thor, the thunderer, gradually
gave way to some attempts at Christianity ; and one of
the first houses built in the land for the followers of the
new faith was at Wenlock, where the splendid ruins of
the additions of a thousand years we lately saw.   But
the savage Danes sacked and burnt it all.   " Jehovah's
vessels hold the godless heathen's wine."   The marauders
got away with aught that was worth the taking and came
again.   What does the ordinary Englishman know or
care to-day about the Danes?   Nothing but the fact
that their butter undersells the local produce in almost
every grocer's shop throughout the land.

When there was peace in Britain, which was seldom
—for " What can war but endless war still breed "—the
country prospered, and even a Saxon prince sought the
solitude and calm of a hermit's cell, which any one may
see near to Bridgnorth.   Its long authentic history of a
thousand years has left it much as it ever was.   Bits
of Saxon work may yet be seen in the ancient churches
with more that is Norman.   Their massive fonts, which
seem to have been made for the total immersion of the
baptized children, are fairly common.   One at Wroxeter
has been hollowed out of the base of one of the largest
Roman columns.   That old stone has gone through
many strange vicissitudes, and looks like lasting a few
more ages and ages again.

Atcham's stately church still stands above the stately
river, where the monks built a bridge of stone for way-

farers. We should want an Act of Parliament and a small fortune spent in law before we could do it now. Here Ordericus, the Norman historian, was born, and sent abroad to be educated in all the wisdom of the church and the Norman. As he himself has written, " I left behind my native country and my parents and all my kin, and they, weeping and bidding me farewell with loving prayers, commended me to Thee, O most High Lord God."

The thoughtful wanderer through the land may often ask himself, " What has become of those strong, able, self-willed Normans who, as kings, lords, and priests, ruled with a rod of iron those who owned the realm before them. There is little remembrance of them left. Even their names are gone. In a few cases a family name like that of Corbet, or a place-name like Haughmond, shows its Norman origin ; but mostly they are plainly Anglo-Saxon. The endurance of the English has absorbed the Norman. Any one who wants to be any one in particular, gets a pedigree showing his descent from William the Bastard or his robber comrades. If the deception pleases them, the antiquary may only smile ; to him the authentic period is generally plain.

There are few indeed if any of the proudest and oldest English families who can prove legitimate male descent from the men of the Norman Conquest. If the qualifying words are omitted the descent is undoubted, and most of the English to-day are distant relations of William the Conqueror ; for arithmetic will prove that, taking three generations to the century, if there has been no in-breeding we must have had 33,554,432 ancestors in his time, and therefore we could not easily escape him. Much less than half the time since the Conquest is the date of the spoliation of the Religious Houses, and yet some historians on the fate of sacrilege have found that, out of six hundred and thirty grantees

P

of the abbey lands, only thirteen have left families who have held and still hold in male descent those pilfered lands.

At Acton Burnell we saw the remnant of the house which held the second English Parliament, when the first English Edward summoned his barons and burghers to meet him there. By it is the roofless Norman castle and the renovated church. The inscriptions in and on these ancient churches perplex the reader of them in more ways than one. If churches were built and lands given that prayers should be offered for the repose of the souls of the founders of those churches and their families, what right have others to appropriate those churches and bequests, and ignore conditions with which they do not agree? Wrong and robbery riot triumphant through our long English history. The stronger has always robbed the weaker and justified its acts by its religion. Why should the inheritor scrutinize the title? Are we not told that a contented mind is great riches?

Hanging up aloft in these same churches which should be temples of peace, are weapons of war, the actual weapons used by Cavaliers against their Round-head brethren, and the still older armour of the fratricidal Wars of the Roses. It is interesting but strangely incongruous to see them—silent incentives to war where all the teaching and preaching should be of peace and love.

What a ghostly country it is, as the phantoms of those who are gone before us are conjured up again by the sight of what they did and where they lived! Since our last great Civil War which settled kingcraft for ever and let the people rule themselves, a deep peace has fallen on the land, agitated only by the tales of foreign wars and by the ravings of excited politicians at election times. In many country districts a hundred years seem to have passed as yesterday, leaving no more mark or waste.

Scores of houses built centuries ago are far healthier and more comfortable, and will long outlast our modern sanitary rubbish. Everything is interesting, the birds and beasts, the fruit and flowers, even our fellow-men. The labourer on the land, the delver of the soil, the hewer of wood and the drawer of water, called by them of old time the husbandman, by townfolk the clodhopper, toils at his daily task in rain, or wind, or snow. Patient and long-suffering as the cow he milks, holidays are unknown to him, and he has nought to save. His thoughts are few and slow, full of the folk-lore of his forefathers, with remnants of heathen customs and prehistoric beliefs. The harvests come and go, but there is little harvest save toil for him. The gleaning has ceased, for in these latter days there is nought left to glean. His solace is to get drunk, and he dimly hopes that some day his children will keep him when age and want have weakened his sturdy frame, for he dreads the poorhouse, and there seems no rest but in the grave.

Other generations come, for mothers nurse their babes and sons help their mothers' age in the sweetest bliss that is known to us. Springtide brings the flowers again when happy children wander bird-nesting, thoughtless of the poor birds or of their granny's folk-lore which tells them not to bring the strings of many-coloured eggs into the house lest evil enter with them, for they are spoils that have been robbed and had there-fore better hang in the outhouse in the garden. Autumn sees the yearly harvest with the sacrifice of fruit in its abundance, when the young are smeared with the juice of blackberries, gleefully going a-nutting; while the old folks like to gather fruit, for another year is passing, and they calmly wait for the time when all shall be gathered in.

It is an awful thing to think of the countless genera-tions who have gone before us. How often even in historic times have those little country churchyards been filled, and filled again, and filled again, and yet are never full! We know it well, for although no trace remains, the body has returned to the earth and the grass that it was, but the spirit which left it even as the mourners watched with doors and windows shut yet saw nothing, where is it?

ASHLEY HEATH

THE BEST OF CHESHIRE

PILGRIMS who would like to see the best of all the rich fair land of Cheshire may, in twenty miles, pass through the famous dairy district, where the countless cows show that here—possibly in a greater degree than anywhere else on earth—is the ideal land which floweth with milk and honey, for the clover that enriches the milk produces honey also, and the bees can go for change to the heather in the forest primeval, while the cows may stand knee-deep in the grass of the old turf land. Here are castles ancient and modern, wooded hills and rocks ablaze with gorse and heather, orchards glowing with fruit, damsons, and blackberries in every hedge. All that nature, art, and wealth can give for man's enjoyment are there, and for those who think of making money only, let them stop in the stinks and smoke of Northwich and the neighbouring towns to make it there.

From Delamere station a broad highway goes straight eastward, crossing the Chester road, where stands the inn called the Abbey Arms. Over its portal is the sign, the arms of the Abbey of Vale Royal, three royal leopards, and the abbot's crook to catch them or anything else by the leg. Then, on the right, is the Fishpool Inn, reminiscent of the quantities of fish that were wanted when the Abbot fasted. Soon is passed the once famous Edisbury Castle, with its prehistoric earthworks and forgotten glories. The narrow lane which leads up to it was resplendent in orange-coloured sand when last I went. Now it is a cindered track ; so I shuddered and rushed on.   Through the forest primeval, where the murmuring pines still feel but little of the stealthy fumes of smoke and filth from neighbouring towns, where the prickly fruit of the edible chestnuts is thick amid the glistening foliage, by a sharp descent and ascent we come to the little village of Cotebrook, with its modern church, which looks so nice and neat that we waive our exceptions to modern churches and stay for inspection.

Of course it is open ; the best kept churches always are.   This one is freer than usual, for the books are in a case by the door, and the only request is for prayer for yourself and others.   Tarporley Church we also visit, which, being an ancient parish church, is necessarily more interesting, especially as it is in some degree a fine art gallery with portraits and sculpture.   High on the wall is a half-length figure of Sir John Done, of Utkinton, in his dress as he lived, that being an interesting feature. He was the last of the hereditary foresters, whom I have previously mentioned, a hard-bitten breed who justified the grinding forest laws and the grabbing of all they could by their self-complacent motto, "Omnia mei dona Dei" (All that is mine is the gift of God).

Another large medallion and evidently contemporary portrait is of John Crewe, the husband of the grand-daughter and heiress of the above.   Helmets and battered breastplates hang round, and, partly hidden behind the organ, is a pretentious monument to another John Crewe, son of the above, which shows the vile taste of the Georgian era, when all things seemed viler than before. This John Crewe is represented in marble the size of life, lying on the ground in his night-gown, with every hair clean shaved off, but in an enormous horse-hair wig.   At his head and feet are little boys in the greatest distress, with big marble tears on their chubby fat cheeks.   They are probably crying because he has been smacking them, for there are others aloft in heaven looking wonderfully pleased that he cannot get up to them there. His toes turn up with excitement, and remind me of an old uncle of mine, who told me his troubles had been so sore that all his toe-nails had dropped off.

There is a beautiful monument to the mother of the above and her sister, the co-heiresses of the Dones of Utkinton. The hall with its central pillar of oak, as shown on page 19, is in the neighbourhood. It would take several pages to give the long laudatory epitaphs on these tombs. No one could be so good as they are represented to be in churches. One of the sisters, named Jane, is described as a Virgin, "remarkably Eminent for Parts" and "of Prudence and Piety unbounded." She seems to have been lawyer, doctor, parson, and everything else to all the countryside, and as they are really two nice-looking women lying down together, I wondered which was which, when, seeing that one had high heels and square toes, I judged that to be the virgin. The other sister has a funny little grandchild with ruffed cap standing by her feet.

Everything about the place seems carefully kept. Adjoining the churchyard is a school-house dated 1636, the gift of Dame Dorothy Done (please pronounce the *o* long in Done). The main street of the town is broad and airy. Gentlemen's gentlemen ride thorough-bred horses from the neighbouring hunting-boxes, and look with contempt on poor cyclists. Life seems very slow and placid. No one knows the way to Harthill, and no one cares. Shopkeepers smoke at their shop doors as if they were quite content, and, therefore, not likely to know much, though they would evidently gossip interminably. Three men are sitting on a corner curb-stone and one standing; all smoking. I ask the way to what, in country pronunciation, is Artel. They all stop smoking and spit. This is evidently an important question. They try to think. That takes time. Then the lower half of one's face drops or opens as, pointing with his pipe, he says, "It's ower 'ere." He tells me to go straight on and keep to the right, but another one says, "Nay, nay; go down yon road and keep to th' left, turn again when yo' come to an 'ouse." I go my own way, thinking I have set them "a nice craddy to threeup on." After crossing a canal with one of the too common steep and narrow bridges, I find some men working on the road who do know the ways about. I wind round the base of Beeston Castle, under its precipitous rocks, and farther on, where black and white cottages are on each side of the lane, a halt is made to view the castle-crowned crag rising so grandly above the woods.

Nearing Tattenhall there is a large burial party walking behind a hearse. Dismounting while they pass, an old familiar smell assures me that they are cheese-makers, whose best clothes are perhaps kept in the cheese-room and infected with the smell of the all-important article. Their talk and thoughts are probably of cows and crops and cheese. On the other side of Tarporley I had talked to a Cheshire dairymaid, who was tending her turkeys from the fox. She was more of the practical than the poetic type. Young and strong, wearing clogs, evidently fed on buttermilk and 'taties, her working weight probably sixteen stone, she was just the sort for some folk.

Past the gate of Bolesworth Castle and by its lordly park, I trudge uphill to the charming little village of Harthill. It seems almost too spick and span, too much the model village of "new riches," though there is much of hoar antiquity about the tiny church; and the site, high up in the wooded hills amid the pine-trees, overlooking Cheshire to the sea, what a glorious vision is here! I doubt whether Ormerod, the historian, or his reviser, ever visited this secluded spot, or they would have more fully mentioned it.

BEESTON CASTLE

Conspicuously carved right across the church porch is a big inscription, "Rondvll Pricket church warden ever since 1606 until 1611." In later years other churchwardens put up their names in much smaller letters. Mr. Randvl Pryckit, who spelt his name differently inside the church, with a shield of arms of three prickits, which I should judge to be peewits, was possibly a bank manager, or pompous official, they being generally the most self-satisfied of men after the parsons. For having great ideas of their own importance in this world, they think by becoming churchwardens they have also a voice in the affairs of the next world, and then they are almost objectionable.

Inside the church there is quite a display of heraldic cognizances, some of them old and genuine, others painfully new. An eminent statesman said heraldry was the most useless of all studies, but after saying that, he turned Tory and wanted a coat of arms and long pedigree. As the parish is very lonely and 428 feet above sea-level, some one, probably the parson, filled up his dull time with heraldic and antiquarian studies. The arms and initials of the Bulkeleys from the small neighbouring manor of Bulkeley are here. One of their ancient race married a co-heiress of the Chedles, making the new name of Cheadle Bulkeley, where X is lord of the shadow and some of the substance.

But, oh! what is this on the rood-screen? Here is a coat of arms which flabbergasts me—the gorgeously emblazoned heraldic cognizance of the Withington Urban District Council, of which I have lately been chairman. It gave me quite a turn, as the old women say, for councils are generally said to have neither souls to be saved nor bodies to be kicked, and what is their warlike shield of arms doing in the church, conspicuously hanging on the screen which separates the nave from the holy of holies? Does our enterprising council intend to take a farm up on these balmy hills for the disposal of sewage, or are they going to grow their own timber, or make their own broken stone, or have a smallpox hospital, or what? Dreadful and perturbing thoughts come crowding on me. What, if Withington were to amalgamate with Manchester or absorb it, would become of their respective armorial bearings? Would they be quartered or impaled? It might cost a deal of money to settle that. The town-clerks would probably get mixed with the arms, they are such funny things nowadays.

Adjoining the churchyard, in the centre of the village, is a real village green, with live long grass and seats under trees, where one can have lunch in peace and quiet, for the necessary children were conspicuous by their absence, and the only sounds were from the neighbouring farm. At this elevation the air is pure and balmy, and the well-earned rest is sweet. With the roses come the thorns, and a thorn has punctured my back tyre while I dreamed of something else. A village wench or maiden tells me, "them things" can be mended at an alehouse down the hill. So down the other side of the hill I go towards Bickerton. On either side the lane are cottages built of stone in classical style, far behind the common ones of Cheshire for beauty. The inn is down below on a main road, up which I turn to the left, after all is fettled up.

Soon I mount again to the high ground of the Peckforton Hills with the rival castles, old and new, before me, and then come miles of gentle descent in the most beautiful country one can wish to wander over. On the left are the hills ablaze with patches of gorse, and heather, and bracken. Here and there are solitary beautiful specimens of firs, or oaks, or birches, some in clumps and some in masses. Every cottage has gardens glowing with fruit and flowers, and far to the right stretch out the dairy lands of Cheshire.

Past the giant oak before the embattled gatehouse of

Peckforton's splendid modern castle, which is perched like an eagle's nest on its almost inaccessible rock, the road winds down towards the time-worn, well-known Beeston. Winding down again to the station, far below, the pilgrim may sigh that his journey ends, for of all the rich fair lands this earth can show, there are few that can with this compare.

FALLOW DEER AT BEESTON CASTLE

CARADOC, CARDINGTON, CHURCH PREEN

ONE of the finest yews in Britain is said by the author of a book on yew-trees to be the one at Church Preen in Shropshire. Its height is given as fifty feet, breadth more than sixty feet, and girth of hollow trunk at ground forty feet. The remarkable fact of these almost everlasting trees having been planted and zealously cared for alongside every ancient building, church, cottage, or hall, as if they were sacred or had some special merit as safeguards, increases our interest in them, and desire to see any venerable specimen. This great tree stands in a country which teems with historical interest and romantic ruins. When at Acton Burnell and Easthope we were within a few miles of the place, but difficulties of access and want of time prevented us from finding it; therefore, in the lovely weather of September, I made a solitary pilgrimage to those lonely hills.

Taking the train to Church Stretton Station, from there I asked the way to Cardington, and found the shortest route as shown on the map was over a mountain and impassable for a bicycle. I went back towards Shrewsbury and then to the right over the shoulder of the steeps of Caradoc, which is the conical hill to the left of the railway as you near Church Stretton. In a few miles the walking uphill began; the air became rarer, the country wilder, with vistas of more distant lands and hills. From the wayside hedge came suddenly a startling peal of laughter, then another and another, as gorgeous birds in green and gold with crimson crests went flashing by. These were woodpeckers, sometimes called yaffles from their cry, and known in song from their "tapping at the hollow beech-tree." Fortunate it is they do their tapping and their laughing in the daylight, for if they did them in the dark, in spite of all their beauty, they would frighten wayfarers to fits.

As one mounts Caradoc the country round is very fine. Picturesque farms and cottages with big stone chimneys good for use, good for show, and good to last, stand in gleaming orchards with guardian yews. On the crab-trees the wild apples hang like ropes of onions, fair to look upon, but sour to the taste, as the proverbial crab. Sour enough to make lads screw up their faces and sadly look sick. The noted cider-apple Foxwhelp is so tart that even the most angelic choir-boy will not steal it thrice. Blackberries are thick as blackberries, and there are nuts for all. On the summit of the pass I eat my frugal lunch as a drove of colts and cattle come by. The white-faced Herefords jostle their thick lumbering bodies against each other as they wonderingly stare at the bicycle, and the drovers touch their hats as if in these unsophisticated regions a cyclist might possibly be taken for a gentleman.

Down a rough and rugged hill I rattle to Cardington, the little town below Caradoc; car or caer being the British name for a fortified hill. The curious little houses have been dropped about at all sorts of angles and many levels. The church is evidently very ancient in those parts of it that have escaped the hand of the destroyer, alias restorer. Some of the round-headed doors and windows have been merely blocked up, not entirely destroyed, and some of the herring-bone stone-work is left. Ancient oaken pews with the names of outlying farms or estates carved on them, names that are interesting from their old-world savour, such as

Ench marsh or Lydley shaies, have been cut up into modern benches, with other needless and senseless Vandalism. A double piscina and carved pulpit are left. The black and white porch is dated 1639. The tower is immensely broad and solid, mostly spoilt and plastered, with narrow slits for ancient windows, and modern clock with two inscriptions, redolent of parish strife.

Outside the church I notice a simple stone to Ann Finch of The Gutter, and inside is a gorgeous monument to " William Leyghton, of Plashe, Esquyer, Cheife Justice of North Wales." He died in 1607, and a glowing account of his many virtues and wives and children ends " Nemo ante obitum beatus " (No one is happy before death). So we may infer that even with either wife he was not happy before death, whatever he might be after with the two together. This pious judge lies on his side in scarlet robe as large as life, laying down the law to lesser images of wife and grown-up sons and daughters. They are all evidently likenesses, even to the cut of the whiskers of the sons. One of these was a poet who doubtless lacked the ability to earn his living. The widow and daughters are in deep mourning, with tremendous flat black head-dresses ; perfect frights the women of to-day would call them ; and the particular woman who cleans the church says she would like to give the whole lot a good scrubbing. She says this pious Chief Justice was " a wicked old beggar," and when I repeat the inscription, says again, " Don't you believe it ; he was a wicked old beggar." Knowing what is the unpardonable sin in a woman's eyes, I ask if he had his two wives both at once. She snorts, " Two indeed ! father could have told you many tales about him. What did he hang the man for in his own chimney ? Oh ! he was a wicked old beggar. If you doubt it, go and look at the chimneys ; they are there to this day. Put up all these lies in the church ! They'll put up

anything for money. You may see the chimneys and
the house too if you go down that lane and keep on.
He was a wicked old beggar."

It happened that the place with the noted chimneys,
named Plash Hall, was nearly on my way to Church
Preen, so I bumped and jolted along two miles of loose
stones to find it. The tradition is that when pious
Judge Leighton was building himself a fine house to die
in, as newly rich men often do, he condemned to death
(they were not particular about hanging a few in those
days) a noted builder, but reprieved him to get the
benefit of his genius in the ornamentation of the new
house, particularly with regard to fantastic chimneys,
which are characteristic of the buildings of that age.
The poor convict put his whole energies, body and soul,
into the construction of elaborately beautiful chimneys,
which are there to this day, and then the rascally old
lawyer, having got all he could out of him, had him
hanged at last, some say in one of the big chimneys.

Of course the house is haunted, not by an odd ghost
or two, but by several. Country folk know that lawyers
do not often die, but that the "Old Lad" fetches them
when they have done enough. It is said that in this
house one dark and stormy Sunday night a party were
playing cards, and the parson was one of them. Perhaps
he had a cold and could not go to church, or there was
no church, or something, but his holiness could not
prevent what followed, for with a great bang that shook
the strong house to its foundations Old Scrat came
and vanished, and with him vanished the owner also.
Nothing was ever seen of that wretched man again, and
the parson denounced gambling harder than ever. A
blood-stained floor is all that is left of some other blood-
curdling tragedy, but it is enough. A man from London
took the place some years ago, and had the blood-mark
carefully painted over. But the stain came again, and

the paint went, and the man from London went also.
If any one doubts these tales let him see the house, a
magnificent house in a lovely country, to be had very
cheap, for almost nothing.   Why?

Across the fields, up hill and dale, and over stiles by
a moated, mullioned farm, it would be a mile or two to
Church Preen, and twice that distance to go by what
they call lanes.   Bad as the so-called roads were, I
thought it better to keep to them than wander over
hills and woods with a bike.   Slowly, painfully, and
carefully I jolted on, until I found a man who pointed
out a distant hall, and advised me to go for a shorter
and a better road through the squire's park.   I went
and found a fine handsome black and white house, evidently an enlargement of a still older one, with a little
church adjoining it, but higher on the hillside.   In
these country places it is common to see the hall and
church close together, and if that old lawyer at Plash
had built a church close to his house it might have been
better for him.   A modern brewer would do it, though
a lawyer would probably say he was not so superstitious.
Even the lawyer might get caught, for when I told my
old aunt that I did not believe in the devil, she replied
at once, " That may be, but he'll have you all the same
some day," and she seemed rather pleased and triumphant, for her Toryism is very strong.

The object of my pilgrimage, the splendid yew, was
easy to see, though all around it were enormous trees.   It
is a female tree laden with myriads of beautifully translu-
cent berries, looking like glowing pink wax, on which innumerable birds were feasting.   It seemed almost wrong to
lean my bicycle against it, but I did so, and went to church.

Ages ago the Cluniac monks of Wenlock built themselves a cell or remote chapel, possibly a tithe barn also,
in these lonely woods, and the walls of the present
church are probably the original walls of their building.

I carefully measured it ; the inside width is four yards, and the length six times the width. There are bits of carved work and a pulpit dated 1646, but round-headed slits of windows in deeply splayed walls are evidences of far greater antiquity. Its very remoteness from civilisation has fortunately preserved it until in our day it has fallen to good patrons who keep it open, as it should be, and well cared for. In a silence as deep as the grave I sat and mused awhile. No sound came through those solid walls. The light through tinted glass and under mighty trees was very dim and sanctified. There were no echoes of the bygone ages when fervent men set up a lodge in this far wilderness. The clang of battle-axe and spear, the whirr of arrows, have long since ceased. The railway's stir and shriek sound not up here. In blessed silence I rested until even the silence became oppressive, and remembering Wordsworth's lines where Death and Time lie in mute repose within the yew tree's pillared shade and on its grassless floor of red-brown hue they lie and listen, I did the same, lulled by the fresh winds of heaven and the peacefulness around. Drowsiness came over me with the monotonous cooing of the wood queece or cushie doos. In endless monotone they coo to one another through the long hours of light.

What can it be they say ?   Let me try and learn their tongue.
First the hen-bird sitting on her two pale eggs would sing :
       Coo, cu coo-oo,
       These eggs won't do-oo.
Then in deeper tones her mate would answer :
       Koo, ku koo-oo,
       They'll both be true-ue—
Solemn pause, to end in tones of plaintive doubt :
       Coo, cu coo-oo,
       Young should be through-ough—
Pause again, but steady faith :
       Koo, ku koo-oo,
       Have patience, do-oo —

Q

Time is flying, life is short :
Coo, cu coo-oo,
I'm tired too-oo.
Faith unfaltering, haste not, rest not ;
Koo, ku koo-oo,
Sit till you're blue-ue.

Happy as a dove in love, they coo till something
wakes me from my reverie, and there is a chattering
squirrel scolding me for lying idle there.   It jerks its
tail, and jumps about, and chatters away as if it would
throw nuts at me.   A black and white rabbit also is
sitting up, with lustrous wondering eyes, only a few feet
away, reminding me of "Alice in Wonderland."   A
brown terrier is curled up in front of the hall, but he
seems too old and sleepy to trouble about trifles.

Am I dreaming still? for it is only six hours since
I left Stockport Station, and the sights and sounds and
smells were very different there.   The apples are done,
and the yew berries look good but dangerous.   It will
soon be tea-time.   From the adjoining stableyard I hear
the sound of voices, and go to consult with grooms about
my way.   They seem as surprised as the squirrel at seeing a bicycle up there.   They say I cannot go over the
hills the short way to Church Stretton, but must go the
other way round by Longville in the dale, where there
is that paradise for grooms and wayfarers—a public-
house.   The best way, of course, is through the park,
whither I turn to go, but the Squire seems to have
heard us.   Voices sound strange up here, and he
abruptly appears upon the scene and asks me where I
am from.   I say "Didsbury."   If I had mentioned some
common places like Cheetham, or Salford, or even Moss
Side, goodness knows what might have happened ; but
as it was, he said, "Oh, do you know the Ashtons of
Ford Bank?—Certainly, go through the park, or where
you like."   So I got off again all right, and went for
miles down a straight road where something far ahead

puzzled me exceedingly. It turned out to be a gipsy caravan, where the loosened asses were rolling in the road, enjoying a dust bath like hens and sparrows, who love to fluff themselves in loose, dry earth. Miles of thistle-down also were there, spreading the thistle crop far and wide. The yellowish soil with much that grew thereon seemed strange to me, a lonely pilgrim with the darkness closing round.

FRODESLEY LODGE

FRODESLEY LODGE

HIGH up, on an outlying spur at the end of the steep hill known as Hoar Edge, about ten miles south of Shrewsbury, there is a curious house or castle standing forth prominently on a precipitous green hill, up which you climb by many steep and narrow steps. Above the lofty gables rise still more lofty ornamental chimneys, and a round tower encloses a circular stairway of broad stone stairs, up which three persons might walk abreast. It is called the old Lodge, Frodesley, the *o* in the name being pronounced short as in Frodsham. I had pronounced it long when asking my way from the country folk, and was continually being sent towards Shrewsbury, for that name the natives call Srowsbury.

In that remote district, three hundred years ago, a house that was half castle might be very useful, and some one spared no trouble or expense in building for himself a lodge from whence he might not only hunt but see the country and all comers for miles on miles. Behind it rises the steep side of Hoar Edge, coloured with bracken and dotted with wind-swept firs. Close to it is the skeleton of an immense dead oak, whose strong bare arms stand out black against the sky, the smaller branches having been long since blown to smithereens by the storms that sweep and whistle through it. Below are gigantic oaks in various stages of decaying age, some of them hollow, one of them apparently sound and solid, as near as I could tell, three yards in diameter— enormous trees, the hollows from whence big limbs were lost being the ideal places for the homes of owls.

My little pilgrimages have taken me to many outlandish nooks and corners and up many strange bypaths, though probably none of them were more curious than this one. The road itself was, perhaps, more ancient than the bleak house to which it led. For about a mile it was perfectly straight, paved in the middle with big squared stones, which might have been put there by the Romans. Ruts had been worn in them by ages of traffic, and here and there a stone was missing. Thistles and burs grew in the way to the height of a man. There were big ditches on each side, hidden with tangled thickets of briars and thorns, growing into hedges twenty feet high and laden with various fruits. It was all uphill, not very steep, but impossible to ride a bicycle, and to trundle one with scratched hands is not pleasant, through thistles as prickly as any Scotchman, and briars with long curved hooks like a lawyer's claws. Now and then, through the high hedges, came glimpses of the far-away house or castle on high, to which this pilgrim's progress was being laboriously made, with as many doubts and halts and fears as are recorded in a much more famous pilgrimage. Often I had to stop, and thought of turning back, but on I went again. There were only cattle to stare at me. What a place to be benighted in! No need to ask or doubt if that grim, weather-beaten hold were haunted. That was plain enough to see, even for the simple.

At last I reached a gate which was difficult to open, and led into a croft where there were big trees under which sheep were lying. The silly sheep stared in amazement, and rushed bleating up the hillside as if they cried, "Whatever is coming now? The butcher has had our lambs, and the wool has been shorn from our backs. Do they want our hearts and kidneys also?" Up an almost precipitous grass bank of great height goes a long flight of narrow steep steps, and on the top of them is a big black dog, just as there ought to be. The dog barks loudly, and I fervently hope it does not bite. An old woman comes out to it, and I shout to her asking if I may go up. She says, "Are you my son?" I answer, "No. I am only a stranger wishing to see the house." She shouts again, "If you are not my son you can't come here." It is difficult to talk when there are fifty or a hundred steps between us, and the dog talking at the same time. He comes down and stands just above me, ready to dispute the passage. What is to be done? I am not going back all at once, but try round about. Thatching a stack in the farmstead is an Irishman, who merely says "The missus is quer." Many things seem queer here. I wander farther round, but the big black dog keeps his eye on me. An old man is found who says he will show me the house if I will not mind the missus. Every one seems frightened of the missus, but perhaps, as the Irishman says, she is only "quer," and I tell him that I am well used to all sorts of funny folks, which, considering the public work one has to do, is very true.

We went inside a noble old house. The missus was giving the Irishman his dinner, something in a bowl, probably buttermilk and 'taties. The dog went to lap at the big tub, something good from the dairy, which made him lick his lips and seem satisfied. Up the broad stone spiral stairs the old man takes me to rooms which are panelled from floor to ceiling with immense panels of finely grained old oak and deeply carved ornamental work, also in oak. From the windows are entrancing views over half the fair rich lands of Salop, and as we talked of them something cold and wet was thrust into my hand and another voice said in anxious tones, "Are you my son?" The woman and the dog had come quietly up the stairs unheard by me, and each in their own way had offered startling greeting. I went on asking the man about the country round, but that forlorn and anxious query came again, "Are you my son, or can you tell me where is my son?" I could but wonder to myself, Is this another victim of the war? Has a son gone forth, and with him all his mother's hope and joy in life? But I went on talking of other things. The man began again of his troubles, and said in a dialect that was strange to me, "Them theer roooms is empty noo." Yes—in the daylight—I could see that. "They ain't no use to we us dwells aboo. It's an awfu' place." Awful enough, no doubt, when the mists shut out the wondrous country round, when the spectral-looking tower rises over its spectral-riven oaks, while the winds howl and shriek

as if the spirits of other days were in them, and one
wonders if the cry comes from an owl, a ghost, a jackdaw,
or a child.

When asked if I would go on to the roof of the tower,
the tale of Lord Derby's fool when the King went on the
tower at Lathom rushed back to memory, and I thanked
my host for having shown me enough.   He asked me to
have a glass of ale, and seemed puzzled at me declining
it, saying, "Are yo one o' them as ne'er touches?"
There seemed to be the sound of a low mocking laugh,
which, let us hope, was not so; and again there came the
yearning query, "If you art not my son, can you tell me
where is my son?"

The dog accompanied me to where I had left the
bicycle, evidently going to see me safely off the premises,
although we were good friends now.   Suddenly he
seemed to see a ghost, for he rushed off with pricked
ears, growling savagely at nothing so far as I could see,
and well I remembered how the dogs at home, when
they slept in the house, used to trouble us with growling
at the ghosts when we took no notice of them.   At the
bottom of the castle mound was a small herd of swine,
looking as their progenitors may have looked eight
hundred years ago, for in the Domesday Book it is
recorded that in the woods of Frodesley there was
fattening for a hundred swine, and their pannage
possibly came from the time-worn oaks which still
are there.   A patriarchal pig, with a snout and hide
like a hornless rhinoceros, led the herd, and I noticed
a younger one gruntingly whisper something in its ear
as if it told it we were near, when the razor-backed
rhinoceros turned and led them to the barley stack, for
well it knew that your barley-fed bacon is better than
the Indian-corn fed reisty bacon of other lands, and the
credit of the tribe must be maintained; for even that
thick-skinned patriarch, lean and lank and long as it
now is, will some day be salted down and given as food
to the Irish labourers in the winter.

The dog and I sat down to talk and think. He seemed sad and sympathetic, as if he could have told me strange secrets, though as one of the family it was not right to do so. There are tracts which tell us all human beings have souls, and are infinitely superior to the beasts or dogs which perish and have only bodies to be kicked. It seems rather strange here. " Poverty," an old proverb tells us, " makes us acquainted with strange bedfellows." It is quite as true if it is reversed. The dog and I were friendly, and would have helped one another if we could. I wanted a photograph of the house, and as there was no chance of getting one and no place from whence one could be taken, I made a drawing of it, and sad reflections again arose, for on this lonely pilgrimage all things seemed sad. I thought of the many happy hours I had spent in painting, studying to be an artist ; how through the many schemes for life the inbred wish to be a farmer had always maintained its hold ; and after all those high hopes and noble aspirations, the failing time of age finds me only a common councillor.

Well, good-bye, doggie, we must jog on. I shall have to walk all down that wonderful paved street, and push my way through the thistles. There was something like a church in the village, and, of course, that must be inspected. But it was only like another nightmare. Instead of one of the lovely, venerable churches, which all over the land our pious forefathers built centuries ago, there was one destroyed, hideous with all the worst horrors of "restoration"—a thing like a Calvinistic barn, where one would expect to hear long sermons on the torments that are in store for the damned, that term including all who differ from the preacher in his narrowness. Precious little has been left of the former building, which was built when men gave of the best they had for the house of their God. Perhaps one of our latter-day parsons thought his preaching would be better listened to if there were no beauties of art, of architecture, or music to detract from it.   I was told this destruction was perpetrated about sixty years since, and that quite lately the beautiful old black and white manor-house, with overhanging storeys and deep eaves, was pulled down to make room for a new red-brick farm-house, with the latest modern "improvements," which stands in its stead.

That night I hurried off to Church Stretton and lying in bed could see the stars in the Wain circling round the Pole Star, and hear the chimes at midnight, for a forlorn and weary face haunted me with its broken-hearted query, "Are you my son?"

CLUN

THE quaint and queer little town of Clun, off in the hills, away from the beaten track of train or tourist, serene in its quietude, redolent of decayed gentility, with ruined castle, stately church, artistic bridge, and garden-encircled mediæval home of rest for age, was so wonderfully picturesque on the summer's eve when I lit on it from the hills of the Welsh borderland, that a second pilgrimage had to be made with X and camera to secure mementoes of bits as beautiful as any foreign land can show.

The Lancashire and Cheshire Antiquarian Society had visited Shrewsbury one Saturday in the splendid weather of September. We then saw the ancient seals and records of the town, its castle and churches, its well-preserved, unmutilated hall of the Drapers' Guild, and many other interesting things. I went on to Church Stretton for the night, and early in the morning was on the Longmynd, the long mound or mountain behind the town. There the sun shone gloriously, while all the country round was wrapped in mists, which, slowly rolling up, gave promise of a brilliant day. Porridge and milk and bacon were all-absorbing till it was time for church as rung out by the bells, though in their sound the conscience-striken natives only hear the mild rebuke, "They eaten more than they getten." Just then an architect, one of our society, who had stayed the night at Shrewsbury, came cycling along hot and thirsty, wanting beer or something wet, and me to cycle with him to Bishop's Castle or over the hills and far away. In forty

years I have not three times missed a Sunday morning
service, and though this time temptation was too much,
yet recompense was made before the night.

> What say the bells of Church Stretton?
> Off to the hills let us get on.
> What say the bells of Church Stretton?
> Weather 'll be fine you may bet on.

There! Whenever I lapse into poetry a strange editor
carefully takes it all out, but as this book cannot afford
the luxury of an editor, the verse may stand as our
excuse for not going to church. We did not wish to be
numbered among the natives whose local rhyme to the
bells of Church Stretton says, " They eaten more than
they getten."

Past the russet-clad hills of Stretton we roll down to
Marshbrook, where we turn westward over the railway
and up a long ascent towards the borderland of Wales.
The roads are arched and bordered with trees, where
every bough is laden with fruit, and every blade of grass
and frond of fern sparkles like diamonds with the dew.
The woods and fields seem to swarm with birds and
butterflies and life in myriad forms. Loud and conspicuous are the brilliant woodpeckers, with their laughing and tapping and rattling noise. The hills become
wilder and steeper, with brawling streams and fertile
fields below, all gorgeous in harvest-tide and the bright
luxuriance of the early Indian summer—the perfection
of a day and journey, when even the spirits and strength
of youth seem to come again.

By many twists and turns we come to Bishops
Castle, a rather faded town with poor brick buildings,
cobbled streets, and poverty-stricken air. An inn stands
on the castle's site. The church is painfully modern.
The streets are steep, and as we hobble on the petrified
kidneys I see some money lying in them. It seems
strange that people cannot take better care of their

money, but there is no good in making a fuss; the simplest thing is to pocket it and go along as if nothing were the matter. We have some lunch, and then on to Clun over a ridge of hills, along a road that is lined with blackberries. From the edge there is a grand view. Far below, in a charming country, is the precipitous keep of an old castle, a landmark to beckon us on our way.

That is all that is left of the ruined fortress of Clun, the scene of many a fierce, deadly struggle between Norman and British, or English and Welsh. Sacked and burnt and blown up and built again, its walls are now ten feet thick and eighty feet high. Beyond is another sheer drop of sixty feet to where was the moat below, and down again is the little river winding, brawling around. Most of the famous legendary heroes of Wales—princes and chiefs, Llewelyn and Glyndwr, all in their

CLUN CASTLE

turn—did their worst with fire and storm to devastate that old stronghold, and still the English built it up again. Time has sapped it, ruin seized it, but still it stands, gaunt, bare, and roofless to all the winds that blow. Now, upon its grass-grown mounds, cattle graze in peace, with no marauding Welsh to harry them.

Above, the daws and shepsters have their windy homes, and when X hears of it he says at once, " A branch of my ancestors, the Fitz–Alans, built it, and Sir Walter Scott wrote of it in ' The Betrothed.' We must photograph it before we die. I wonder if it's on sale."

It being Sunday afternoon as the architect and I neared the uncommon-looking, impressive church, there came from it a sound as of revelry and music. So we left our bikes outside, peeped in, and entered. We were just in time for the collection. Then I knew why that money had so providentially been put in my way at Bishops Castle. It had not come from a fish, but it went in the bag, a very small bag considering the size of the church. A sort of children's service with processional hymn was going on, and I was glad to rest and feel satisfied. It is a noble church. The columns are round and thick, with coloured bands of stone, evidently Norman, and yet the arches are pointed with zigzag mouldings, and on the capitals are ornaments with heads or animals or the remains of them. Above, the clerestory windows are deeply splayed with rounded arches, and the whole effect is of a spacious, light, and beautiful church. High above the altar is a rare old oaken canopy. The pulpit is carved all over, with sounding-board and back, and round the walls, as dados, are placed the old carved backs of pews. The seats, we are told, were sawn up into three, and then were strong enough to bear the folks who use them now.

Outside the church is very singular. There is a deep and spacious porch of stone, with a black and white chamber or parvise over it. An extra aisle on the south side has lately been taken away. The tower stands on ten yards square of land, and has a double-louvred, curious top. The western door is almost hidden with gigantic hinges, bolts, and nails, and possibly there may be under them bits of the skins of Welshers, for in olden

CLUN CHURCH AND INN

times they flayed them and nailed their skins to the church doors, as gamekeepers, even now, stick up the vermin they destroy.

Six bells are there, for that is the name of the inn, and a lot of knocking and banging it takes to get the door opened, for we are on the borders of Wales, where Sunday opening is not indulged in. At last we are admitted. Every one was out, or had gone to sleep. We assure them we do not want intoxication ; we have come a long distance, and want tea. We get it in the best parlour, any amount, two fresh eggs apiece, maiden honey, as much currant tommy, if we had cared for it, as a policeman could eat, and then the bill. Tell it not in Gath, publish it not in the streets of Lancashire, lest the cyclists rejoice and the Philistines devour the substance of the unwary. Would the gentlemen think ninepence too much ?

Then we go to seek the Hospital of the Holy and Indivisible Trinity, which is the somewhat extravagantly grand name of some Almshouses, or Homes of Rest, for aged folk. Through a lofty gateway in a quaint garden stands a chapel and a cloistered house. Through another great archway is a large square grass plot or lawn within square walks, and on each side the lowly dwellings of the poor. Beyond is yet another archway, and there are the gardens which each may till and call his own. An air of deep peace and quiet rest broods over all. Every one is very old, as if death came slowly here. Time itself almost stands still, for this is as it has been for three hundred years.

I was much impressed and interested, and glad to be in the company of one whose knowledge comprised architecture and building, and the by-laws of our local councils. He soon upset all my little schemes by saying somewhat as follows : " There is not the least chance of our local authorities letting you or any one else build a place anything like this. Quadrangular courts, with houses round and gardens back and front, are beautiful in idea and fact, but the authorities will say sanitary considerations are the chief thing. Never mind comfort or pleasure. You must have paved streets before each row of houses and flagged passages behind. A court with grass or gardens front and back would never be allowed. The rooms here are low and cosy ; that would never do. There are no steps or stairs for the old folks to tumble down, and possibly no drains. That is why they live so long. There is a pump. Our inspectors would probably analyse the water, and paste up a notice, ' This water is not fit to drink,' as on a noble lord's pumps at Withington, but the water would be drunk just the same. Thatched roofs did you say ? "—then he burst out laughing—" thatched roofs are certainly warmer in winter and cooler in summer than any other roofs, but your councils would not allow them at any price. Why? Because they care nothing, and often know nothing, about comfort, or pleasure, or beauty. They have cast-iron rules and hide-bound officials. They chatter about health with ignorance appalling and—and you are one of them ! "

The name of the Hospital of the Holy and Indivisible Trinity speaks of age, and also shows us how the meaning of words may change. At the present time the word hospital means a place for the temporary treatment of the injured or diseased. Originally it meant a place where hosts or strangers could have free relief of needs or hospitality. In the shorter or more modern form of hostel or hotel it still has its original meaning, only the strangers pay for what they have. At Clun the hospital is a spacious court of lowly houses where aged folk may freely rest in peace and till their little gardens. When I asked the way to the alms-houses no one knew what I meant, and one would

HOSPITAL OF THE HOLY AND INDIVISIBLE TRINITY, CLUN

shudder to call it a poor-house or a bastille.   Whatever
the name may be, the place itself is a quaint and charming specimen of old-world homes and charity.

Twilight was coming on as we rolled down the well-
kept road along the valley of the Clun.   Below us was
the river, wandering between rich meadows that gradually rose up to the wooded hills.   Above all were
cloudless sky and balmy air.   All the perfections of
cycling were there, when suddenly my back tyre got
punctured, and blowing it up was of no avail.   I cannot
mend my own machine or imperfections, but take my
chance and trust in Providence.   The friend in need
was there in my companion, who soon took off the tyre,
and found in it two thorns making four punctures, which
he mended easily, thereby showing I was very helpless
not to be able to do my own work.   Shortly afterwards
there was suddenly a great clatter, as if a load of scrap
iron had been upset on the road.   His machine seemed
to be coming to pieces, with the chain and a crank loose,
but he ingeniously mended it with a bit of string, and on
we went again.   At the next hill there was a terrific
clatter.   It was now getting dark, and another load of
scrap iron seemed knocking about all over the road.
The string was not strong enough, so his pocket-handkerchief had to be used instead.   When I saw the
architect mending his bike with his handkerchief by
lamplight, I thought of the old proverb, " It is a fine
thing to be a scholar."   We went like Agag, delicately,
that means gingerly, and like him unavailingly.   The
rag got worn through, and the clatter began again,
frightening things to fits.   It was then decided that he
would walk on to Craven Arms, stop the night there,
and I should come again for him in the morning.

The remaining ten miles of my journey might have
been very pleasant, but at that time of the year it was
dark at seven, and, being Sunday night, there were

R

lovers all along the road, and they do not carry lights
as cyclists do.   If they had been to church they might
have heard the text, " They loved darkness rather than
light, because their deeds were evil."   They were all over
the road, so totally absorbed in their own delicious soft-
ness as to be oblivious to aught besides.   If a cyclist,
nearly upset by them, did mar the heaven of their repose, the woman would scream, and the man would
want to fight.   It was a mercy there was no blood
shed.

My second pilgrimage to Clun was soon taken.   X
with his camera and I with more plates went by express
to Craven Arms, and cycled up the valley by the river
of Clun, to the town, honour, and forest, all of Clun—
the natives seem to pronounce the word as if it were
Klon, and in some degree it reminded me of the German Koln or Cologne.   In former days the name must
have been freely applied to the district, for other villages
on the route are partly named the same—

> " Clunton and Clunbury, Clungunford and Clun,
>   Are the drunkenest places under the sun."

As far as I could see, we could give them many points
at drunkenness nearer home, but then they have not so
many political clubs as we have.   They have abundance
of apples, which in some places are lying in the fields
apparently ready for any one to help themselves.
Every one seemed to be eating them, crunching and
munching, and even toothless age and babes in arms
suck the sourest, acidest, juicy fruit.

X is as delighted at finding another of his long-lost
ancestral castles as a poor man would be with a rise of
wages.   He seems afraid the lofty, weather-worn old
pile will drop into its depths below, or the sun disappear
before he can get it photographed.   All around it is
quiet enough now, though it was an exciting place when

CLUN BRIDGE

his ancestral lords sorted out the heads of their friends and enemies, and sent them in sacks to Shrewsbury to know if they were the right ones. Property, especially castles, does not always go to the rightful heirs. His Grace of Norfolk, England's premier peer, has now for second title, Baron Clun.

Then we go for the bridge, one of the most artistic bits in England. A solid, low, old stone bridge, with five irregular, unequal arches, and recessed projecting buttresses, over a little river, where the steep streets wind down on either side. The village children are in ecstasies. They swarm upon the parapet and frighten away the ducks. A higgler in his cart stops to stare. A farmer's boy with horse at smithy door gorps open-mouthed at the camera. A lurry is already soaking in the water. It is as well to get all you can for your money. The pity is for the children, who cannot see over the wall, but most of them are taken in one of the best of photographs.

A local proverb says, "Whoever crosses Clun bridge, comes back sharper than he went." So we crossed it again. The chairman of one of our banks tells me that when he had an estate in this neighbour-hood the local half-breeds of the Welsh borderland were so much too sharp for him that he sold all up and retired. That is high testimony to their abilities. When we put our bikes in the inn yard I found a copper on the stones, and as on the previous visit I had found money in the street of Bishops Castle, it looked as if the country folk were careless about their money or put it in the wrong sort of bank. This bit went in blackmail to the child at the inn, who would chatter at us as we had our tea. It was given to her if she would "shut up," but she took the money and went on talking. A cynic might say that was the fault of her sex. X, who suffers patiently and is very charitable, says she is very young; perhaps she will be better some day. Perhaps? Outside, the children were a nuisance. X and his camera charmed them as if he had been the Pied Piper of Hamelin. In the shrillest of shrill tones they screamed to one another all over the town and hills, "Here's the fortygraf man. Come an' be took."

The lych gate is one of the most beautiful ever made. It is four gables of simply carved, unvarnished oak, roofed with mossy, lichen-clad stone. It is photographed from above, with the street going steeply down beyond; and from below, where is the hill with market cart at door, the road branching right and left with rugged picturesque firs on banks, and beyond all the fine old church and yews. Another from an altar-tomb takes the double-storeyed stone and timber built porch near by the massive tower, and the last must be for the Hospital of the Trinity.

Here is an epitaph worth copying, though I have only space for the last verse. It is on a gentleman whose birth was joyous, and whose cradle shone with wealth—but

> " His wine was finished and he ceased to brew,
>   And fickle friends then hid them from his view,
>   Unknown, neglected, pined this man of worth,
>   Death his best friend, his resting place the earth."

This year we have sought out, found, and photographed in the fair county of Salop some of the most picturesque bits that can be imagined. Stokesay's well-kept mediæval grandeur, Acton Burnell's parliament house, castle, and cedars, and the glories of Tong with its splendid images of its bygone lords and ladies, are each, in their own way, entrancing. Much Wenlock has wonderful ruins and houses, but Clun, in its simple variety, is as charming as any. The newest thing

LYCH-GATE, CLUN

about it seems to be its Homes of Rest, with greensward
in the courtyard and gardens round about, and they
were built nigh on three centuries ago.

To go further would only be to get into the hills,
and darkness would be on us by six, about the time
to catch the train at Craven Arms. Therefore we
turned for home. The stubble-fields were thronged
with feathered fowl innumerable. All the homely
poultry of the farm, with pigeons, wood-pigeons,
pheasants, and peewits in hundreds; coveys of par-
tridges, waterhens, and smaller fry innumerable. The
birds from the wooded hills were there, and miles upon
miles of trees were resplendent with the first bronzy
tints of autumn. The breeze was at our backs. The
road was good and mostly downhill. The machines
would go by themselves, and in the exhilarating air
X began to coast and try gymnastics, quite forgetting
all about his wife, his family, or his ailments. Fortunately nothing happened but a happy time, a most
successful day, without even a punctured tyre.

When we came to where the grey old tower of
Clunbury was far away below us, we turned down
a steep and twisting lane; went over the river by a
low bridge, through orchards gleaming with fruit,
amid farmsteads, to the very curious old church, which
is particularly worth seeing, for it not only has windows,
doorways, and arches of what I take to be Saxon work,
but the walls of the church itself are built like the sides
of the arches or doorways, that is, they slope outwards,
something like the sides of an overturned boat or a
round-headed coffin reared up, and therefore the inside
width of the church at the eaves is probably some feet
more than it is on the ground.

At Hopesay, a valley up the hills, is another of
these very ancient, uncommon churches, whose remoteness from new riches has probably proved to be

their salvation.   Here are big pears on the rector's wall inside the churchyard, showing how good or how superstitious the natives are.   A big round house by the roadside with all its chimneys in one stack in the centre of the building attracts our notice, but we have to hurry on to catch the express at Craven Arms, for darkness closes over all.

HEREFORD COW AND CALF

DIDDLEBURY — MUNSLOW — MILLICHOPE — ONE OF ENGLAND'S OLDEST HOUSES

IT may be remembered that my companion the archi-tect, who ingeniously tried to mend his bike with his pocket-handkerchief, as we were returning from Clun, had to be left at Craven Arms while I cycled, in the dark, back to Church Stretton. The next morning I returned for him, fortifying myself for another long day's jaunt with a good breakfast, begin-ning with the homely porridge and working up, through common bacon, to the modern hotel delicacy of wasps in marmalade, served by little German waiters.

As I neared Craven Arms, the roads were thronged with herds of Hereford cattle and flocks of Shropshire sheep, which were being driven to one of the great sales by auction. The hotel was crowded with farmers and drovers who had mixed with the cattle, been reared with them, and lived with them until they were like them in their ways and almost in their speech. Strong in jaw and bone, resolute and hard-bitten they must be if their farming is to pay, for their lot is to work from morn till night from the cradle to the grave. What use is "book larnin" to them?—if they try to read they drop off to sleep. To be fruitful and multiply and keep the pot a-boiling is the oldest order known to man ; the latest is—Mind how you vote : for even beasts know which way the wind blows, and the weather eye must needs be kept open.

Here is a smart agriculturist in straw hat, sitting with easy hunting-seat on dark-brown hunter, while he drives before him four haltered couples of enormous,

well-groomed Shropshire rams. Then comes a drove
of long-horned Hereford oxen, each one weighing nigh
upon a ton. Next is a pitiable sight, a poor woman
driving two little white-faced calves and her flock of
turkeys. What would happen to that lot if a rampaging
beast came charging down the lane? At the inn, the
ostler tells me that the gent with the broken bike has
gone to get it mended, there being two shops where
that could be done—one is a barber's, the other a
jeweller's. What a nice assortment of occupations!
and, after all, he went to the blacksmith's and did the
repairs himself. We missed one another, and I went on
alone, still meeting droves of cattle and sheep, all of
the prevalent type, the seemingly endless droves of the
surplus stock of a rich country, for the well-tilled lands
around and the fat and panting sheep all told their own
tale of prosperity.

After a few miles of good cycling on the road to
Wenlock the map showed me that Diddlebury was near,
and down below, on the right, was a grand old tower
that had evidently been there for ages. Most of the
ancient churches are on high ground, but this is in a
vale down a steep and narrow lane, which ends in a
river and a churchyard. There are three ways of crossing the river to get to the church. The broad one in
the middle is to wade through the water. The one to
the left is by a narrow, low bridge, and the one to the
right over a plank footbridge. The absent-minded or
the flabby might be puzzled as to whether it is the broad
or the narrow way which leadeth aright, and if the
sermon should be more than usually muddling, some
might in their confusion involuntarily suffer the total
immersion of a Latter-day Saint.

The church is very curiously built, indisputably rare
old work, for all inside the north wall is herring-bone
Saxon stonework—flat stones set zigzagly upwards with
striking and peculiar effect. Above them are carved

taken from
The Pilgrimages in Shropshire
by Fletcher Moss
of
Didsbury Manchester
1901

DIDDLEBURY

heads for corbels. There is one row of pillars which are square at the base, then octagonal, with rounded capitals. Many bits of ancient carving and interlaced work are built in the walls. A Saxon window and doorway have their sides sloping wider to the rounded arch. Tombs of the historical families of the Baldwyns and Powells. One of the former, whose folks owned Diddlebury for centuries, was set to mind the captive Queen of Scots, and met the fate of all who had aught to do with that unlucky race.

The ancient tower is of enormous strength. Its great buttresses have stone enough to build a modern house. The western doorway is more than a yard deep, with many-shaped concentric round-headed arches over it. Apparently the crushing weight above has pressed all out of shape, and various custodians have used various kinds of stone wherewith to mend and prop. Weather-worn shields of arms and heads of beasts are on it, flowers and lichen grow aloft in its crevices, and the whole is a venerable relic of antiquity. Built into the church wall outside, by the tenth son Hector, is a memorial of Elizabeth Fleming, who had thirteen sons and six daughters. Well done, Betty!

So much for Diddlebury. When trying to learn anything of the ancient history of Diddesbury I had wondered whether there was any connection between it and the Shropshire village, but could not find any. Their name is now shortened to Delbury. One old spelling was Dudesbir, which would do for either place, and after many changes we have settled on Didsbury, but now there is a railway station, the porters contract the name still more and call it Bry.

Farther on the road is a picturesque inn, the Swan, built of stone with black and white gables, overhanging sign, and long steep steps. Across the road is another timber-built, projecting house, and there is a gig-house without doors, so that any one might go off with the gig ;

but perhaps it is not worth much, and there is a watch-dog on the step. Then another inn, the Hundred House, so named because it was the old courthouse for the Hundred. Here I ask for lunch. "Cider? Yes, sir, twopence a quart. Oh, well, if you have only a pint, and want the best, it will be a penny-halfpenny. Bread and butter a penny. What, half of this? It's all our own making." When a man takes his ease in his inn his thoughts are apt to wander, and I thought of X, who was, like the good apprentice in the parable, piling up the money, while I, a wanderer and a vagabond, was spending my time and substance in a public-house. A prodigal in a far country, though twopence for dinner is not very riotous living, but when the Good Samaritan left that sum for the man who fell among thieves it was evidently expected to last some time. The landlady tells me cider is more intoxicating than ale; at least hers is—"it flies to the head more." I was afraid it might affect me somewhere else, but her directions for me to cross the park at Millichope and find my way to the old forester's lodge were certainly more confusing than my head could carry or compose. So we talked about "tekkin a farrum on a by tek," until I jogged on with all the world before me.

Up a pretty lane at Munslow is another most interesting church of many styles and dates. The timbered porch is formed of interlacing arches carved in oak. The windows are deeply splayed with real old glass, their sides and arches being formed by irregular projecting stones, singularly primitive or rude, and yet beautiful. None of the windows or arches or doorways resemble another, and the enormously massive pews or benches are carved all over into chess-boards, triangles, or coats of arms. Some of the seats after ages of wear are still three inches thick of solid oak, and there is ten times more to note than I have space or time for noting. Over a tomb by the porch is some-

MUNSLOW CHURCH PORCH

thing like a lych-gate's top, all smothered with clematis. Enormous yews and firs and oaks are in the spacious churchyard, where the tombstones lean in all directions, wreathed with woodbine and garlanded with roses. The rectory lawn slopes to the pool where the water-hens are croaking, and the grass of the neighbouring orchard is thickly strewn with apples gorgeous in scarlet and gold. A garden of Eden with no serpent or woman to beguile me—yet I fell.

MUNSLOW CHURCH

Next comes the adventurous part of the journey, which is to find the ancient forester's lodge at Upper Millichope. It is said to be about a mile and a half off across the park. There are endless ways, delightfully romantic if only there were some one to lead me aright. The simplest instructions seem to be to go along a grass-grown lane until it ends in the park. Then follow the park wall until there is no wall. Then follow the

fence until there is no fence. Then keep to the track
(if there is one and it does not go down a rabbit-hole).
Then go through the thick wood, and when you get
out, Upper Millichope is far down below you.

Well, the day was fine, and I had plenty of (cheap)
apples in my pocket. So I cycled carefully up the lane
until I was soon crushing and squelching through a lot
of big red plums. " Oh, help yourself," an old lady said;
"take as many as you like." Fortunately I had a
poacher's pocket in my coat, one that would hold a peck
of apples or a couple of rabbits. Lawyers say these
big pockets are for deeds and documents, but even
those gentlemen are not too particular what they put
into them. So I took about half a peck of plums, and
when I got in the park they seemed so heavy with their
stones and skins that it was obviously better to eat the
pulp and throw the rest away. If those old ladies had
sent their plums to Manchester to be sold they would
only have had more to pay than they would have got,
as I know some had to do, so we did one another a
good turn. In the park and round about were hundreds
of tons of rabbits, mushrooms, and blackberries, mostly
going to waste. I fared better than I expected on my
way, though one needed all one's faith to push a bike
through a thick and steep wood.

On re-emerging into daylight there was a long broad
hillside shedding from me, on which at least a thousand
pheasants were feeding, and far below was a tiny hamlet,
probably the place I sought. Thither I clambered
down, holding back the bicycle, from which a toe-clip
had got broken somewhere. Doubtless it was the first
machine that had ever gone down that trackless hill.
The first little farm was empty, with pheasants all about
the fold and garden, but beyond it was evidently the
house I had journeyed far to see.

It is unmistakably very ancient, a small rectangle of
stone with steep roof, having a Norman doorway with

ball-flower ornament and one tiny window. With that doorway blocked the bottom storey is a little castle with nothing to burn. The walls are six feet thick, of solid stone, with stone stairs, and in the upper rooms stone-mullioned windows with stone sockets for bars. Enormous oaken beams, almost touching one another, support the floors, and in the attic is a fireplace of oak. The

THE ANCIENT FORESTER'S LODGE, UPPER MILLICHOPE

gables are built of massive timber. The whole is one of the oldest houses known, supposed to have been built for the hereditary forester of the King there in those far-off lonesome hills and dales, to guard the deer, hang wanderers like myself, and mind the savage forest-laws.

A country wild and lonesome enough for any one or anything even now. What must it have been six or seven hundred years ago, or even a short time since, when trains and bicycles were unknown? Not that either of them is of much use within miles of the place, for I had to trudge up an apparently old Roman road-way, perfectly straight and steeper than the roof of a house, for a long mile and then down on the other side, still too steep to ride. Here I met several carts and waggons laden with coal for the hall, being dragged up the frightful hill by teams of five or six horses. There is any amount of fruit for everybody by the roadside, blackberries, plums, and apples. By Rushbury, another ancient church, I make for train and home, well pleased with an adventurous journey through a wild and primitive country where bicycles were seldom or never seen before.

The place name " hope " that is so common in this region seems to be another form of " slope," meaning a valley in the hills ; and Millichope, I read in learned books, is in British or Celtic the high valley of the mill or of the violets.

STRANGERS AND PILGRIMS

WE have met such funny folk upon our pilgrimages, have seen strange sights and heard such queer tales, that now our wanderings are o'er, the winter's night may be beguiled by setting down some record of the curious folk who have amused, amazed, or vexed us, in their turn.

On a fine day in September, when X could not go with me, I went by train to Crewe and then cycled by the hall, not to the Barthomley side, but straight on to Betley through that beautiful old-world village where, on the spacious road, there is every style of house but the present ; and where the hall— famous for its stained-glass window of the morris-dancers, with its tremendous Latin inscription, encircling stables and pigeon cots—looks like a workhouse with worn-out paupers wearily sweeping up the fading

BETLEY

leaves they soon must join in death. The road runs past Betley Pool, which is in two counties, two parishes, two dioceses, two archbishoprics (what a holy place it must be !), with a grand old yew alone in the park,

and cottage gardens gorgeous with autumnal flowers.
Then it goes up the hill to the right through the
wood for Madeley in Staffordshire, known to readers
of Izaak the immortal fisherman, by the dedication of
his book, and where he chiselled his initials on the
stone.   This village is still more charming than the last,
for the road divides the waters of the tranquil pool
from the gardens of the quaint old timber-built houses,
one venerable specimen of which has the inscription,
" 16.   Walk knave what lookest at.   47. $_I{}^S{}_B$," as may
be seen in the accompanying photograph, 1647 being
the date, and the initials those of the builders.   Elsewhere have I written of the jewelled caul that hid the
face of the future Lord Mayor of London when he came
into the world, and now holds the luck of the Crewes so
long as it is not concealed nor sold by any.   As I am
nearing the homes of my fathers the folk-lore and
legends rise again.

At Madeley Station on the right-hand side as the
traveller towards London enters the station, there may
be seen a handsome column standing in some garden
plots.   As they were the first allotment gardens I ever
knew, and are probably held in connection with some
neighbouring almshouses, I visited them again, thinking
to learn the rents or terms of tenancy.   Where could
there be a more convenient place to eat one's apples
than on the seats by the time-worn, mouldering, beautiful
monument of Annabel Hungerford Crewe?   The pious
mottoes around it are tumbling to decay.   Rust has
consumed the iron dolphins' jaws and tails.   The gorgeous coats of arms are as faded and worm-eaten as
are those who once were proud to bear them.   Even
the sun-dials cease to tell the sunny hours.   The water
drearily drips from what remains of the dolphins' slob-
bering mouths.   All else is silent save when a train
whirls swiftly by.   Even the stones on which I sit are
crumbling to decay, poverty-stricken in the midst of

IN MADELEY, STAFFORDSHIRE

boundless wealth. Suddenly the clock strikes twelve, and like a ghost I start, for here comes a man.

He has not come to turn me out, it seems, for he gropes and pokes about the water from the fountain; so I get plucky again and ask him if he can tell me whether there are any garden plots to let, and the rent of them. It seems a sore subject with him. He says they have no right to charge any rent, it is a robbery of poor folk, and he has waited for years and cannot get a plot even by paying for it; rent five shillings a plot of eleven rods. Assuming the rod to be Cheshire measure, I mentally reckon this to be 704 square yards, or approximately the seventh part of an acre. Therefore, that is about thirty-five shillings an acre rent, which is the value of land in that part. But the man says they have no right to any rent; so I go back to the inscription on the monument and find it there recorded, " Given to the poor."

Then with difficulty I learn that he is looking for a frog. He reiterates repeatedly that he wants a frog, because he has a child with the frog. This is puzzling. I should prefer a sum in algebra or double practice to this puzzle. When the Mormon from Salt Lake City wished me to give him the names of as many of his ancestors as I could, so that he might be baptized with total immersion for each one of them separately when he got back to Salt Lake, it was very astonishing, and now a man wanted a frog to cure the frog. Gradually it dawned on me that he wished to cure some ailment, and I remembered the thrush in a horse's frog. He said this was thrush or frog in his child's mouth, and gave me the valuable information that if any one has a child with the frog and will hold a live frog in the child's mouth while it sucks it all away, the child will be cured.

Outside the garden gates, waiting for their father, there were four children, aged about seven, six, five

S

and four. They were pale and bloodless, with sunken cheeks and big flat mouths like frogs. They all hopped about on their hind-legs just like the pictures of the dressed-up frogs in the children's picture-books, and they all cried in chorus as if they were ravenously hungry, " Dadda, av oo got a fwog? Dadda, av oo got a fwog?" It was a horrible sight, enough to make one shudder if there had been any shudders left.

Here was a poor peasant hunting for frogs for food for his froggy children, yearning after a bit of land that he might till for his own little garden, half starved in the midst of a wealth beyond his wildest dreams, where the long trains constantly whirl up and down the great trunk line through the rich red earth of Staffordshire, where the lord of the land has miles after miles of estates, well kept and well cared for, but all the land our English laws ensure to the poor peasant is six feet of earth to bury him when he is dead! " He that increaseth knowledge increaseth sorrow."

Sadly I turned from the froggy chorus to go up the steep and narrow lane to the land I knew so well. In five miles I should pass from the watershed of the Mersey to that of the Severn and to that of the Trent. On the Maer hills a weather-beaten old woman, with a tin can on one side of her girdle and a basket on the other, with long nut-hook in hand and short petticoats, gathering wild fruits, asked me if it had "gone noon." I replied that in that land it seemed to me to be always afternoon. She looked curiously and half scared at the glitter of the bicycle, though otherwise hard-faced enough for anything. I pushed on to see my aunt once more, knowing she would tell me all about everything, and sure enough I soon had my ignorance lightened. Frogs are sometimes eaten by country poor folk, and even snails when they are in a decline. Why, old Betty Howes, of the Cuckoo's Nest, had a lad who would eat all the frogs he found in the harvest field, and he did well on them.

THE ALLOTMENT GARDENS, MADELEY, STAFFORDSHIRE

Considering the old lady, like her twelve brothers and sisters, had a dose of rue tea as soon as she first looked out on to the world and has survived it nearly ninety years, she knows a thing or two. My education was defective, for I was brought up a strong Tory when a college education taught that only Frenchmen ate frogs and Englishmen ate beefsteaks, that being the cause why any Englishman could " lick " three Frenchmen.

Another day I was travelling to town by train as usual, when an ex-churchwarden deigned to say that he did sometimes read my articles in the *City News*, adding, " You seem to think that all churches should be open on week days, so that cyclists may go in any time." I admitted that was my opinion. He said again, " What would become of all our prayer-books and hymn-books if such goings-on were allowed ? " My reply was, " If all your old books were collected together and tipped in the road, very few cyclists would stop to pick any up." " Oh ! if that is the way you discuss the matter I must decline to discuss it any further, but I should like to know what right cyclists have in a church." " The rights of any other sinners." " I maintain that no sinner, as you call them, or any one else, has a right to go in a church unless the minister is there to conduct the service and teach them how to pray, or some official in authority to see no wrong is done. We don't want our books stolen." What a life of drudgery to petty details this respectable skinflint must have had—used to save, and scrat, and screw, suspicious of all, until his soul is as narrow as his useless body !

Having visited nearly all the ancient or pre-Reformation churches in Cheshire and its neighbourhood, it gives me pleasure to write that the majority of them are free and open to all comers, and the key can easily be obtained to those which are locked. There are two exceptions, namely, Didsbury and Gawsworth. Many people ask me about the key to Didsbury church, quoting the notice at the churchyard gates, which the church authorities know to be untrue. At Gawsworth the case is worse, for at p. 69 is the photograph of the parson's gate locked, with a big notice board, " Trespassers will be prosecuted."

From the church to the public-house is an easy step. Generally they are neighbours, though the keepers of them are anything but neighbourly, for excepting at election times the un-Christian language in which they speak of one another is something awful. A well-known brewer in the city lately told me that he did not believe I had ever been refused tea by a licensed victualler. Here are two recent cases. On July 7 I was cycling alone in the Wirral, and at Parkgate saw a large sign, "Good accommodation for cyclists," on the Chester Castle Hotel. I went in and asked for tea, but was told they could not be bothered with teas. On Friday, October 19, X and I called at The Windmill, Tabley, about four o'clock and asked for tea, but were point-blank refused. At The Smoker, Tabley, we had before been told that we might get tea if we waited half-an-hour. Unfortunately there are whole villages where the temporary owner's influence has caused them to become noted for the inhospitality and hindrances shown to tourists.

We wish to thank the many strangers who have invited us to tea. Their invitations have necessarily come months too late, but that is not their fault. The account of the Easthope and Acton Burnell journey, when we went nigh on twenty miles without seeing a public-house, and the solitary farmeress at Easthope refused us tea, brought an invitation from Skimblescott, which was as near to there as any place with such an extraordinary name could be to anywhere else. If we had gone, X would have fallen into the arms of another of his numerous unknown relatives, and the local newspaper at Bridgnorth, which copied the account of our journey thither, and accused us of drinking in the only slum in the town, said it was a pity that X could not get a better companion.

THE FOREST

In revising the writings and choosing the illustrations for this book, the evenings of my first lonely Christmastide have been greatly cheered and lightened, and it happens that the end is reached on Candlemas day, a day to which so many quaint old folk-lore proverbs refer ; a memorable day for Manchester, when I, as one of the procession from the Town Hall to the Cathedral, may be said to have gone on pilgrimage to the old church to join in the service of respect to the memory of the dead Queen.   In that old church was my mother christened ninety-two years ago, and there she was wed ; and now within a few days of the first anniversary of her death, it seems to me that in their last days, when strength and life steadily ebbed away, there were many points of resemblance between my beloved mother and revered Queen.   Both women did their

life's work well.   Princes and powers with unnum-
bered common people mourn for the one.   Very few
ever heard of the other.   She had outlived her generation and most of the next.   In the great sorrow of
my life I could merely send to friends a plain memorial
card with a little photograph of her sitting in the old
parsonage garden with the grey tower of the church
beyond, as if it and the churchyard also were part of
the garden, a sprig of rosemary, the time-honoured
symbol of remembrance, and these lines—

> " She looked well to the ways of her household,
>   Even at the great age of ninety years.
>   Her eye was not dim, nor her natural force abated,
>   And when strength failed, sleep came the more,
>   Until in sleep she calmly passed away."

And now that she is gone, my loneliness is lightened by
"the glorious lady with the eyes of light," who dowered
Macaulay with the power to think and dream and
write—

> " I brought the wise and brave of ancient days
>   To cheer the cell where Raleigh pined alone :
>   I lightened Milton's darkness with the blaze
>   Of the bright ranks that guard the eternal throne."

THE OLD PARSONAGE, DIDSBURY

Index

Printed by BALLANTYNE, HANSON & Co.
Edinburgh & London

Folk-Lore

OLD CUSTOMS AND TALES OF MY NEIGHBOURS

48 Illustrations.   Pp. xvii–332.   Price Half-a-guinea.

The Times

"Mr. Fletcher Moss, of the Old Parsonage, Didsbury, the author of several volumes of local history, has sent us a large volume, entitled 'Folk-Lore.' . . . His pages, miscellaneous, garrulous, egotistical, and autobiographical, are fairly entertaining, but their interest is rather psychological than anthropological."

The Athenæum

". . . The book contains a few notes of value, and a certain indication of things that will never be again, for which indication we should be grateful.   The ordinary histories disdain such phases of life, a life well worth relating. . . . Mr. Frazer will probably like to hear of the version of the last sheaf on p. 54 ; Mr. Hartland will be interested in the very singular evidence of a kind of couvade belief and custom noted on p. 6 ; Mrs. Gomme will appreciate the description of the burial cakes on p. 28. . . . It is a pity Mr. Moss did not extend his notes in many instances."

Notes and Queries

". . . Most of the beliefs, customs, &c., he chronicles are familiar to readers of *Notes and Queries*, but there are some which will be strange.   Here, for instance, is a custom of which we never heard.   'My Aunt who still lives at Standon Hall, and is long past the fourscore years, has all her long life religiously taken the first pancake on Shrove Tuesday and given it to the gamecocks.   It is supposed to make the hens lay. . . .' Mr. Moss's book we unhesitatingly commend to our readers.   It will be useful to some and agreeable to all."

The Scotsman

"A handsome and beautifully illustrated book.   There are chapters on the customs connected with birth, death, and marriage ; on festivals, ghosts, and family legends ; on flowers, animals, and the weather; with the myths and observances of the people . . . curious and valuable."

The Journal of American Folk-Lore

"The non-commercial character of this beautiful volume gives it an additional charm.   It is liberally illustrated with presentations of such scenes as only England can furnish ; quiet parish churches, ample halls, noble oaks, landscapes from the tranquil fields of Cheshire.   It is impossible for an American to examine the book without a sigh over the deficiences of his own land."

The Manchester Guardian

"This handsome volume is readable, entertaining, and what Charles Lamb styles matterful. . . . To industry he adds a sense of humour, so that the casual reader may find amusement where the student of folk-lore will find instruction or matter for debate."

The Manchester Courier

"The chief charm of the book is that it supplies in a handsome form a record of old people, old places, and old customs, compiled with equal skill and sympathy. Only a true lover of his neighbours and of his country could have entered so truly into the joys and sorrows of rural life, and only a true literary artist could have given the themes their proper setting."

A History of
The Old Parish of Cheadle in Cheshire

And the Hamlet of Gatley in Etchells

Profusely Illustrated.   Price 7s. 6d. Nett.   Postage 4½d.

The Times

"A popular history of an interesting parish, well illustrated, and dealing, as all such histories should, not merely with church and buildings, with personal and historical associations, but with local folk and folk-lore, and with local natural history."

The Athenæum

"It is difficult to know exactly what to say of 'A History of Cheadle in Cheshire,' by Mr. Fletcher Moss. . . . As a son of the soil he has had means of accumulating information on diverse subjects which would never have come to the ears of one who, in many other respects, might have been far better fitted for the work. . . . We gather from various good stories which Mr. Moss tells . . . a pathetic story about a witch named Bella, told in very good dialect. . . . We can speak with unmixed praise of the series of photographs of the old half-timber houses by which the book is illustrated."

The Manchester Courier

". . . The whole of the volume is a proof of the large amount of valuable material waiting for conversion into such fascinating literary chapters as are given in 'The Chronicles of Cheadle.' But the author must not lack the keen observation, sense of humour, above all, the vigorous and inherently picturesque style of the writer who has done so much for the southern suburbs of Manchester."

The Manchester City News

". . . Excellent accounts, admirably illustrated, follow of the church and halls, with a mass of curious and interesting information concerning them. The concluding chapters·deal with the folk of the district and its natural history, the last most excellent. Mr. Moss's book will probably remain the standard authority on the subject, . . . and the illustrations, varied and well chosen, are an attractive representation of an interesting neighbourhood."

The Cheshire County News

". . . Simply invaluable to all who care to know the history of the village. The book is well got up with the highest workmanship, full of humour wherever humour is possible ; there are witty raps at abuses and evils, trenchant criticism, and good temper pervades the whole volume."

A History of Didsbury

Also

Didisburye in the '45

Price 6s. each Nett.

The Manchester Guardian

" There are few places whose history will not be found interesting, if only you are lucky enough to meet with some one who knows all about them and is willing to impart his knowledge. These qualifications Mr. Moss undoubtedly possesses as regards Didsbury. . . . If there be such a thing as the genius of the place, he is probably better entitled than any one else to be considered its incarnation. . . . The book is, moreover, full of salt—touches of homely and sometimes rather pungent humour expressed in racy vernacular. We rather like the flavouring."

The Manchester Courier

" . . . Pleasant, chatty, and entertaining, and cannot fail to be interesting to Lancashire men generally, . . . brightened by the numerous anecdotes, wise sayings, and old rustic phrases of the people."

The Manchester Examiner

" . . . Pleasant books of one of Lancashire's oldest villages, free from personal bias, free from misstatements, and free from tediousness. . . . A vivid picture of life in Didsbury in the times which are rapidly passing away."

The Manchester City News

" . . . More delightful he could not possibly have been, nor could he have produced anything more racy or more genuinely characteristic in the description of the old-fashioned natives. Whilst the record is delightfully chatty and free and unconventional, there is no lack of the solid information which goes to the making of a trustworthy history. . . . He brightens his narrative with abundance of anecdotes, particularly the odd sayings of the ancient natives. Almost every page tempts to a quotation. . . . We take leave of a charming book with reluctance, . . . and higher praise we could not give."

The Cheshire County News

" . . . . Intensely attractive. Who has not longed for a real history that would tell us how the people talked and felt and lived ? . . . Full of interest to the lover of local lore and to the England of years ago."

Any of these books may be bought from the Author. The Set of four, sent carriage paid, for £1, 10s.

AUTHOR AND PUBLISHER—

FLETCHER MOSS, THE OLD PARSONAGE, DIDSBURY.